THE EVERYTHING
HOMEBREWING BOOK

Dear Reader,

For most of the 5,000-plus-year saga of people and beer, the beer you drank was the beer you brewed. Everyone drank beer. Everyone was a homebrewer.

Over the last several hundred years we've handed off our beer to companies with their own thoughts on what we'd like to drink. Driven by profit over taste and tradition, they reduced beer to a narrow commodity, differentiated more by mascots and ad slogans than taste.

In the 1970s intrepid men and women woke up to the idea that beer wasn't just the pale yellow sparkling soda foisted on them by a handful of brewers. Beer could, they found, have substance and taste. Scouring old brewing texts, traveling to beer culture capitals, cozying up to brewers, and experimenting endlessly, they unraveled the lost art of making real beer at home.

Today, if you can make a pot of soup, you can make beer. I started on my kitchen stove with my stockpot and within three weeks cracked open my very first bottle of beer. Ten years later, I still get the same thrill pouring my latest.

So how about it? Are you ready to take back your suds?

Drew Beechum

Welcome to the EVERYTHING Series!

These handy, accessible books give you all you need to tackle a difficult project, gain a new hobby, comprehend a fascinating topic, prepare for an exam, or even brush up on something you learned back in school but have since forgotten.

You can choose to read an *Everything*® book from cover to cover or just pick out the information you want from our four useful boxes: e-questions, e-facts, e-alerts, and e-ssentials.

We give you everything you need to know on the subject, but throw in a lot of fun stuff along the way, too.

We now have more than 400 *Everything*® books in print, spanning such wide-ranging categories as weddings, pregnancy, cooking, music instruction, foreign language, crafts, pets, New Age, and so much more. When you're done reading them all, you can finally say you know *Everything*®!

QUESTIONS?
Answers to common questions

FACTS
Important snippets of information

ALERTS!
Urgent warnings

ESSENTIALS
Quick handy tips

PUBLISHER Karen Cooper

DIRECTOR OF ACQUISITIONS AND INNOVATION Paula Munier

MANAGING EDITOR, EVERYTHING SERIES Lisa Laing

COPY CHIEF Casey Ebert

ACQUISITIONS EDITOR Katrina Schroeder

DEVELOPMENT EDITOR Brett Palana-Shanahan

EDITORIAL ASSISTANT Hillary Thompson

Visit the entire Everything® series at *www.everything.com*

THE EVERYTHING HOMEBREWING BOOK

All you need to brew the best beer at home!

Drew Beechum

Avon, Massachusetts

This book is dedicated:
To my lovely Amy, who endured the endless beer facts, simultaneous
move, and book. Now where's that beer I promised to make you?
To my mom, my sister, and my grandmother, who fostered my bookish
ways and somehow knew I'd end up writing one of my own.
To the fine folks of the American Homebrewers Association
for their encouragement and support.
To the members of the Maltose Falcons Homebrewing Club, for their mentoring,
advice, years of beer (both good and bad), and being silly enough to have
elected me president more than once.
To homebrewers and brewers everywhere for being generous and inquisitive.
There are no "secrets" in brewing; only truths we haven't shared yet.
And finally, to you, the reader for taking a step to better brew days for you.
(To your significant others, I apologize for leading you down the primrose path.)

Copyright © 2009 by F+W Media, Inc. All rights reserved.
This book, or parts thereof, may not be reproduced
in any form without permission from the publisher; exceptions
are made for brief excerpts used in published reviews.

An Everything® Series Book.
Everything® and everything.com® are registered trademarks of F+W Media, Inc.

Published by Adams Media, a division of F+W Media, Inc.
57 Littlefield Street, Avon, MA 02322 U.S.A.
www.adamsmedia.com

ISBN 10: 1-60550-122-0
ISBN 13: 978-1-60550-122-2

Printed in the United States of America.

J   I   H   G   F   E   D   C   B   A

Library of Congress Cataloging-in-Publication Data
is available from the publisher.

This book is available at quantity discounts for bulk purchases.
For information, please call 1-800-289-0963.

Contents

Acknowledgments

Thank you to the following folks for reviewing and making this book better: Derreck Bourdon, Rob Coffey, Matt Crill, Mike Dietz, Charlie Essers, Bill Herlicka, S'ven Kinsey, Jonny Lieberman, Alex Macy, George Mahoney, John Palmer, MB Raines, Paul Schultz, and Jamil Zainasheff.

Extra pints to Derreck for helping review, tweak, and enter a number of recipes, and John for his tremendous help with water chemistry.

On the recipe front, thank you so much to my fellow brewers for lending their recipes. Without their help, the book would be far more one-sided. Great brewers share and help others learn from their successes and failures.

Thank you to Gina and Katrina for sheparding this book from a jumbled mess of stuff upstairs to a real book.

And lastly, a big thank you to John Daume, owner of the Home Beer Wine and Cheesemaking Shop in Woodland Hills, California, for starting my brewing career.

Top 10 Tips for Homebrewers: Novice to Pro

1. There are no bad batches, just less successful ones. Even a less successful one can inspire great ideas.

2. Beer happens! Mankind brewed beer for thousands of years without understanding what they were doing!

3. Brew constantly. You learn with every batch! When you have enough beer stockpiled, throw a party with friends or take the breathing room to brew bigger, bolder beers.

4. Have patience—time fixes many problems. You don't have to worry about selling your beer quickly, so squirrel it away and visit the beer at a later date.

5. Take risks: It's only five gallons and you may just surprise yourself.

6. Support your local homebrew shop. You may find cheaper prices online, but your local store can provide support and rescue you when things go terribly wrong.

7. Know your local brewer. The professionals have been there and done that. They are a valuable source of knowledge. If you're nice, you might even get yeast and grain from them!

8. Be proud of your brew, but be humble too.

9. There are twenty different ways to do anything in the brewery. Eighteen and a half of them are right. Brew with other folks and see what crazy things they do!

10. Your friends all love your beer? Enter a competition and see what the judges have to say. You may just walk away with the gold!

Introduction

▶ UNLESS YOU'VE AVOIDED beer for the past twenty years, you've seen changes come at the taps and shelves of your local bar, grocery store, and liquor store. What used to be a lineup of monochromatic monotonous brews has sprung into riotous life. Strange old names like Porter and India Pale Ale crop up like long-forgotten adventuring uncles. The sheer variety of new beers daunts even old hands.

If you've never tried these new brews, stop right now. Put this book down! March to the corner store and try a new beer, something unfamiliar, something not called a "true pilsner." Prove to yourself—and to those who still say, "But, I don't like beer!"—that the beer spectrum doesn't end with "lite" beer.

The newfound multitude was born out of a beer desert by folks like you. Travellers roaming the wilds of Europe knew there was something missing at home and set to changing the situation. These early homebrewers worked with scant information and scanter ingredients. The early accepted wisdom and myths were tested, discarded, polished, and refined. The fiscally brave among them jumped at the chance to reintroduce Americans to the taste of real beer. They continue to expand the beery horizon and even now many of their successors start as homebrewers.

So why brew when you can enjoy the new American beer oasis? Maybe you want a creative project, to work with your hands. Maybe you want to recapture the fun of your childhood chemistry set. Or maybe you just want to try your hand at learning a skill that's always been fundamental to civilization. No matter the reason, there's an indescribable thrill of pride when you open a beer for friends and they look in wonderment and ask, "You brewed this?" That's the moment you'll be hooked and wonder why you never tried this before.

Brewing offers a chance to explore skills you never knew you had. You can learn the biology of yeast, the chemistry behind mashing, or the detective skills needed to track down obscure bits of brewing history. All while enjoying the gustatory pleasures of delicious beer. Some brewers get juiced by recipe development;

others by creating labels and crazy names; and others by endlessly tinkering, soldering, and welding to make their next great gizmo.

You'll find a new world of friends and odd fellows open up when you brew, from the beer enthusiasts hunting the next great brew to your fellow brewers discussing their latest exploits. You might even get to know your neighbors when they find out you make great beer.

Homebrew clubs have sprung up all over the country, and even those without one nearby can find camaraderie in numerous online forums. Talking with experienced brewers is the fastest way to learn. One lesson you'll quickly discover is that there really is no wrong way to brew. Get four brewers together in a room and you'll find at least five different brewing techniques, and they'll argue why three of them are "wrong."

Compared to even ten years ago, homebrewers have access to an embarrassment of riches. The selection of ingredients and equipment has exploded. Today homebrewers use the same high-quality ingredients as the big boys and have adapted and built the gear needed to make great beer. Veteran brewers shake their heads in disbelief.

All of this has made it possible for a new brewer to make a great beer the first time out. Long gone are the days of porcelain crocks, weird yeasty odors, and busted bottles that showered your clothes in beer. In just a few batches, you'll find homebrewing in your thoughts. You'll dissect the beer before you and figure out how you could make your own version. You'll toss recipes around in your head, deciding how exactly you want to create a new taste.

This is an exciting time to be brewing. There's a growing back-and-forth with pro brewers. They watch and feed on the creative output of the homebrewing community and return the favor with their own exciting twists.

So, grab a kettle and make a beer. It's your first step on an endless exploration and your chance to continue the brewing lore.

CHAPTER 1

Beer Basics:
Your Primer to a
Sudsy World

Beer, the gloriously frothy and quenching beverage, punctuates life's moments. No summer party or football season is quite complete without it. Wandering down the megamart beer aisle you may marvel at the vast array facing you. With this plenty why would you ever want to tackle the messy task of creating your own? Read on and you'll find it's not that crazy an idea.

Why Brew Your Own Beer

These days there's not enough time to relax. Brewing provides a perfect excuse to spend a few hours chatting with friends and the "research" time sampling different brews. An old brewer's maxim states, "Brewing is an hour's worth of work 'crammed' into three." Throw some burgers on the grill for an impromptu party!

Curiosity about a favorite pint leads many to the hobby. Where wine lovers obsess over a vineyard's tiniest details, many brewers obsess over a new brew. What kind of hops? What techniques are used? How do they get that wonderful flavor? Solve the puzzle and crack the key. The endless ways to brew and to tinker means the search never ends.

For others, the modern workplace leaves a quiet dissatisfaction. Unlike their fathers, the end of the workday comes with no physical achievement. No fields are plowed, no cars are built. Brewing satiates the need to create something real, something mechanical yet poetic.

Lastly, though, the real reason: pouring a pint and watching eyes crinkle in anticipation and close in rapturous enjoyment. From the first time a friend looks incredulously at you and says, "You brewed this?" you will be hooked. Nature's high!

QUESTION?

Can I brew beer more cheaply than I can buy it?
It all depends on how you look at it. Your typical ingredient costs are much less than an equivalent amount of micro/imported beer. Don't forget to factor in the costs of equipment, bottle, kegs and, most important, your time.

Is It Legal?

If you rent, or have a nosy neighbor, don't be surprised if someone involves the local police force. Almost every state permits amateur brewing. Even in the few forbidden states you find homebrew shops and clubs.

Federal law was changed in 1979 to return to pre-Prohibition traditions. Unless prohibited locally, each brewer can produce 100 gallons per year or 200 where there are other adults in the household. Relevant information about your state's laws can be found online at *http://beertown.org/homebrewing/legal.html.*

Of course, that doesn't mean you won't find someone convinced that you're cooking up methamphetamine or moonshine! Be polite, and explain what you're doing and why that big copper coil isn't actually part of a still. Your neighbors are probably just curious and want to try your beer!

The government doesn't go after the run-of-the-mill homebrewing scofflaw, but selling your beer will get their attention quickly! The law strictly forbids homebrewers from selling. Distillation of alcohol is another no-no.

The Myths, Legends, and Hype of Beer

It comes as no surprise, given beer's long history, that an endless sea of myths and legends swarm around it. Here are some commonly told tall tales. If you believed any of them, don't fret! You are not the only one to fall victim to the misinformation.

Dark Beer, Strong Beer?

Name the darkest beer you find in many bars. Guinness, right? Now name the least alcoholic beer in that same bar. Bud? Bud Light? Nope, Guinness! Shock your friends when you reveal that the "dark, thick stuff" is a mild kitten. Conversely, some of the world's strongest beers are the color of newly minted gold.

Color comes from the brewer's choice of grains and doesn't indicate the relative strength of the beer. How else do you think an old Irishman stands at the pub all day drinking pints?

Cold to Warm to Cold Disaster?

No doubt, you've heard a friend dismiss an offer of leftover beer, because it was cold and then warmed up again. The reheating cycle isn't as bad for beer as people think. You don't want to store beer at sweltering summertime temperatures, but the average bottle will do just fine moving between the fridge and the warmth.

Imported Beer Is Supposed to Smell That Way!

"Skunking" a beer requires large doses of ultraviolet light and hops. The light energy strikes dissolved compounds from the hops. The molecule is cleaved into two chemicals. One reacts with other chemicals and creates 3-methyl crotyl mercaptan, the same chemical sprayed by odorous skunks.

The average consumer experiences this flavor drinking green-, blue-, and clear-bottled beers. The reaction is so sensitive that the bright fluorescent lights of a beer fridge can trigger it. Now you know what that "imported taste" really is. One major domestic brewer avoids the problem by using light-stabilized hop extracts in their clear-bottled beer.

Label Confusion—Malt Liquor/Bock/Ale/Porter/Beer

Ever been confused by the terms you see on labels? Why do some lagers get labeled "ale"? Or even worse, why is a hefeweizen labeled "malt liquor"? Blame outmoded classification systems in states like Texas, with labels based solely on alcohol content. In Texas, beer is a malt beverage less than 4 percent alcohol by weight (ABW). Conversely ale and malt liquors contain more than 4 percent ABW.

Malt liquors are strong American lagers, ranging between 6 and 9 percent ABV. They contain a vast quantity of cheap adjuncts (corn, rice, corn syrup, sugar) and are fermented rapidly. They're cheap, potent, and punishing with their headache-inducing fusel alcohols.

FACT

An old joke about American beer and canoes implies all are weak. Even before microbreweries, most American beer was stronger than British beer and equivalent in alcohol to German and Czech beers. Today, Boston Beer Company holds the record for strongest beer with their 25-percent ABV Utopias.

Bock—Gunky Beer

Did your mom tell you the story of bock beer as told to her by her father? Every spring the breweries empty their tanks and scrap them clean. The brewers concoct a thick sweet beer called bock from the gunk.

In the post-Prohibition era, breweries did promote bock to celebrate winter's end and the Easter holiday, but that's the only nibblet of truth. Bock beers are sweet, malty traditional German lagers. Brewing requires constant cleaning; tanks aren't left with syrupy sludge. Spoetzl Brewery's Shiner Bock is a remnant of this Americanized tradition.

Some Quick Terms to Know

Every field has a specialized vocabulary. It's human nature to define one when a task gets specialized. Here are some of the more common things you'll hear brewers talking about.

- **Alcohol by Weight (ABW) and Alcohol by Volume (ABV)**—Measurement of the amount of alcohol in a drink. Since alcohol weighs less per ounce than water does, the ABW will appear less than the equivalent ABV—for example, 3.2 percent ABW (a classic blue law in some states) is 4.0 percent ABV. Until recently, American beer was always expressed in ABW, while the rest of the world used ABV. American breweries now use ABV to sell their beer.
- **Alpha Acid (AA)**—Expressed as a percentage, it's the amount of bittering acids available from a hop. Dissolved in the boil, they give beer bite.
- **Final Gravity (FG)**—Measurement of the remaining sugars and solids in a fermented beer. The difference between this and the OG (see below) is "apparent attenuation." Using that difference, you can calculate an approximate ABV and verify that your fermentation was healthy and complete (see Appendix C).
- **International Bittering Unit (IBU)**—Measurement of the amount of alpha acids dissolved. The scale runs from 0 bitterness to the human tasting threshold of 100+. Beer can be found anywhere on that scale.

- **Original Gravity (OG)**—Measurement of the amount of sugar dissolved in unfermented wort. Homebrewers talk about this in units of "specific gravity" while professional brewers use Plato.
- **Standard Reference Method (SRM)**—A value that indicates the relative darkness of a beer sample. Common pilsner-style beers range between two to five, with the dark stouts of the world weighing in at over thirty-five. SRM has mostly replaced the older Lovibond scale.
- **Trub**—The leftover protein and yeast sludge found in a fermenter.
- **Wort**—The brewing term for unfermented beer.

What Is Ale?

Until the dominance of the lager movement in the late 1800s, if you had a beer, it was ale. Pale ales, browns, porters, and stouts were the daily tipple of the thirsty. Ale yeasts (*Saccharomyces cerevisiae*) work at warmer temperatures (60°F to 70°F) than lager yeasts and are naturally suited for most climates. They express greater fruitiness and leave more residual body than lagers. The more robust and hearty ales sustained the populace through hard labor. Many ale styles, recently on their deathbeds, have seen a revival in the turn to older traditional flavors.

What Is Lager?

Ask the average punter about lager: "Lager is white-headed, pale yellow, and easy to drink!" And they'd be right, about pilsner lagers, but they're missing out. The German word *lager* means "storage." Two factors distinguish a lager from other beers: a period of cold storage and the yeast.

Lagering is a simple practice, but the change it introduced to the brewing world is profound. Starting about 500 years ago, brewers discovered that their beers became cleaner and brighter, and lasted longer, when stored in the cold caves found around the breweries. Beer would last through the endless nonbrewing summers. The process slowly changed the barreled beer: Off-flavors and sulfur would vanish and the drier beer had a more refined carbonation.

Lager yeasts are a different breed, mutants born out of the cold. *S. Pastorianus* and *S. Uvarum* ferment at colder temperatures (45°F to 55°F). This cold ferment produces less of the fruity esters, phenols, and fusels that flavor ales—hence the clean descriptor given to lagers. The characteristic crispness comes from their unique ability to ferment raffinose and other large sugars left untouched in ales.

Major Brewing Cultures of the World

Since the Sumerians formalized the world of beer, suds have flowed from every corner. There are places so beer crazy that no one is surprised when you step off the plane and say you're there for beer.

The UK and Ireland

The British and the Irish love their pub time. Trading rounds is so deeply ingrained in the culture that failure to respect the round is a grave faux pas.

Traditional "session ales" lubricate the long pub chat without high alcohol dragging the crew to oblivion. Even with their lower punch (3.0 to 4.5 percent ABV), the traditional Irish stouts, British bitters, and milds pack rich character. Look for traditional "real ale" for the full experience of old-fashioned, hand-pumped draught ale.

QUESTION?

Do the British serve warm and flat beer?
Not by a long shot. Traditional British ale is served at "cellar temperature," around 50°F. Carbonation is controlled by careful cellaring of a cask. Blame the warm, flat beer myth on American servicemen. American lager beer is served highly carbonated and ice cold, about 37°F.

The much-feared British "lager lout" comes, in part, from an abandonment of the old pub culture. Increasingly, Brits turn to industrial lagers and cider, which are more than a full percent stronger than the old stuff. Fighting this tide, Britain's Campaign for Real Ale (CAMRA) and Cask Marque seek to safeguard and encourage the exploration of real ale.

Germany and the Czech Republic

Germany is renowned for the biergartens and the massive Oktoberfest in Munich. Per capita, the Czechs drink more beer than anyone. Together, the two shaped much of the world's beer consumption. In the town of Pilsen, the Czechs (with a German brewmaster) created the pale lager beer known worldwide. As German brewmasters learned the secrets, they spread across the world and brought their pils beer with them.

FACT

With Germany's inclusion in the European Union (EU), the Reinheitsgebot is no longer the law of the land since it would restrict the sale of other EU members' beer in Germany. However, many brewers proudly claim to cling to the tradition of "Hops, Water, Barley, and Yeast."

Beyond pils, there's a cornucopia of regional favorites to explore. The Czechs have beautiful dark lagers beaten only by the German schwarzbier. And not one can forget the sweet banana, bubblegum, and clove flavor of a Bavarian hefeweizen, one of Germany's few ales. Bocks, alts, Berliner weiss, rauchbiers, and more dot the countryside. All of this happens, under Germany's strict "Beer Purity Law," the Reinheitsgebot.

Belgium

Where the Germans are strict, the Belgians flaunt the boundaries of beer. Styles are mere whimsy or, as New Belgium Brewing's Peter Bouckaert explains, "In Belgium, there are no styles." The 10.5 million residents of this Maryland-sized country can choose from an astonishing array of more than 1,500 beers. In comparison, for the United States' 300 million residents, there are just over 1,400 breweries.

The Belgians favor stronger ales. Many brews contain more than 8 percent ABV. Despite the massive strength, the Belgians strive for "digestibility." Unlike other strong ales and lagers with sweet finishes, the varied Belgian ales finish bone dry, perfect with a plate of cheese.

Where Does the United States Rank as a Beer Culture?

The postwar, post-Prohibition phase of American history nearly killed any hope for American brewing. Beer was simplified to a cheap product. The beer culture was pale, watery, lifeless, and on the skids. Thanks to the growing craft-brewing revolution, things have changed dramatically.

The late beer writer Michael Jackson wrote in his final book (*Beer: Eyewitness Companions Guide*), "Today, neither European brewers nor most drinkers on either side of the Atlantic have yet grasped that tomorrow's most exciting styles of beers will be American in conception." The past decade marked incredible achievements in brewing, with brewers executing American riffs on classic beer styles.

CHAPTER 2

Your First Batch

Ready to take the plunge? You're sitting just a few short weeks from homemade beery bliss. All you need is a kit, a pot, some malt, and a dash of gumption to pull it together. Be warned, though! Once you start fermenting, you won't want to stop.

The Most Important Resource: Your Local Homebrew Shop

It's possible to fulfill all your brewing needs online. With a mouse click, supplies whisk to your doorstep. However, there is no single greater resource for the new brewer to cultivate than their local homebrew shop.

Tucked in cramped quarters, the average homebrew shop is a spartan affair. Chaotic shelves and bins collide with refrigerators overwhelming your senses with strange, unknown items. Every visit reveals new trinkets stuffed in a corner.

Choosing a Good Shop

In the midst of the clutter, how do you sort out the good shops from the places to avoid? Look around. Is the place clean and semiorganized? (Ignore the dust that gathers anywhere grain is milled.) Check out the grains and extract. Stores that only have a few grains to choose from limit your brewing options. Great stores allow you to dive into grain bins for a sample to smell and taste. While checking for freshness, you learn a grain's flavor. High marks to those allowing the purchase of any amount of grain, not just pre-weighed amounts. The extract selection isn't as important as the speed with which it flies from the store. Better beer comes from fresh extract. Beer kits, important when you begin, fade when you get the hang of creating recipes.

Top shops stuff fridges with different hop varieties. Cold preserves hop aroma. Each hop type has unique characteristics. Don't get locked into a limited selection.

In the bad old days, shops stored hops in paper bags at room temperature. These stale yellow cheesy hops made bad beer. If you find a store that doesn't keep their hops cold, find another shop!

Next to the hops will be yeast. Variety and freshness count. Check the expiration dates to avoid old dead yeast. Between the two main yeast suppliers there are nearly a hundred choices available to you.

Gadgets are great, but they don't make a store worthwhile. Delving deeper into the hobby, you'll discover a handful of items you need. Don't be tempted by the shiny widgets. Save your pennies for the good stuff.

Watch the clerks. How do they interact with customers? Are they answering questions without dogmatic answers? At a great shop, the crew manning the store is deeply immersed in homebrewing lore. Ask questions about things you don't understand. Reward their kindness with a bottle and get honest feedback to make your beer better.

Several companies sell no-boil, cheap brew kits or "beer-in-a-bag"-type setups. They are frequent gifts by well-meaning loved ones to the beer enthusiast. With some luck, you can produce a vaguely beer-like product. The basic starter kit is more expensive, but well worth it.

Why Shop Local?

No small shop can match the prices of the big online purveyors. So why shop local? Because on brew day, short a crucial ingredient, you need them there. A virtual retailer can't pull your fat from the fire, but your local one can! If your shop treats customers poorly or fails to supply your needs, don't hesitate to take your business elsewhere.

How Expensive Is It?

Your basic brew kit will set you back $100 to $200. And that's if you need every bit of gear. You'll always need bottles, cleaners, sanitizers, bigger kettles, and so on, and there's always another gadget you can buy. However, your per-batch costs are predictable. For each batch you'll purchase grain, extract, hops, and yeast. That's less than $40 for fifty handcrafted bottles. With microbrews ranging from $6 for a six pack or $10 to $20 for special bottles, eighty cents a bottle is a great savings. Experienced all-grain brewers can manage a batch for less than twenty cents a glass.

FACT

Every shop carries a basic starter kit. For around $100, you get the most basic gear and your first beer. The precise contents of the kit vary, but standard items include a fermenter (a bucket), a glass carboy, siphoning gear, a bottling bucket, a bottle capper, caps, and chemicals for cleaning and sanitizing. To start brewing you'll need a large pot (20 quarts) and fifty bottles.

The Four Types of Brewing

There are four types of brewing: extract, extract with stepped grains, partial mash, and all grain. Here are the basics of each type.

Extract

Brewing at its most basic is slightly more complicated than making a can of soup. Concentrated malt syrup or powder dissolved in water becomes beer. Despite the limitations of a single ingredient, beginning brewers can practice core skills with a modicum of expense and equipment.

This is how your grandfather brewed. The old recipes (and current recipes in some other countries) called for cans of malt syrup and pounds of sugar and a sprinkling of bread yeast.

Extract with Steeped Grains

Instead of relying on extract alone, spice things up with freshly cracked malt soaked in hot water. The tea is strained and mixed with the extract to form the wort. For the price of more time and a colander, you create fresher and more varied beers. Plenty of veteran brewers have continued to brew this way for years. They find it the perfect balance of brewing time and quality family time. Extract brews medal in competition far more often than elitist brewers like to admit.

Partial Mash

Partial mashing recipes derive most of their sugar from malt, with extract providing the final gravity boost. A partial mash is possible using almost all of your extract equipment. As you edge closer to all-grain brewing, partial mash batches get your feet wet by allowing you to practice new techniques without a mess of gear.

Experienced brewers sometimes revert to a partial mash for larger beers. The extract prevents a long brew-day and ensures achieving the monster target gravities.

All Grain

Professionals don't mess with the expense of malt extract, and neither do legions of obsessed homebrewers. Instead they start with large piles of barley, crush it, mix it with hot water, wait for mash magic, and rinse. All-grain beer requires more gear and more time to get a beer in the fermenter. Complete brewing freedom is your return on investment. No beer is out of reach.

Batch costs drop considerably because the fresh grain costs a fraction of extract. A five-gallon batch of regular extract beer may cost $35 to $45. The same recipe all grain costs about $15 to $20. With all that extra cash, you can buy some new gear. An added bonus is that you're no longer dependent on extract manufacturers.

Step-by-Step Instructions to Get Your Beer Fermenting

Take a deep breath! It's time to get started. This first batch may not be perfect, but it will be beer. Focus on learning the process. Prepare for the day by gathering six to seven gallons of filtered water. If you don't have a filter system, buy bottled drinking water or visit your local water store. Chill three to four gallons. When using a Wyeast pack, smack it the day before.

New equipment usually only requires a good rinse, but examine them closely. Fermenters need to be clean of all dirt before you try to sanitize them. Cleaning ahead of time saves you brew-day hassles and keeps you focused. Sanitation, on the other hand, must be done at the last minute. Clean everything, hoses, airlocks, test tubes, funnels, and anything else you'll use for brewing.

Fill a twenty-plus-quart pot with three gallons of unchilled water; put on high heat. Remove the yeast from the fridge to warm up. If you're using liquid malt extract, put the syrup in hot water to loosen the syrup. Add water salts when the water boils. Remove the pot from the heat and stir in your extract. Mix thoroughly. Extract resting on the bottom scorches, ruining the beer.

Return the kettle to a boil. When the boil is roiling, add your first hop addition and start a timer. Add additional doses of hops and clarifiers according to the recipe.

FACT

Kettle additions are always specified for the time remaining in the boil. For instance, a hop addition labeled as the "15-minute" addition is added after the kettle has been boiling for 45 minutes with only 15 minutes before the heat is shut off. Convert times by subtracting the time specified from the boil time. The "15 minute" addition happens 45 minutes after the first addition (60 mins −15 mins = 45 mins).

As the wort boils, mix enough sanitizing solution to fill the fermenter. Your store has some fantastic chemicals for this, but the cheapest is a tablespoon of unscented regular-strength bleach per gallon of water. Let this soak for 20 minutes with your airlock and other gear, rinse thoroughly and air-dry completely, upside down.

After an hour's boil, turn off the heat and tightly cover the pot. Settle it into a sink full of cold, just running water or ice water and cool to around 90°F. When ready, add two gallons of chilled water to the fermenter and then the lukewarm wort. Top up with chilled water to reach five gallons.

Close the fermenter and place the airlock in place. Rock the fermenter back and forth for 10 minutes to thoroughly mix. Take a sanitized wine thief or turkey baster (unused for poultry) and draw enough wort to float a hydrometer in your jar. Record the original gravity for your records.

Open the yeast pack (with sanitized scissors if necessary) and pour ("pitch") the yeast into the waiting wort. Close up the fermenter and fill the airlock with vodka or sanitizer solution. Put the vessel somewhere cool (between 60°F and 70°F preferably) and wait. Within twenty-four hours the airlock should bubble, slowly at first and then like a machine gun. Congrats. Sit back with a brew and wait patiently.

To help keep your brew day organized and on track, make a copy of Appendix E—Extract Brewing Checklist.

Getting Bottled (Or, How Long Before I Can Drink It?)

In a cool corner, your first beer burbles away, taunting you with impending deliciousness. The anticipation of sweet nectar kills you. So just how long do you have to wait before the beer is finally yours to enjoy?

The answer is, it depends. Some projects can take years to complete. Fortunately, this chapter's recipes require approximately a week before they are done fermenting. Wait until the beer ceases bubbling before proceeding to bottle unless you want an exploding bottle rhythm section!

Bottles exploding? Don a pair of goggles and gloves and get to work. You can uncap the bottles and release some of the pressure. Alternatively, shuttle the bottles carefully to a fridge. The cold retards the yeast, preventing more carbonation. Drink quickly though!

Once the beer ceases fermenting, clean and sanitize the bottling bucket and siphoning gear. Pay close attention to any bottling wands or spouts. Failure to clean these can ruin all the hard work you've done. Wash out fifty bottles. Drop the bottles into the bucket full of sanitizer. After the appropriate soak, drain the bottles and cover with foil.

To a cup of water, add ¾ cup (4.4 ounce by weight) of priming (corn) sugar and bring to a boil for 10 to 15 minutes. Add to the bottling bucket and keep covered. Carefully siphon the beer out of the fermenter into the bucket. Siphon from above the yeast layer to keep the beer fairly clear. Let the beer swirl through the sugar syrup. Thorough mixing is the key to consistent carbonation from bottle to bottle.

Attach a hose and bottling wand to your bucket's spigot (or a siphon-ready racking cane—see page 91). Press the wand to the bottom of each bottle. When the beer reaches the top of the bottle, pull the wand out. The remaining space is perfect. Cover the bottle with a cap and move on. Once the bottles are filled, break out the capper and crimp the caps firmly to the bottle. Press multiple times, rotating the bottle each time, to ensure a solid seal. If you have a brew partner, they can cap while you fill.

Save yourself a lot of work before your next bottling day! After you pour a bottle into a glass, immediately rinse it out and let dry. This prevents hard, scrub-resistant deposits, and you can then sanitize your cleaned bottles. Cap dry, sanitized bottles firmly with foil and use in a day or two.

Set the bottles in a warmer spot (70°F) for two weeks, then place a bottle in the fridge to chill. When you the pop the cap you should hear a reassuring hiss of escaping CO_2. Decant the beer in one smooth pour to avoid adding the accumulated yeast in your glass. If you don't hear a pfft, check the remaining bottle temperatures. Wait another week and check again.

Your First Beer

Every brewer needs a recipe to start. The following are classic recipes perfect for the first-timer. The only thing you need to worry about is staying calm and focused. Take your time, relax, and learn each step.

A beer recipe is different than a food recipe. The recipe tells you the beer style and in brewer's terms how strong (OG, ABV), how dark (SRM), and how bitter (IBU) it is. Ingredients are separated by type. Grains, sugar, and extract provide the body and potential alcohol, while the hops and spices provide the aromatic and bitter kick to tame the sugar. Other ingredients include clarifying agents, yeast nutrients, and water salts for the boil pot. Often multiple yeast strains are listed; choose one or more to ferment. Appendix D's mash schedules and instructions cover the brewing and fermenting process.

Both recipes contain only extract, so you can concentrate on everything else. If you're feeling more adventurous, check Chapter 9 for more advanced extract recipes.

Dead Simple Hefeweizen

There's a reason this is "Dead Simple." The longest part of your brew day is boiling the beer. This is an ideal first beer since you can focus on preparing the equipment and process.

Style: German Wheat Beer (Hefeweizen)
Brew Type: Extract
For 5 gallons at 1.048 OG, 6.4 SRM, 12 IBUs, 4.7% ABV
60-minute boil

Directions

Follow the Steeping Grains and Extract Process starting with 6 quarts of water at Step 6 (page 283).

Extract
6.60 pounds Wheat (Weizen) Liquid Malt Extract (LME)

Hops
0.5 ounce Tettnanger (4.5 percent AA) Pellet for 60 minutes
0.5 ounce Czech Saaz (3.5 percent AA) Pellet for 5 minutes

Yeast
White Labs WLP830 Hefeweizen IV, Wyeast 3650 Bavarian Wheat

Plainweiser Pub Ale

To suppress the naturally fruity character of ale yeast, ferment this beer at cool temperatures—low to mid-60s—for the first couple of days of fermentation.

Style: Blonde Ale
Brew Type: Extract
For 5 gallons at 1.037 OG, 2.6 SRM, 8 IBUs 3.7% ABV
60-minute boil

Directions

Follow the Steeping Grains and Extract Process starting with 6 quarts of water at Step 6 (page 283).

Extract
5.0 pounds Pale Liquid Malt Extract (LME) (Pilsner preferred)

Hops
0.25 ounce Hallertauer Tradition (6.0 percent AA) Pellet for 60 minutes
0.25 ounce Czech Saaz (3.5 percent AA) Pellet for 5 minutes

Yeast
Wyeast 1007 German Ale

Malt, Extract, and Grains

Malted barley provides beer's soul and strength, backbone, and color. Each variety uniquely impacts beer's flavor and body. Explore the varieties and other options available to you.

3

Barley: The Staff of Beery Life

Barley (*Hordeum vulgare*) was one of the grains cultivated at humankind's first settlements. It's a hardy, drought-tolerant crop that grew alongside another core grain, Emmer wheat. Barley grasses are found almost globally.

Brewing barley grows in two major family varieties, two- and six-row. The rows are the lines of barley kernels gathered around the central stalk. Two-row has fat plump kernels with room to grow and is the norm in Europe. Six-row has more starch conversion power in smaller, tough kernels.

A kernel consists of a large protein starch matrix called the endosperm surrounded by a thin coat, the aleurane. At the base of the kernel is a rootlet. Surrounding the seed is a papery husk, useful to brewers as filtering material. All of these structures change when barley is readied for brewing.

FACT

Approximately one-quarter of all the barley grown in the United States meets maltsters' exacting standards. Livestock feed on more than half of the barley grown. The growing Chinese and Indian markets are putting strains on the available global supply. The resulting rapid price increase (20 to 30 percent over a year) currently squeezes a number of America's craft brewers.

What Is Malt?

Barley converts its starch into sugar, but its starch-converting powers need coaxing to appear. Their secret weapon? Potent enzymes tuned to break starch molecules into component sugars. Malting develops sufficient enzymes to convert more than just the barley's starch. Smart brewing cultures leveraged barley malt's ability to use other grains such as spelt, wheat, rye, and rice.

Malting as a controlled, studied process began with the Egyptians during early pharonic rule. Previously, brewers depended on the inherent enzymes in the barley or accidental malting. Today, a handful of maltsters handle breweries' needs. They examine a farmer's crop, seeking a careful balance of flavor, kernel plumpness, starch, and protein content. Too much protein and the beer will be hazy. Too little plumpness, the beer will taste steely and harsh.

Malt Making

Making malt requires a few steps, time, and manpower. Malting is the controlled sprouting of the barley embryo. The sprout, "acrospire," triggers the aleurane layer to release enzymes into the starchy endosperm, breaking apart the starch matrix and creating the amylase enzymes crucial to brewing. The plant is making the starchy food available for new growth. The maltster's goal is to stop the growth at the ideal level of enzyme production and starch availability. Allowing too little conversion creates "undermodified" malt, which requires extra brewing steps to use successfully. "Overmodified" malt results from lengthy sprouting that consumes too much starch. Today's malts are "fully modified." Here are the basic steps to malting:

1. **Soaking**—Barley is wetted continuously with freshly aerated water for forty to fifty hours to activate the enzymes and embryo.
2. **Germinating**—For the next five to fourteen days, the barley is laid in aerated beds and allowed to sprout and grow. The temperature is kept cool and the grain is turned regularly.
3. **Kilning**—Hot air is blown through the green malt to stop the germination and dry the grain. Temperature-controlled roasting alters the character of the final malt. Light-colored malts are kilned at a cooler temperature to prevent browning, while dark-roasted malts are blasted with heat to create blackened kernels.

FACT

Until the eighteenth-century development of indirect kilning, most malt was dried over wood fires. A smoky campfire aroma permeated the malt. Brewers in Bamberg, Germany, carry on the traditional flavors of smoked beers with their ham and bacon rauchbiers. The powerful "Aecht Schlenkerla" lineup includes smoked Weizen, Marzen, and Ur-bock.

You can make malt from most raw cereals, barley, wheat, corn, and oats. Some obsessed brewers even grow their own barley for truly homegrown beer.

Extract: A Beginning Brewer's Best Friend

New brewers use small amounts of malt—not nearly enough to make strong beer wort. Malt serves as an accent and top note to the brew. Maltsters make these first batches easy with their malt extracts.

Extracts start with mashing the malt to produce full-strength wort. Instead of producing beer, after a brief boil the wort is transferred to a series of vacuum boilers. Water's boiling point drops under a vacuum. The lower temperature for evaporation prevents the wort darkening and caramel formation you'd get boiling in a regular kettle.

To create Liquid Malt Extract (LME), a significant percentage of water is removed to create gooey caramel syrup that is canned or loaded into drums. Dry Malt Extract (DME) is a heavily concentrated (90 percent water removal) wort, sprayed as a fine mist into tall heated chambers. The extract dries to powder by the time it hits the floor thirty feet below.

Both types have advantages and disadvantages, and most brewers settle on what works for them. The recipes in this book are formulated around an extract base of LME. Fresh LME retains more malt character. However, stale LME can ruin a beer with metallic twangy flavors that won't disappear. If you're in doubt about the freshness of your LME, choose shelf stable DME. See Appendix C to convert between LME and DME.

When choosing extract, find a packaging or best-by date to avoid bad extract. Buy bulk LME from drums only if the shop flushes the drums with nitrogen or speeds through a drum in a few days. Avoid extracts with sugar added. If your extract choice comes with free yeast, throw it out, or throw it into the boil as free yeast nutrient.

Common Types of Extract

Maltsters use several terms to describe their extracts. Most reflect the color; some indicate the composition of the extract. This book's recipes specify varieties of extract that replicate the all-grain version of the beer.

Malt Extract Types (Ordered by Color)
- **Light/Pale/Xtra Pale**—Pale malt-based extracts that will serve as the primary workhorse in your extract brewery. Great base for a beer and for converting a recipe to all-grain and back.

- **Pilsner**—Pale extract based on pilsner malt, instead of pale ale malt.
- **Wheat/Weizen**—Replicates the wheat/barley ratio of wheat beers, which consist of 40 to 60 percent malted wheat combined with pale malt. Golden color with a bready sweetness.
- **Amber**—Extract with added crystal or toasted malts. Useful for building a stronger finishing sweetness with a bit of toastiness.
- **Munich**—Based on a mixture of pale and Munich malts. Produces reddish tinged beers with an intense, yet not sweet, malt character.
- **Dark**—Adding a dose of roasted malts to an amber extract yields a dark extract suitable for use in a porter or stout.

Hopped Versus Unhopped Extract

A choice facing a brewer is the use of hopped or unhopped extract kits. Extract manufacturers add hop bittering extract to their syrups for bite. Some cans use pellets for a fresher hop character. Hopped kits are perfect for the casual brewer living far from homebrew resources.

Read the labels closely to ensure a good shelf grab. Cans labeled with a style (e.g., "IPA" or "Stout"), are more often prehopped kits. Most hopped extracts originate from Britain and Australia, so pay extra attention when looking at those.

When calculating gravity for recipes, extracts are fairly consistent. LME is calculated as giving 37 points per pound per gallon (pppg), while DME is calculated using 46 points. Replace these generic numbers with specifics for your brands.

Choose unhopped extracts when you can. Formulating recipes around hopped extracts can lead to frustration when a manufacturer switches hops based on availability or adjusts the bittering.

Major Extract Brands by Country of Origin

Every extract brand affects the aroma and flavor of your beer differently, The primary factor in your extract decision is country of origin. Since manufacturers produce extract with local malts, consider an extract from the same region as your target style.

This list of major extract brands is ordered by country. For each country, possible ingredients are listed. Due to manufacturers' secrecy, the ingredients lists are speculation in them.

EXTRACTS

Country American

General Notes Made from North American two-row or six-row barley. Designed for fermentability since brewers no longer use large infusions of sugar.

Brand Alexander's Sun Country

Types Liquid

Notes Designed by the famous brewing scientist Dr. Michael Lewis of UC Davis. Good fermentability. Uses Klages-style two-row for a neutral clean taste.

Brand Briess

Types Dry/Liquid

Notes America's only vertically integrated maltser. Briess produces a variety of extracts blending two-row and six-row. Known for their "CBW Pilsen Light" extract, the lightest colored LME on the market. 80 percent fermentable. (Also packaged as "Northwestern" or "Stone")

Country Australian

General Notes Bastion of "Kit & Kilo" brewers, recently Australia's homebrewing community took off like a rocket. Their brewers are flaunting the "rules" of brewing and producing a good jug of beer. Extracts are from two-row varieties like Franklin, Harrington, Schooner, or Stirling.

Brand Coopers

Types Liquid

Notes Unlike other extract manufacturers, Coopers is an active brewery (Cooper's Sparkling Ale) and some of their kits replicate their commercial product.

Brand Morgan's

Types Liquid

Notes Developed for export from Australia to America, Morgan's is less commonly available than Coopers. Morgan's specifies the basic recipe for each of their extracts.

Country German

General Notes You can trust the Germans to ensure the quality their beer ingredients. Made from German pilsner malt, they bring a grassy, toasty, "Continental" graininess to your brews.

Brand Bierkeller

Types Liquid

Notes The most widely available German malt extract. Comes in several hues built on a base of lager and Munich malts.

Brand Ireks

Types Liquid

Notes A major malt manufacturer supplying bakers and brewers around the world. Sadly, their 100-percent wheat extract is lost to homebrewers.

Brand Weyermann

Types Liquid

Notes Major German maltster. When looking to make German styles, reach for Weyermann. Most of their syrups are decocted to replicate traditional German processes.

Country United Kingdom

General Notes British beers start with the classic malt base, like Maris Otter or Golden Promise. Their fresh-baked biscuit quality is not found in American malts. Check the ingredients for any sugar.

Brand BrewMart

Types Liquid

Notes A Scottish line of extract kits that focus on "lagers of the world."

Brand EDME
Types Dry/Liquid
Notes Founded in the 1880s, EDME (English Diastatic Malt Extract Company) is a sister company to maltser Crisp. The gem of the company lineup is the EDME Diastatic Malt Extract (DMS). Grains steeped with that extract will convert to sugar like they were mashed.

Brand John Bull
Types Liquid
Notes Ubiquitous brand of extract kits. Reportedly discontinued by EDME so be warned that this will be older extract and therefore stale.

Brand Iron Master
Types Liquid
Notes Scottish company focused on hopped extract kits for the casual brewer. Includes a kit for making an "American Light"

Brand Munton & Fison
Types Dry/Liquid
Notes Of the British extracts, M&F ferments the most completely. Widely available in both liquid and dry, the dry malt finishes lower than the liquid. The extra light reportedly uses sugar or other additives to ferment down.

Base Malts: Building a Beer Foundation

Base malt is the foundation for beer. It provides the majority of gravity and enzymes and the major flavor notes. Base malts include the pale, the pilsner, and some toasted malts.

KEY BASE MALTS			
Malt Name	**Origin**	**Gravity (pppg)**	**Description**
Two-Row Pale Malt	American	36	The standard American pale ale malt. Neutral base with great enzymatic power for tackling an additional 25 percent of malt. Lacks malt complexity.
Six-Row Pale Malt	American	35	Uniquely American and used by larger brewers. Its small kernels pack the larger enzymatic punch of any malt. The extra husk material aids lautering sticky additions of wheat, oats, or rye. Taste can be husky and rough depending on the maltster.
Maris Otter/ Golden Promise	British	38	Archetypical British malt (and its Scottish cousin). Kilned hotter than American malts, MO has a snappy toasted-biscuit flavor perfect for ales.
Mild Malt	British	36	More highly kilned variety of pale malt gives more body and malt flavor to smaller ales.
Munich	German	36	Toasted malt that many brewers treat as specialty malt. Used as a base malt, it gives a rich melanoidin-driven malt biscuit character.
Pale Ale	Belgian	36	A crisp, cracker-and-grass flavored malt found in Belgian pale ale and other styles
Pilsner/Lager	Various	36	Every variety of lager malt is pale and low in haze-causing proteins. Domestic versions carry very little flavor. European lager malts carry a distinct "Continental" grassy flavor.
Vienna	German	36	Similar to Munich malt. Lighter in color and effect than Munich, it comes across less malty and more toasted.

Think of base malt as the spaghetti in a bowl of marinara. All the attention is ladled on the sauce, but a bad pasta choice or poor cooking can ruin the whole meal. Like pasta, base malts have a definite character and effect on your final beer. Don't get distracted by the flashy specialty malts. Many world-class beers are built on base malt and little else.

Mash all base malts to convert their starch before moving on to the boil. Extract brewers, keep the steeping temperature in the low 150°Fs for an hour and the starch will convert.

When composing a grain bill, base malts comprise 40 to 100 percent of the grist. The lower end of the spectrum is dominated by wheat and rye beers since those grains contain just enough power to convert their own starch. Mostly the base malts must provide the conversion power for the remaining grist. Generally 75 to 80 percent of the grist is a combination of base malts.

Specialty Malts: Beer Accent

Specialty malts, the malt world's spices, bring color, aroma, and flavor to the kettle. To create these unique characters, a maltster varies the kilning heat and moisture. They produce specialties from chewy pale crystals to nearly carbonized black kernels.

Highly roasted malts retain little starch through the roasting phase. As the malt color (SRM/Lovibond) increases, the contribution to gravity drops.

To learn a malt variety's flavor, pop a few kernels in your mouth and chew. Hold the malt for a minute or two and taste the changing flavor. The amylase enzymes in your saliva perform the same magic mash conversion.

Exposed to new tools, it is tempting to throw in everything. You can ruin a meal by throwing in the spice cabinet and you can do it to your beer with too much specialty malt. Keep them down to 25 percent or less of the grist. Veteran brewers rethink their recipe designs when crystals rise over 1 pound for 5 gallons.

Crystal/Caramel Malts

After germinating, the grains are moistened in a drum roaster and held at 130°F to 150°F until the starches convert in the husk. Effectively, the maltster mashes the barley in the kernel. The sugary grain is then dried and roasted pale or dark. Crystal malts are named for their color contribution in Lovibond.

Chew on a grain of crystal malt. Notice how it's rock hard compared to pale malt? That's the sugar crystals locked inside the husk. When you crack it, the sugar dissolves into the beer. This is why crystals make great steeping fodder.

Brewers often refer to a specific crystal malt by the abbreviation "C [Malt Color]." For example: Crystal 60L is shortened to "C60."

The Belgians and Germans name their crystal malts differently. While you'll still hear brewers talk about German C60, it helps to know that is CaraMunich III. The common German names start with "Cara" like Cara-Hell, CaraMunich, CaraFoam, or CaraRed. Belgian maltsters are a bit more straightforward, but common ones are Caramel Pils (C8) and Special B (C220).

As the grains darken, two effects happen: the amount of sugar decreases and the flavor transforms. The light crystals offer extra sweetness, but not much else. Climbing the color ladder yields stronger caramel flavor and eventually strong roasted nut and coffee flavor. This culminates in the darkest and most intense crystal malt, Special B. Used sparingly, the malt wraps roasted flavors in a cocoon of plums and raisins, great in darker beers with depth. It is very easy to overdo it, so be sparing.

Roasted Malts

Before the 1817 invention of the direct-fired drum roaster, slightly charred brown malt was the darkest unburned malt. Brewers wanting darker beers turned to questionable additives including burnt grain husks. The roaster brought the first dark roasted but unburned malt: black patent malt.

Very black beers were now possible for low cost. With pale malt's adoption, brown malt quickly fell out of favor. Very few producers make a true brown malt.

Black patent may have the first roasted malt, but others have appeared, each emphasizing different flavors. The intense heat of the roasting process renders much of the starch unusable for fermentation, but that's fine since you want their flavor and color.

Other Roasted Malts

- **Chocolate Malt**—Chocolate malt provides less color than black patent, but it also provides less of black patent's tongue-clucking acrid flavor. Gives subtle chocolate and coffee tones to the brew.
- **Carafa**—A German chocolate malt variety in several strengths denoted as I, II, or III. Smoother than the other chocolate malts are the "special" dehusked variants. Removing the blackened husk takes away the acrid roast character leaving a powerful dark toffee and chocolate–flavored malt.
- **Kiln Coffee**—A product of one maltster, Franco-Belges, Kiln Coffee isn't super dark, but it carries a potent espresso flavor that can sex up dark beers, especially porters and stouts.
- **Roasted Unmalted Barley**—A stout cornerstone, roasted barley uses raw, unmalted barley to provide a foam-positive and body-boosting protein and massive color.

American use of raw rice and corn is responsible for the development of the American cereal mash process. For a description of this technique, see the recipe for Dougweiser on page 241.

Other Malts

A mishmash of different malts remains to be explored. When you encounter new grains, chew on them and read about their traditional use. These malts generally need mashing or steeping with base malt:

- **Acid malt**—"Sauer malt" is a crafty German way of circumventing the Reinheitsgebot. Acidifying brew water increases efficiency of a system. Brewers acidify their water with small additions of food-grade acid. The Germans can't, so they soak malt long enough to activate natural barley lactobacillus, producing natural lactic acid that dries on the malt. Small additions of this malt can acidify the mash or add a light sour tang to the brew.
- **Aromatic malt**—This pale malt is a different take on Munich malt similar to Melanoidin that in small quantities—less than 10 percent of your grain bill—can provide powerful malt aromas and flavors to your brew.
- **Biscuit**—A pale malt that should be used sparingly due to its potency, biscuit adds fresh-baked bread or cracker character to your beer.
- **Carapils Dextrin Malt**—Found in numerous homebrew recipes, carapils gives beer a boost of long-chain dextrin sugars. These unfermentable sugars remain, adding a sense of fullness and body. Handy for extract brewers needing a little boost. Most varieties, with the exception of Briess, can be steeped.
- **Honey Malt/Brumalt**—Produced by manipulating oxygen levels during the malting process, honey or brumalt gives distinct honey flavor and sweetness. Provides a boost in apparent body. Due to its intensity, it's recommended for 15 percent or less of your total grain bill.
- **Melanoidin**—Supercharged Munich malt that produces a red color and intense maltiness. Used to replace some of the flavors attributed to decoction mashing.
- **Victory**—An American malt variety similar to biscuit and aromatic, victory gives maltiness and dry toasted bread qualities to your brew.

Other Brewing Giants

Even today, barley isn't the only cereal invited to the beer party. Major American brewers famously use rice and corn. Steeping these grains leeches extra starch into your brew, perfect for bacteria. They must be mashed with barley to convert the starch. Don't use these in anything less than a partial mash.

ALERT!

Because many of these grains lack a hull or husk by the time they reach brewers, they can gum up the works for all-grain brewers. The worst offenders include rye and oats. To combat this and keep your lauter flowing, invest in a pound of rice hulls. The cheap addition adds no sugar or character, but can ensure an easy sparge.

Many grains need to have their starches "gelatinized" before a brewer can access them. This means they need to be precooked. This is not a concern for any grain that's been malted or flaked. Flaked grains are steamed and pressed between heavy steel rollers. Other grains need to be boiled first before adding to the mash. Here are some of the common grains that can be used in beer:

- **Corn**—Corn found its way into beer in an attempt to reduce the harsh hazy tannic qualities of American six-row. Leaves a faint, sweet corny flavor and aroma to the brew.
- **Oats**—A very popular adjunct, particularly with darker ales, oats add unctuousness to beer. You will find a number of extract-steeping recipes with flaked oats. Provide plenty of time and base malt, but be careful of infection. Steeping oat malt provides much of the same character without the starch worries.
- **Rice**—Rice is a plentiful, low-protein, low–water content, high-starch grain that serves as a staple worldwide. When used in brewing, it leaves a crisp finish due to the almost completely fermentable sugars.
- **Rye**—Spicy and intense, rye in all of its guises has almost completely disappeared from the brewing world. Worts heavy in rye (20-plus percent) feel slick and viscous, almost oily. The Germans produce

a rye dunkelweizen called Roggenbier. In America, breweries produce hoppy rye pale ales, IPAs, or even DIPAs.

- **Wheat**—The most popular alternative grain for homebrewers. Lends a sweetness and breadlike quality to the brew. The protein levels in the beer help produce better foam, so small additions of wheat can be found in a number of nonwheat-style ales.

Other Grain Extracts/Syrups

- **Corn Syrup**—Corn syrup is a readymade sterile sweetener for meads, ciders, and fruit wines.
- **Rice Solids**—Unlike wheat solids, rice solids contain no barley, only rice sugar. Useful for replicating American or Asian lagers.
- **Sorghum Extract**—Due to the rising numbers of celiac sufferers, this gluten-free grain is being explored as an alternative beer base. Both red and white extracts are available for experimentation.

Walls Scottish 80

The Walls family is an Orkney Island offshoot of the Wallace (as in William) clan. This recipe was brewed in honor of the family's heritage and tries to capture the simple beauty of malty Scottish ales.

Style: Scottish Ale
Brew Type: All grain
For 5.5 gallons at 1.042, 11.9 SRM, 22.0 IBUs, 4.0 percent ABV
60-minute boil

Directions

Follow the Multistep Brew Process (pages 284-285).

Malt/Grain/Sugar
6.50 pounds Maris Otter Malt/Golden Promise Malt
1.25 pounds Crystal 55L
0.40 pound Cane Sugar
0.25 pound Torrified Wheat
0.05 pound Carafa

Extract (for 5.50 pounds of Marris Otter Malt/Golden Promise Malt)
4.00 pounds Pale Liquid Malt Extract (LME)

Hops
0.40 ounce Wye Target (10.6 percent AA) Pellet for 60 minutes
0.50 ounce Fuggle (5.1 percent AA) Pellet for 15 minutes

Other Ingredients
1 tablet Whirlfloc
1 tablespoon Yeast Nutrient

Yeast
WLP028 Edinburgh Ale

Mash Schedule
Saccharification Rest 154°F 60 minutes

CHAPTER 4

Hops: Putting the Bitter In

"Eww! Bitter Beer Face!": The punch line to beer commercials you may remember. But what causes bitter beer face? Why is some beer bitter? And is that always a bad thing? The short answer is no, because there's more to hops than a bitter bite.

What Are Hops?

Hops, loved in the world of brewing, are the flowering cone of a vine (*Humulus lupulus*). Bright green with sticky flecks of yellow, they resemble a soft baby pine cone. Crush and rub them between your hands to get blasted by pungent perfume.

The term *lupulus* (meaning "wolf") was first applied to hops by the famous Roman admiral and naturalist Pliny the Elder. He observed that wild hops grew among the trees and forests like a wolf hiding. At the modern hop yard, hops grow on long vertical poles and run 6 to 50 feet long.

The sticky yellow flecks found under the bracts of a mature cone are the lupulin glands, source of the oils brewers covet. For centuries, herbalists used lupulin to cure or ease delirium tremens and anxiety, and as soporific to cure insomnia.

Hops' central role is a relatively new one. From the time of the Sumerians until the thirteenth century, beer was brewed with spices including hops. Slowly hops gained a foothold as a primary beer flavoring. The rise of Protestantism helped drive the adoption of hops. Since the Catholic Church controlled most of the secret spice blends, Protestant brewers adopted hops to break free of the onerous fees charged for the gruit herbs.

Toxic effects of different herbs used by brewers helped push hops. Some common herbs, such as heather, carried psychoactive and hallucinogenic properties. If you plan on doing old-fashioned spiced ales, make sure your spices are safe.

These days, thanks to modern agriscience, hops grow globally. Traditional centers lead the way, if not in acreage, then in the properties bred into hops. The top producers include the Hallertau Valley of Germany, with concentrated production of noble aroma hops and the Yakima and Willamette Valleys of Washington and Oregon.

Why Are Hops Used?

Brewers covet the magical properties of the hop and in particular their mix of acids and oils. The powdery lupulin consists largely of complex molecule chains called "humulones," collectively named "alpha acids." In addition there are aromatic essential oils.

Beer's bitter bite is derived from these acids, but there's a challenge. Alpha acids won't dissolve in water. With the application of heat the molecules isomerize (rotate) into isohumulone. Basically, a chunk of the molecule flips around, allowing it to bind with water. Wort's roiling boil dissolves the acids by inefficiently extracting a maximum of 30 percent of the available humulones even after 120 minutes of churning.

QUESTION?

Why does beer get that skunky aroma?
A reaction between ultraviolet light and isohumulone is responsible. Light causes the isohumulone molecule to decompose into 3-methylbut-2-ene-1-thiol, primary component in skunk's infamous "spray." The effect is more noticeable in beers bottled in clear or glass bottles that block less UV. One major American brewer uses stabilized isohumulone extracts, preventing skunking in their clear bottle beers.

Malt and sugar's strong, sweet flavors explain the need for a bite. Even after an efficient fermentation, there are residual sugars left. Great for richness and body, the resulting beer tastes toothachingly, sickeningly sweet. The bitterness cuts the remaining sweetness, increasing a beer's drinkability.

Experiment by mixing extract and water, boiling briefly, and transfering to a jug to ferment. After a week's time, take the beer, measure the final gravity, and taste. Notice how the beer lacks zippiness or punch?

In addition to the bitterness, hop oils contribute aroma: pine, woody resin, flowers, grassiness, spices, citrus, cattiness, and more. The variety and amount of oils diverge widely, based on hop type and location grown, which is important to remember when shopping for hops. Using Argentinean Cascades in place of American Cascades yields disappointing results, as the Argentinean crop is herbal and spicy, lacking the citrus character of American Cascade.

Before there was microbiology, brewers knew that beer soured quickly. The beers with hops lasted longer and stayed pure. Hops have a secret property, a limited antibacterial effect that is particularly effective against lactobacillus, beer's biggest natural predator. This is also why you don't have to worry about sanitizing hops when dry hopping. Hopped beer pours clearer because hop tannins bind with haze-causing proteins.

Putting the Bite in Your Beer

When and how you toss the hops into your boil kettle matters. Add them early and you get a blast of bitterness. Add them later and you perfume the brew. How do you know just when to add them and how your beer will turn out? The longer the hops are boiled, the more alpha acid converts to isohumulone. The additional bitterness comes at a cost; the boiling action drives off or destroys the delicate oils that create the aroma and flavor. Hop additions named "bittering," "flavor," or "aroma" describe the goal of the addition, but even "bittering" hops add flavor.

The basic hopping rules of thumb: Boiling hops thirty to ninety minutes adds bitterness. The fifteen-to-thirty minute mark promotes hop flavors. You can capture aroma by adding hops between zero to fifteen minutes.

ALERT!

Don't boil hops more than ninety minutes. The hops break down creating strong vegetal favors. If you need more bitterness, add more or stronger hops.

Other Hop Uses

There are more places to hop than the boil, each with different end effects. Each is designed to boost hop presence without boosting bitterness. In order of addition:

- **Mash Hopping**—Brewers can toss a couple of ounces of hops into the mash bed. The actual effect is subtle and may not be worth the extra cost.

- **First Wort Hopping**—An old German technique revived by home-brewers. It involves taking flavor additions (twenty minutes) and putting them in the kettle during mash runoff. The resulting flavor and bitterness rates favorably in blind tasting panels.
- **Dry Hopping**—Widely used to boost hop aroma, dry hopping involves adding fresh hops during secondary fermentation. Over several weeks, fresh hop aroma suffuses through the beer. Dry hopping imparts no additional bitterness.

Hop Packaging

There are different hop packages that you need to sort out. Each has advantages and disadvantages:

- **Whole flower**—The cones are picked straight from the vine and dried in a hop roast to prevent rot. Many swear by them, but they can oxidize quickly even in vacuum-packed bags and bitter less per ounce than pellets.
- **Pellet**—Most brewers use pelletized hops. Dried whole hops are passed through a hammer mill that crushes the flower and lupulin glands into powder. They are pressed together into tight pellets. They store better than whole hops and bitter more efficiently. Purists contend the aroma is inferior to whole hops. This book's recipes are formulated for pellets.
- **Plug**—A medium between whole flower and pellets, plugs are lightly crushed and compacted into half-ounce tablets. Developed for the British cask beer industry for easy dry hopping.
- **Extract**—The "better living through chemistry" solution of hop oils. Brewers choose a bittering or aroma extract, measure, and add. Before you dismiss the notion completely, several top-flight, award-winning microbreweries use bittering extract to reduce wort loss to hops.

Calculating Bitterness

When brewers talk about beer bitterness they talk about "IBUs" or international bittering units. This measure corresponds to bitter compound levels in the beer. The higher the number, the more bitter.

Alpha Acid Units/Homebrew Bitterness Unit

Alpha acid levels change between crop years. When you find a recipe, you must adjust for your hops' different AA levels. Calculating IBUs on the fly is a math headache. To save brain cells, homebrewers devised the "alpha acid units" (AAU) or "homebrew bitterness unit" to scale hop additions of varying strengths. It does not calculate actual bitterness, just potential bitterness.

To find the AAU of an addition, multiply the weight by the AA percent.

AAU = Weight (hops) × AA percent (recipe)

To scale to your current hops, divide the AAU by the new AA percent.

Weight (needed) = AAU / AA percent (hops on hand)

For example: Your recipe uses a half ounce of 8.1 percent AA Cascade. You can buy them at 5.4 percent AA.

AAU = 0.5 × 8.1 = 4.05 AAU

You'll need:

Weight (needed) = 4.05 / 5.4 = 0.75 ounces

With these calculations in hand, you can quickly adjust.

FACT

Unless you have access to a spectrophotometer, your actual IBU levels remain a mystery. Small breweries often don't know the true IBU content of their beers. If you have access to a spectrophotometer, look to either the ASBC's methods by Rigby and Bethune or Moltke and Meilgaard.

Calculating IBUs

Several formulas exist for IBU calculation, with different results. For brewers, calculating consistently with the same formula means more than the number. That way you know how 60 IBUs tastes for your system and calculations.

The Tinseth method of calculating IBUs starts with the AAU and a table of hop utilization. The utilization figure estimates how much bitterness you extract. The percentage decreases for whole hops and as the beer gets stronger and as the hops are boiled less. Higher gravities impede the isomerization process, so heartier beers need heartier doses of hops.

$$IBU\ (addition) = (AAU \times Utilization\ percent \times 7490) / Volume\ (beer)$$

Utilization factors can be found in Table C-1 in Appendix C. A constant to scale AAUs calculated by ounce weight is 7490.

Double Trouble Double IPA

This DIPA contains a lot of malt and low cohumulone hops to soothe your bitten tongue. The numerous hop additions and techniques spread hop flavor through the whole beer experience. The small dose of Chinook adds a raspy bitter edge that enhances the beer. Use a healthy yeast starter to ferment this bigger beer.

Style: Double IPA
Brew Type: All Grain
For 5.5 gallons at 1.087, 10 SRM, 99.9 IBUs, 9.3 percent ABV
90-minute boil

Directions

1   Follow the Single-Infusion Brew Process (page 284).

2   Add the dry hops in secondary and age for at least 2 weeks.

TIP

If you keg your beer, you can add a second dose of dry hops in the keg to provide an even fresher hop aroma. To get truly insane fresh hop aroma, build yourself a "draft hopback." Look online to learn how to build your own.

Malt/Grain/Sugar
7.50 pounds Domestic Two-Row Pale Malt
7.50 pounds Maris Otter Pale Malt
0.75 pound Crystal 55L
0.75 pound Munich Malt
0.50 pound Wheat Malt
0.25 pound Biscuit Malt

Extract (for 15.0 pounds of Pale Malt)
11.00 pounds Pale Liquid Malt Extract (LME)

Hops
2.00 ounces Cascade (8.1 percent AA) Whole—Mash Hops
0.50 ounce Cascade (8.1 percent AA) Whole—First Wort Hopped
0.50 ounce Simcoe (13.7 percent AA) Pellet—First Wort Hopped
0.75 ounce Centennial (9.1 percent AA) Pellet for 60 minutes
0.25 ounce Chinook (10.8 percent AA) Pellet for 45 minutes
1.00 ounce Crystal (4.0 percent AA) Pellet for 30 minutes
0.50 ounce Cascade (8.1 percent AA) Whole for 30 minutes
0.50 ounce Warrior (15.6 percent AA) Pellet for 15 minutes
0.50 ounce Amarillo (8.9 percent AA) Pellet for 5 minutes
0.50 ounce Simcoe (13.7 percent AA) Pellet for 0 minutes
1.50 ounces Cascade (8.1 percent AA) Whole for 0 minutes
1.50 ounces Cascade (8.1 percent AA) Whole—Dry-Hopped

Other Ingredients
1 tablet Whirlfloc
1 tablespoon Yeast Nutrient

Yeast
Wyeast 1056 Chico Ale/WLP001 California Ale/US-05

Mash Schedule
Saccharification Rest 152°F 60 minutes

Not All Bitterness Is the Same

An IBU is an IBU, right? Not quite. As it turns out, different alpha acids impact flavor uniquely. Using Amarillo hops creates a pleasant grapefruit taste. Brew with Chinook instead and the beer tastes harsh, catty, and raspy. This effect is due to the essential oils as well as the alpha acids.

- **Humulone**—The primary alpha acid found in hops. The bitterness from humulone is smoother and softer.
- **Cohumulone**—In descriptions, direct measurement of cohumulone is sometimes given. Both supported and disproved by blind testing, brewers believe that cohumulone-derived bitterness is harsh and raspy. Newly developed hop varieties are often marketed as "low cohumulone."
- **Adhumulone**—Found in small amounts in hops. Its impact is unclear.

Some of the low "coho" hops seem to lack the hop "punch" that makes bitterness noticeable. The need to push the bitterness envelope sometimes requires a boost. Adding small amounts of a high-cohumulone hop like Chinook provides that beer-popping backbite.

Hop Aroma and Flavor

Essential oils are volatile hydrocarbons easily vaporized by boiling. Found in small fractions in hops, very little stays in the beer, but those tiny amounts make huge impacts.

Major Flavor Sensations
- **Citrus**—Ranging from lightly orange to massive, face-slapping grapefruit character, they appear in a number of American ales.
- **Floral, Grassy, Herbal**—Associated with the classic British hops, these milder tones can be overshadowed by other potent aromas.

- **Noble "Spicy"**—Hop growers throw the term "noble" around. Technically the term refers to a set of German and Czech hops, Hallertau, Tettnanger, Spalt, and Saaz. The noble hop character is spicy with additional complexity from oxidized oils and beta acids
- **Piney**—Common in American-style beers. While the Europeans heavily use the British/German/American Northern Brewer hop, it is more woody than piney.

Essential Oil Groups
- **Cadinene, Citral, Limonene, Myrcene**—Citrus notes, often found in well-known American hop cultivars such as Cascade or Centennial.
- **Caryohyllene, Humulene**—These provide the spicy herbal charge for many German and European beers. Noble hop cultivars mostly contain humulene. Both oxidize easily, contributing to the "noble" profile.
- **Nerolidol, Pinene, Terpineol**—Woody, piney, and resinous, found in hops like Chinook and Northern Brewer.

Choosing Winning Hops

There are dozens of varieties from several countries, all with different flavors. How do you pick the right hops for your beer? Why, follow these simple rules:

- Think about the flavors and aromas that you want and choose hops that express those characters.
- Some styles have characteristic hops, like California Common and Northern Brewer or American Pale Ales and Cascade.
- For a cleaner beer with fewer vegetal flavors, use the minimum amount of hops necessary. Choose a low-cohumulone, high-alpha hop to provide most of the bittering.
- Remember the rule of origin and pick hops that are regionally accurate when attempting a style.

What to Look for in a Hop

Ignore variety for the moment. If all hops were the same, how should you avoid bad hops? When hops go south, they impart an oxidized, stale, cheesy aroma through the brew. Focus on the freshest hops when choosing. They retain better flavor and aroma. Less of the acids and oils have degraded, meaning a better bittering character.

To preserve freshness, keep hops in the coldest section of your freezer. If you can, put packages in a zipper bag with ice. This stalls oxidation and slows the degradation of alpha acids.

Pick hops stored cold and dark. Small amounts vacuum-packed in barrier bags are ideal. Bulk hops should be stored in oxygen-barrier canisters. Seal them immediately after weighing.

Check hop color before picking. Bright or dark green with flecks of yellow are preferred. Avoid hops with large blotches of brown or sickly yellow bracts. Give the hops a sniff, and throw them back at the slightest whiff of cheese.

Hop Varieties

Here is a list of some major hop varieties organized by country. Each variety includes basic profiles. If a hop is listed as an aroma hop, you can still bitter with them. Bittering hops can also be used for aroma and flavor. The designations have more to do with general perception of a hop's strengths. Since the hop market constantly changes, it pays to check out the hop dealer websites for the new information.

When hops go bad, don't throw them away. Sour Belgian lambics use old oxidized hops for their antibacterial purposes. If you get a hankering to brew a lambic, ask your local shop, odds are good that they'll have old hops stored to give away for precisely this purpose.

American brewers don't see as much variation in foreign hops due to importers waiting until a hop is well established before pushing it to the domestic market.

AMERICAN HOPS

Name	Type	AA percent	Description
Ahtanum	Aroma	5.7–6.3 percent	A citrusy hop with pine tones. Similar to Cascade.
Amarillo	All	8–11 percent	A recent well-received addition to the hop scene. Screaming grapefruit aroma and flavor with clean, low-cohumulone bitterness
Brewer's Gold	Bitter	8–10 percent	Old-school American bittering hop with a rough attitude.
Cascade	Aroma	4.5–8 percent	The classic American hop. To American beer drinkers it smells of piney oranges. Foreign brewers complain of catty tones.
Centennial	All	8–11 percent	A workhorse of the craft-brew scene. The profile can be summed up by its nickname "Super Cascade."
Chinook	Bitter	10–14 percent	The spicy, piney, catty hop that defines raspy bitterness.
Cluster	Bitter/Flavor	5.5–8.5 percent	Once the preeminent American hop, this has fallen into serious decline. Flavor of blackberries mixed with some cattiness.
Columbus/Tomahawk/Zeus	All	14–16 percent	A newer American high–alpha acid hop with multiple names. Herbal and slighty piney with a clean bright bitterness.
Crystal	Flavor/Aroma	3.5–5.5 percent	An American Hallertau hop with the spicy aromas that suit it for Continental beers.
Galena	Bittering	12–14 percent	One of the first true high–alpha acid hops. Used by a number of older microbreweries to provide the initial bittering charge.
Glacier	All	5–7 percent	Released in 2000, this new hop has an herbal and citrus edge to its low-cohumulone bittering charge.
Horizon	All	11–13 percent	A floral and spicy hop that gives clean bitterness.
Liberty	Aroma	3–5.5 percent	A new American herbal, spicy "noble" hop based on the legendary Hallertau hops.
Magnum	Bittering	12–14 percent	A popular German hop that's growing in popularity in America. Very little aroma character, but it gives impressive and smooth bitterness.
Mount Hood	Aroma	5–8.5 percent	A Hallertau derivative with some of the noble spicy character with a pungent resiny backbone.
Northern Brewer	All	7–10 percent	An old stalwart hop of the American brewing scene. Best known for an intense woody and peppermint aroma.
Nugget	Bittering	10–14 percent	Used by many brewers for its bittering potential. Can have a bit of a carry bite.
Perle	All	7–9 percent	Clean, spicy hop that carries some of the noble characters from its German heritage.
Simcoe	All	12–15 percent	New hop with strong grapefruit and sandalwood aromas
Summit	All	17.5–19.5 percent	A proprietary "dwarf" variety hop released in 2003. Amazingly high alpha acid leads to low kettle loads for bittering. Aroma and flavor impacts are still being defined, but aroma characters include orange, grapefruit, and green garlic.
Sterling	Aroma	4–9 percent	An American "Super Saaz" hop, spicy and herbal.
Ultra	Aroma	3.5–5.5 percent	A Hallertaur derivative that has noble spicy notes. Considered to be a very clean version of the German hop character.

AMERICAN HOPS—*continued*

Name	Type	AA percent	Description
Vangard	Aroma	5.5–6 percent	A squeaky clean new Hallertaur-style hop.
Warrior	All	14.5–18.5 percent	New proprietary super-high-alpha hop with very clean and soft bittering even at high IBU levels.
Willamette	Aroma	4–6.5 percent	An American Fuggle derivative, widely grown for use by all American brewers.

BRITISH HOPS

Name	Type	AA percent	Description
Admiral	Bittering	13–15 percent	A new bittering hop with high–alpha acid potential.
Challenger	All	5.5–8.5 percent	Dual-purpose hop. Clean bittering with grassy herbal tones.
East Kent Goldings	Aroma	3.5–6 percent	One of the true classic English ale hops. Mild, floral aroma.
Fuggle	Aroma	3.5–5.5 percent	The other classic English hop. Mild, grassy, and herbal.
Progress	Aroma	5–7 percent	Aroma hop bred to replace Fuggle. Fuggle-like characters with extra alpha acid for bitterness.
Soverign	Aroma	4–5 percent	New aroma hop with fruity and soft peach aromas.
Target	Bittering	9–13 percent	Herbal aroma, intense, mostly used for bittering to conserve kettle losses.

EASTERN EUROPEAN HOPS

Name	Type	AA percent	Description
Lublin (Polish)	Aroma	3–5 percent	A low-alpha, spicy hop used primarily in pilsner-style lagers.
Saaz (Czech)	Aroma	3.5–5 percent	The classic hop of Zatec (Saaz in German), provides the herbal and minty bite of Bohemian pilsner.
Styrian Goldings (Slovenia)	Aroma	4.5–6 percent	A genetic cousin of Fuggles. Mild and delicate. Used in a number of Belgian Brewers.

GERMAN HOPS

Name	Type	AA percent	Description
Hallertauer Mittelfruh	Aroma	3.5–5.5 percent	The classic German noble hop, harder to find now as other hops supplant it.
Hallertauer Select	Aroma	4–6 percent	A disease-resistant replacement for Mittelfruh and Spalt.
Hallertauer	Tradition Aroma	5–7 percent	A disease-resistant replacement for Hersbrucker.
Herbrucker	Aroma	3–5 percent	Mild aroma, not as pronounced as the other noble varieties.
Magnum	Bittering	12–14 percent	Germany's biggest high–alpha acid hop. Very clean bitterness, neutral aroma.
Northern Brewer	All	7–10 percent	Dual-purpose hop with a woody aroma.

GERMAN HOPS—*continued*			
Name	Type	AA percent	Description
Perle	All	6–8 percent	A higher–alpha acid noblish hop variety with better bittering characteristics and acceptable aroma.
Spalt	Aroma	4–5 percent	A traditional, very mild noble hop. Very limited production, but in use by even some major American breweries.
Tettnang	Aroma	3.5–5.5 percent	Noble German variety grown in the Tettnanger region. Very spicy profile makes it stand out.

NEW ZEALAND AND AUSTRALIAN HOPS			
Name	Type	AA percent	Description
Nelson Sauvin	All	12–14.5 percent	New variety released in 2000 carries an unusual fruity grape character similar to Sauvingon Blanc.
Pacific Gem (Organic)	Bittering	14–16 percent	Many of the New Zealand hops imported to the United States are organic. Pacific Gem has a woody flavor.
Pride of Ringwood (Australian)	Bittering	7–10 percent	The hop that Foster's built. Found across much of the Australian brewing industry to provide bitterness. Aroma character is herbal and "interesting."

Hoppy Test Brewing

The best way to discover hops' characteristics is to brew with them. Use a recipe with a medium malt profile and neutral yeast and brew the living daylights out of it. Target what you want to learn: aroma, flavor, or bittering. Adjust your additions accordingly. The Monocle Single-Hop Extra Pale Ale recipe on page 45 explores all hop aspects. If you don't want 5 gallons with the same hop, split your wort into multiple kettles and hop each one differently. Ferment in gallon jugs and treat them like any other beer.

Monocle Single-Hop Extra Pale Ale

Extra Pale Ale is an emerging West Coast style. All the hop blast of an IPA wrapped up in a more imbiber-friendly package. Monocle consists of a barebones malt scaffold to hang hops from. If you're going all-grain, substitute about 8.5 pounds of American Two-Row malt and mash at 152°F.

Style: Extra Pale Ale
Brew Type: Extract with Steeped Grains
For 5.0 gallons at 1.047 OG, 4 SRM, 49 IBUs, 4.7 percent ABV
60-minute boil

Directions

1. Follow the Steeping Grains and Extract Process (page 283).

2. Fermentation should take less than a week. If the yeast is dropping clear, skip the secondary on the beer and package right away.

TIP

Substitute hops of your choice to get a feel for them. Remember to keep the bitterness about the same. If you're not calculating IBUs, use the AAU rule of thumb to adjust the sixty-minute bittering charge. (1.5 ounces × 5.5 = 8.25 AAU.)

Malt/Grain/Sugar
0.50 pound Belgian Crystal 8L (Caramel Pilsner)

Extract
6.0 pounds Pale Liquid Malt Extract (LME)

Hops
1.5 ounces Cascade (5.5 percent AA) Pellet for 60 minutes
1.0 ounce Cascade (5.5 percent AA) Pellet for 20 minutes
1.0 ounce Cascade (5.5 percent AA) Pellet for 0 minutes

Other Ingredients
1 tablet Whirlfloc (or 1 teaspoon Irish Moss) Added at 20 minutes

Yeast
Wyeast 1056 / White Labs WLP001 / Fermintis US-05

CHAPTER 5

Water: Ninety-Five Percent of Your Beer

Water, water everywhere and—comprising 95 percent of a beer—oh so important to your drink. Water's composition profoundly affects the final flavor of your beer. Understanding how water interacts with ingredients and a drinker's palate can unlock truly great homemade beer.

Why Water Is Important

For most of brewing history, water has been ignored. It was wet, it dissolved the beery goodness from barley, and it quenched thirst. Any understanding was intuitive. Bad-tasting water made bad tasting beer. Too much iron, your beer tasted bloody. A crisp, pale lager in one town produced an insipid beer in another town. Dublin, London, and Munich's carbonate-rich water made perfect dark beers where Burton Upon Trent's sulfate-laden water provided extra hop punch to Pale Ales.

The impact of your water depends on its source and the conditions it traveled through to get to you. The combination of water source, time of year, and the state of your plumbing affects what you brew best.

What You Must Absolutely Know about Water

The flat out, most basic rule of brewing water: If you won't drink the water, you won't drink the beer. If your water is deplorable, invest in a reverse osmosis system to strip it or buy water from a reliable source. The later sections teach how elements in brewing water affect flavor. Hoppy or dark beer lovers, learn how to use gypsum and calcium chloride to improve those beers.

With decent tap water, your main concern is chlorine. Even if you can't taste or smell it, all municipal water is disinfected, and you must eliminate the disinfectant before introducing the malt.

Using Tap Water: Getting Rid of the Chlorine

Sanitation prevents dangerous bacteria, mold, and fungus from the faucet. Before water reaches your home, the local water supplier doses it with numerous chemicals, including chlorine. While the odor and the taste are objectionable, a small amount stops drinking water from killing you. Today, most city systems have moved away from unstable chlorine to the stable and odorless chloramine.

Disinfected water can't be used for brewing without a little magic. Malt contains aromatic compounds called phenols. Normally, they form pleasant aromas associated with beer. Combined with chlorine, they become potent, medicinal-smelling chlorophenols. New brewers often forget the chlorine problem, while veterans can easily smell and diagnose the cause.

Chlorine is a snap to remove. It wants out and back to a gaseous state. That's why you can smell it so readily. To dechlorinate your water, either let it sit overnight or boil and cool.

Chloramine proves trickier. Since it's naturally liquid, it won't outgas and it survives boiling. You have several options. Activated carbon water filters are a common solution. Designed for light home usage, filter pitchers and add-on water faucets are not practical. Use an undersink or whole-house model to supply your water. Add hose barbs to the input and output and attach it to an RV water hose for outdoor usage. You must run slowly—under a half-gallon per minute—to ensure removal. Since the first stages are carbon, reverse osmosis systems work well.

Sodium or potassium metabisulfite, wine sanitizers, effectively tackle chloramine. Shops carry either powdered meta or the tablet form, campden. To drive off the chloramine, use one-quarter teaspoon of powder or one crushed tablet to clear twenty gallons of water. Stir and dissolve the powder into your water and wait five to ten minutes for the chloramine to react.

ALERT!

If you're worried about your success, buy chlorine/chloramine test strips from your local pet or fish store to verify removal.

Buying Your Water

If you have truly awful water that no amount of filtration will fix, you can always buy seven or eight gallons of dechlorinated water. You want that extra water on hand to deal with evaporation, absorption, and accidents.

Skip over the mineral waters and the distilled water except when brewing pilsners. Distilled water contains virtually no minerals. Minerals are needed to accomplish or encourage some brewing reactions. If you use these options, read ahead for advice on adding minerals to the blank slate.

Water machines outside the corner store provide a cheaper option. You can choose your filtration types. Using a machine means trusting it's been well maintained. Buy your water from a dedicated water store instead.

Basic Water Chemistry

You know H_2O? Basic water class dismissed. Unfortunately, water is never just water. Dissolved solids including chalk, calcium, salt, and others alter water's basic chemical properties.

Hardness and Alkalinity

Years of soap commercials have promoted the term "hard water." Water hardness measures dissolved calcium and magnesium ions. The reason soap companies care is because hard water interferes with soap's cleaning ability, requiring more soap and causing residual soap film and scale.

Don't use water passed through an ion-exchange water softener. It works by exchanging sodium or potassium ions for calcium and magnesium. The end result is too much sodium or potassium to make palatable brewing water.

Alkalinity measures dissolved bicarbonate and carbonate. These powerful buffering agents interact with dissolved calcium and the acidity released from dark malts. Carbonate-rich brew waters make fantastic bases for stouts and porters.

Generally, not all the carbonates are needed to buffer the mash reaction and grains. Residual alkalinity (RA) is the measure of how much alkalinity remains. For pale beers, too high an RA can interfere with the flavor, requiring hardness additions to balance it out. Conversely, areas of water too low in alkalinity will require the addition of minerals like calcium carbonate to bring up the alkalinity for darker beers.

pH: Hydrogen Power

The scale measuring a solution's balance between acid and base is called pH. It is the ratio of hydrogen ions (H+) balanced by hydroxide ions (OH−). Greater amounts of hydrogen ions mean a lower pH.

The scale runs from 0 to 14. Numbers lower than 7 indicate an acidic solution, numbers higher than 7 indicate a basic or alkaline solution. Distilled water measures a neutral pH of 7. Battery acid is pH 0, bleach is around pH 13. Beer is typically served between a pH of 4.3 and 4.5.

ALERT!

If your water is fairly normal and you want to ensure a nominal mash pH, Five Star Chemicals has a product called 5.2, which can help adjust your mash into the optimum range without a lot of thought.

To all-grain brewers, proper pH ensures complete grain conversion. Optimum conditions require a mash pH between 5.2 and 5.8. This is not your unmixed water's pH. Brew waters settle close to this mash pH range mixed with normal grain bills, so water pH only matters in extremes. With extremely pale or dark grain bills, you want to pay attention to the mash pH and where it settles during conversion. To measure your pH, purchase pH paper strips that measure in the range between 4 and 9. Follow the instructions to read the results.

Flavor Impact of Water

Not surprisingly, the minerals dissolved in your water have a profound impact on your beer. These ions do everything from adjust the chemistry of the mash to boosting hop and malt flavors. Where older brewers restricted their styles to those that tasted right with their water, you can adjust your ion levels to meet your needs.

The Major Water Elements

- **Bicarbonate (HCO_3^{-1})**—The dominant form of carbonate. A powerful acid buffer, carbonates neutralize the acidity of dark-roasted malts and reduce hardness by binding with calcium when boiled. If your water is too high in carbonates (200+ ppm), see below to treat it for paler beers.
- **Calcium (Ca^{+2})**—Lowers the mash pH naturally by binding with malt phosphates and is the primary component of water hardness.

It has no flavor impact and extract brewers don't need to add it. For all-grain, calcium is a vital catalyst for mash reactions.

- **Chloride (Cl - ^{1})**—One half of table salt. Has no chemical impact, but leaves your beer tasting fuller and accentuates malt character. Don't overdo it.
- **Magnesium (Mg + ^{2})**—Reduces mash pH, but less than calcium. Yeast need a small portion (around 20 ppm). Too much adds sour and harsh tastes. Malt generally provides enough.
- **Potassium (K + ^{1})**—Blocks enzymatic reactions in the mash. Usual metropolitan levels fine for brewing.
- **Sodium (Na + ^{1})**—Boosts apparent flavors. In heavier concentrations, makes beer taste salty. When combined with hop boosters like sulfate, bitterness is very harsh.
- **Sulfate (SO$_4$)**—Normally bound to calcium, sulfates boost the perception of hop bitterness in levels under 400 ppm. The beer tastes crisper and zippier.

Taste Testing

After tasting grain and hops, it's time to taste the water. For each salt, add a gallon's dose to a quart of distilled water. Bring to a boil with one-third cup of DME and a few hop pellets. Strain and cool the wort. Set aside in sanitized jars and make a whole panel. Pour each sample into clean plastic cups and take notes on the differences. If you don't have any DME, just boil the water without hops.

Calcium carbonate, is tough to dissolve. Add a milliliter of lactic acid to your water if you're using no DME before boiling.

Using Municipal Tap Water

For all the bottled water people drink, you'd think your tap water is gruesome, foul-tasting stuff teeming with dangerous creatures ready to kill you. A great achievement of the modern era has been the clean and safe water supply. Beats schlepping buckets from a foul well.

Can you use your municipal water for brewing? In almost all cases the answer is yes, but it might take adjustments to perfect. Excepting soft water styles, only skip the tap where you have high iron or copper concentrations. As long as the water is drinkable, you can use it. With a filter, some salts, and a little distilled water you can easily hit your mark.

Know Your Water

To start, you need your water's composition. Your standard mineral levels affect the adjustments you make. The Environmental Protection Agency mandates annual water analysis reports from suppliers. These reports are always available to the public. The report covers your area's water sources, mineral content, bacterial loads, and disinfection and safety processes. Keep a copy with your brew library. To find your report, search online for your water company's name and "water report."

The water district's report provides general water knowledge for your area. To gather more information in a brewer-friendly format, you can purchase testing kits from your local hardware store, but for the most accurate information, send your water out to a testing lab. Ward Labs (*www.wardlab .com*) shows you how to gather a sample.

Adjusting Water

With your report data in hand, water additions cease being mysterious. Recipes often list water additions. Once you're comfortable with water chemistry, treat those instructions as guidance. The brewer is suggesting water effects. Some recipes, even if they don't list them, assume you know a few baselines. Dark beers do best with more alkaline water. Hop-forward beers sing more with sulfate, whereas pale lagers want low alkalinity waters with more chloride.

To hit a critical water profile, reduce the amount of ions in your water by diluting or starting with distilled water. See "Reducing Bicarbonate Water" for more information on that technique.

Adding Water Salts

Your store carries powdered minerals to bump your water to the target. None of these are pure elements such as calcium or sodium, but are instead safe and common mixtures. When you plan additions, remember you're changing multiple ions at once.

Purveyors sell "Burton Water Salts," a mix of potassium chloride, Epsom salts, and gypsum. Proponents say X teaspoons per five gallons perfectly emulates Burton on Trent water. Don't buy the hype! Figure out the correct amount of water salts to add to achieve Burtonesque levels from your water.

The table below shows how many ions come from adding one gram of each salt to five gallons of water. Add that amount to the known quantity of ions in your water. For instance, your water has 100 ppm of calcium and 25 ppm of chloride. Adding one gram of calcium chloride to five gallons yields water with 114 ppm of calcium and 50 ppm of chloride. The real tango comes in balancing the ions. Add gypsum to increase the calcium in the mash and suddenly the sulfate is through the roof.

If the addition is too much for you, brewing software programs contain water profilers to aid your efforts. Also check online for websites that help calculate needed additions. Most of these additions are targeted for the mash.

WATER SALTS		
Salt added	Effect Description	Chemical Effect (ppm per gram/five gallons)
Calcium Carbonate— $CaCO_3$	Add to the mash to boost alkalinity to buffer for dark beers. Raises the pH.	21 ppm Ca, 32 ppm CO_3
Calcium Chloride— $CaCL_2 \cdot 2H_2$	Added to lower the mash pH. Extra chloride ions help enrich the malt flavor and smooth the beer.	14 ppm Ca, 25ppm Cl
Calcium Sulfate (Gypsum) — $CaSO_4 \cdot 2H_2O$	Lowers mash pH. Sulfate accentuates hop character ala the classic "Burton" water.	12ppm Ca. 29ppm SO_4
Magnesium Sulfate (Epsom Salt)— $MgSO_4 \cdot 7H_2O$	Magnesium slighty lowers mash pH, but becomes harsh in amounts over 50 ppm. Adds sulfate-like gypsum.	5ppm Mg, 21 ppm SO_4
Sodium Bicarbonate (Baking Soda)— $NaHCO_3$	Raises mash alkalinity (and pH) by adding bicarbonate. Easier to dissolve than chalk. Careful of sodium addition	15ppm Na, 38ppm HCO_3
Sodium Chloride (Kosher Salt)—NaCl	Adds sodium and chloride to the beer for flavor effect. Use only noniodized salt and use sparingly.	21ppm Na, 32ppm Cl

Adjusting pH

When your natural water is too acidic or alkaline to achieve an optimum mash pH of 5.2 to 5.8, give it a helping hand. Two easy methods exist to bring your pH in check:

- **Salts**—Naturally acidify the mash through the addition of calcium salts like gypsum. Calculate the theoretical amount needed via software or stir in small doses (½ teaspoon) of the needed salt and measure the pH.
- **Lactic/Phosphoric Acid**—For water that is seriously alkaline, bring in the heavy guns—food-grade lactic or phosphoric acid. Same approach as the salts, add small doses (a few milliliters), stir, and measure. This is great for acidification of sparge water (around 5.7).

Reducing Alkaline Water

Sometimes acid just isn't enough when you're dealing with heavily alkaline water. When this is the case you have a few choices. Boiling and cooling will cause some of the carbonate to settle out, but usually more drastic measures are needed.

The easiest method to deal with overly alkaline water is to dilute your water with mineral-free distilled or reverse osmosis water. Figure out the effect of adding pure water to your beer by averaging the mineral content. For instance, you have three gallons of water with 300 ppm alkalinity and you add 3 more gallons of distilled water. Your new alkalinity number is $(3 \times 300 + 3 \times 0) / 6$ or 150 ppm. Just remember, the effect applies to all your ions at the same time, so you may need to add some minerals back.

For larger batches of water, dilution may not be practical. Treating your brewing water with slaked lime $Ca(OH)_2$ and monitoring the pH removes much of the carbonate. Look online for further instructions if you feel this is the course of action for you.

Soft Water Sources

What about brewing beers like pilsner? You need soft water. Some sources of soft water include:

- **Rainwater/Snow Melt**—For the most part, fresh snow and rainwater are soft waters. Generally they carry a light mineral load, roughly like Pilsen water. Have your rainwater tested before use and don't use without boiling.
- **Distilled Water**—One of the few legal uses of a home still is to produce clean water. Readily available with other bottled water, distilled water is as pure as water gets. Because of the lack of any minerals, salt additions provide character and needed mash catalysts.
- **Reverse Osmosis**—Slow and ponderous, RO systems are carbon filtration on steroids. Produces water almost as clean as distillation. Plan to start collecting water days ahead of time for your brew depending on your system's production rate. Flush the filters routinely to keep them effective. Treat like distilled water.

All-grain brewers desiring a more thorough explanation of water issues, check out John Palmer's *How to Brew*. The first revision copy is freely available online at *www.howtobrew.com*.

Water-Dependent Recipes

Both recipes that follow depend on certain water profiles. Boho the Hobo is a Bohemian pilsner that needs low-mineral-content water à la Pilsen. Hop Chameleon IPA, on the other hand, wants an extra kick in the pants from the sulfate. Prove to yourself the value of appropriate water additions by switching things up and making a sulfate-filled Boho the Hobo or a soft-water Chameleon.

Boho the Hobo Pils

Modeled after the beers from the town of Pilsen itself, you'll notice this is a slightly strong and hoppy pilsner compared to what you may expect. The soft Pilsen water not only works well with pale malts, but it allows a larger dose of hops without the beer seeming harsh. Brew this beer with German ale if you don't have lagering capabilities.

Style: Bohemian Pilsner
Brew Type: All Grain
For 5.5 gallons at 1.056, 2.9 SRM, 42.5
    IBUs, 5.5 percent ABV
60-minute boil

Directions

Follow the Decoction Brew Process
(page 285).

TIP

If you want a stronger hop bitterness, add sulfate to your normal water supply or try and mimic the Dortmund water profile. A significant part of the difference between Bohemian pilsner and German pils lies in the water chemistry.

Malt/Grain/Sugar
12.00 pounds Pilsner Malt

Extract (for 11.0 pounds of Pilsner Malt)
7.50 pounds Lager Liquid Malt Extract (LME)

Hops
3.50 ounces Czech Saaz (3.0 percent AA) Whole for 60 minutes
0.50 ounce Czech Saaz (3.0 percent AA) Whole for 5 minutes

Other Ingredients
1 tablet Whirlfloc
1 tablespoon Yeast Nutrient
8 gallons Soft Water

Yeast
Wyeast 2278 Czech Pils

Mash Schedule
Protein Rest 125°F 20 minutes
Intermediate Rest 148°F 20 minutes
Saccharification Rest 153°F 60 minutes

Hop Chameleon

A beer with this many hops doesn't really even need a hop boost, but it's great to make a hop head's eyes shine when they get the first sip. Even if you have a higher than expected final gravity, the sulfate forces a drier perception.

Style: American IPA
Brew Type: All Grain
For 5.5 gallons at 1.066, 12.2 SRM, 70.8
    IBUs, 6.5 percent ABV
90-minute boil

Directions

Follow the Single-Infusion Brew Process (page 284).

TIP

Again, switch to a different water profile like Pilsen and watch how the hops soften up and seem less aggressive.

Malt/Grain/Sugar
14.00 pounds Pale Malt Two-Row
1.00 pound Crystal 55L
0.50 pound CaraMunich Malt

Extract (for 14.00 pounds of Pale Malt)
8.50 pounds Pale Liquid Malt Extract (LME)

Hops
0.35 ounce Columbus (15.5 percent AA) Pellet for 90 minutes
0.25 ounce Chinook (15.7 percent AA) Pellet for 60 minutes
0.25 ounce Columbus (15.5percent AA) Pellet for 30 minutes
0.25 ounce Simcoe (13.7 percent AA) Pellet for 30 minutes
0.25 ounce Simcoe (13.7 percent AA) Pellet for 15 minutes
0.50 ounce Simcoe (13.7 percent AA) Pellet for 1 minute
0.50 ounce Columbus (15.5 percent AA) Pellet for 1 minute

Other Ingredients
1 tablet Whirlfloc
1 tablespoon Yeast Nutrient
Gypsum to 450ppm sulfate

Yeast
WLP001 California Ale

Mash Schedule
Saccharification Rest 150°F 60 minutes

CHAPTER 6

Yeast: The True
Beer Makers

"Brewers make wort. Yeast make beer." There is no denying the fundamental truth behind the old saying. No matter how great your wort, poorly chosen or prepared yeast can sink the whole tank. Fortunately, you can easily tame and train your yeast!

A Close Look at the Beasts

Yeast is a member of the fungus kingdom. Like mushrooms, they turn out to be very useful to human cooks. Most of the critters that you control are varieties of *Saccharomyces cerevasiae*, Greek and Latin for "beer sugar mold." The little (mostly) asexual budding microbes conjure the real magic in the craft. Look at a yeast cell under a microscope and you'll see a simple, single-celled creature that shares so many cell structures with animals that scientists extensively study them to gain a better understanding of more complex cellular systems.

Reflecting the long association between bread and beer, bakers use *S. cerevasiae* to give bread its lift. Their breeds are slow fermenters and give very distinctive yeast characters to the dough. In the past, homebrew was fermented with cakes of fresh bread yeast.

In the presence of oxygen, yeasts get their groove on, making building blocks to prepare for fermentation. Abundant sugar and depleted oxygen triggers fermentation. Cells reproduce rapidly. When yeast saturates the wort, they consume available sugar. As it is metabolized, yeast creates ethyl alcohol (ethanol) and carbon dioxide. They secrete a host of flavorful compounds. Every yeast culture produces unique concentrations of flavors based on conditions, including fermentation temperature. Brewers exploit these fermentation characteristics to transform barley malt and hops into a universe of beer.

Ale Yeast Versus Lager Yeast

S. cerevasiae isn't alone in the pool. As brewers in cold climes discovered, its close cousin *S. pastornius* (nee *S. carlsbergensis*) ferments at colder temperatures. They can consume raffinose, a large sugar, making drier beer.

Traditionally brewers refer to ale yeasts as "top fermenting" when they clump together (flocculate) and rise to the top. Skimming efficiently recycles the yeast for another batch. Bottom-fermenting lagers throw less krausen and the yeast settles directly.

Dried Versus Liquid

Should you choose from the vast multitude of liquid yeasts or from the limited simple world of dried yeast? Each has positive and negative traits.

Liquid Yeast

The sleek refrigerated packaged promise of variety tempts you. Breweries previously ran independent yeast banks to meet their needs. Unless you needed commercial quantities you were shut out. Even if you got your hands on samples, they were packaged for labwork.

Today, Wyeast Laboratories and White Labs both offer practical and convenient liquid yeast. For a few dollars, you can purchase strains appropriate to virtually any beer style. To encourage experimentation, they release seasonal cultures.

ALERT!

Purchase fresh yeast only. Pack labels carry a best-by date. Choose tubes that are less than three months old. You can regrow a viable culture from one- to two-year-old packs following the starter instructions on page 63.

Liquid yeast's strengths are freshness, variety, and a sanitary nature. A number of styles are possible only with liquid strains. As you explore the available selection, you can find a strain that produces beer you love.

The primary downsides are sensitivity to mishandling, volume of yeast, and risk of infection. Liquid cultures should never be exposed to freezing temperatures or hot summer sun. Either extreme will kill the cells. Toss a dead pack into the boil as yeast nutrient.

Manufacturers claim to provide enough yeast for five-gallon batches. However, a single pouch contains less yeast than ideal for bigger brews. Using less viable yeast boosts infection risk, stress induced off-flavors, and final gravity. Smart brewers grow yeast in small batches. These "starter" beers are covered later in the chapter and are a good tool.

Always take care, when pitching yeast, to sanitize everything touching the yeast or packaging before opening the yeast to pour into the beer. Pitching, ideally, happens in a clean, draft-free location. The cautious use of a burning blowtorch over the carboy opening can create an updraft, keeping dust and bacteria from the wort.

FACT

Both Wyeast and White Labs provide yeast to commercial breweries, including your local one. Replicating the house yeast may be as simple as buying a tube from the store. However, they produce only a small selection of strains for homebrewers. Ask nicely and the brewery might part with yeast slurry.

Dried Yeast

Remembering the dark ages of homebrewing (ten-plus years ago), hardened veterans denigrate dry yeast. The dried yeasts on the market were dreadful. In articles from the 1980s, brewers report finding *Pediococcus* and *Brettanomyces* contamination in packets of dried yeast. Exposing your beer to airborne yeasts and microbes was cheaper and equally as good.

Why consider dried yeast then? First, dried yeast is one-fourth the price of liquid. Second, the yeast amount in a sachet blows the doors off a liquid tube. Dried yeast is also easier to use. Just rehydrate the yeast and go; no starters needed. Finally, liquid yeasts have a shorter lifespan. Dried lasts years with no loss of viability.

Recently, dried yeast manufacturers stepped up quality. Better drying technology led to purer packs, free of contaminants. Strain selection improved as well. Previously restricted to a single "ale" or "lager" strain, you now have access to a simple style range.

To prepare dried yeast, boil a cup of water with an optional pinch of yeast nutrient for fifteen minutes. Cover with foil and cool to around 100°F. Cut open the packet of yeast with sanitized scissors, pour the yeast on, and gently swirl. Let sit covered for five to fifteen minutes before adding to the beer. Rehydration gives cell walls time to strengthen before hitting the sugar-rich wort.

Many report vigorous fermentations in hours with dried yeast. Fermenting at lower temperatures produces better flavor, aroma, and attenuation.

Always keep dried yeast in the fridge as an emergency backup. A handy sachet has saved many batches from yeast disasters. Replace the pack yearly.

The Starter: Kick Starting Your Brew

Why spend additional time and money making wort that is never drunk? First, you verify that your yeast source is ready to go. Imagine a session's work in jeopardy because your yeast was too old. A starter that refuses to grow gives you advanced warning to prepare another culture.

A starter grows a strong yeast army, not flavorful beer. Different goals mean different fermentation procedures than those used for maximizing flavor. Successful starters taste oxidized (cardboard, stale) or estery (apple, cherries). Importantly, creamy yeast covers the bottom. The yeast cells will have thick walls, large reserves of energy, and the fundamental building blocks ready for more cells.

Preparing Starters ahead of Time

Save time and energy by preparing starters ahead of time. Extra wort from a brew day can be frozen in muffin tins, popped into Ziploc bags, and then boiled and cooled for use in a new starter. With a pressure cooker, you can sterilize wort at 15 psi for fifteen minutes and have starters at the ready.

All-Purpose Easy Starter

Designed to give maximum yeast growth, the gravity is perfect. Some texts suggest increasing the gravity to around 1.060 (4.8 ounces of DME) for yeast training for high-gravity beer. Don't use sugar instead of extract.

For 1 quart at around 1.040

Directions

1. Sanitize a vessel and foil. A half-gallon growler is ideal.

2. Mix DME, nutrient, and hops with a quart of filtered water and bring to a boil for 15 minutes. Cover and chill in an ice water bath or your freezer until cool.

3. Flame the vessel's mouth and pot edges. Pour the wort into the jug. Open the yeast, flame the openings, and add to the wort. Cap with foil. Shake vigorously.

4. Shake the jug 4 or more times over the next day to encourage growth.

TIP

A magnetic stir plate's continuous stirring action increases the amount of yeast three to six times. Find stir plates on eBay or build your own out of a spare computer fan and rare earth magnets.

Ingredients
3.2 ounces (by weight) Light DME (roughly ½ cup by volume)
1 pinch Yeast Nutrient
1 pellet Hops (optional)

Yeast
1 packet your source culture

Larger Starters and Settling

For higher-gravity beers and lagers, starters larger than a quart are recommended. Prepare your starter as before. The next day prepare another 4 to 10 pints of wort and add to your starter. The new food and larger volume allow greater growth.

Start distressed or old yeast packs with small starter sizes (½ cup) and step up from there to nurse the limping critters along to healthy brewing strength.

To avoid adding that stale starter beer to your beer, you need time to settle. Crimp tightly the starter's foil covering and place in a fridge for a day. The yeast settles out, leaving a growing band of clear wort. Before pitching, sanitize the vessel and pour off the beer, reserving some. Swirl the yeast into suspension before pitching the smaller amount.

Don't overdo the starter size. You want some reproduction happening in your brew for the flavors secreted by reproducing yeast. For normal-gravity beers, don't exceed a quart.

Choosing Your Yeast Strain

With the wide variety available, how do you narrow your options? Yeast companies publish statistics and blurbs for each product. Together they give you a rough idea of performance and what to expect in the final beer.

Yeast Statistics

- **Attenuation:** Expressed as a percentage, measures how much sugar is consumed. For example yeast listed at 70 to 75 percent attenuation usually ferments a 1.050 beer to 1.013 to 1.015.

- **Flocculation:** Measures the tendency of a strain to clump together. Highly flocculant strains mean quickly clear beer, but they leave extra sugar and aromas of sulfur, diacetyl, and so on. Less flocculant yeasts hang around leaving hazy but well-attenuated beers.
- **Fermentation temperature:** The range of temperature where yeast operates best. Cultures produce unique flavors at different temperatures. Some yeasts drop immediately after a too-hot or too-cold day.
- **Alcohol tolerance:** Ethanol is yeast's toxic waste; they can only ferment so much before succumbing to the poison. Very large healthy starters can push further than the number suggests.

Consider these traits. Is the yeast sourced from the locality best known for the style? A number of strains are named for a style. Charts provided by Wyeast and White Labs offer their advice to steer your decision.

Weigh all these factors to decide. For instance, for an Irish dry stout (Guinness), you'd do better choosing an Irish ale yeast over an English ale strain. The more attentuative Irish ale (69 to 74 percent as opposed to 63 to 70 percent) means a drier, less fruity beer with a hint of yeastiness, due to its lower flocculation.

This chapter closes with a couple of examples of the same basic wort transformed into radically different final beers by yeast choice. Brew batches big enough to split, pitch multiple yeasts, and put another beer on tap while learning the often subtle differences between strains.

Some tricky European breweries don't use their fermentation strain for bottling. If you notice that the ale yeast acts oddly, you may have run into a beer bottled with lager strains.

Using Yeast from Your Favorite Brewery

Everyone eventually finds a brewery that turns into an obsession. The inner brewer awakens, pronouncing the yeast the trick behind the beers' profiles. If the beer is bottle-conditioned, a fine layer of beige gold awaits the frugal.

Seize it for your projects: buy two bottles; pour most of the bottle into your glass. Pour a cup of starter wort into a jug and add the bottle dregs. Make sure to swirl the bottles to grab everything! After a day or so, check for signs of growth and add more wort. Stay patient, growth may take a week before ready for use. When buying a source beer, choose the brewery's freshest, lowest-alcohol beer for healthier starting yeast.

Reusing Yeast: Big Cakes, No Dough

Buying new packets of yeast quickly becomes an expensive proposition. Cleaning your primary fermenter, you've washed massive amounts of yeast and gunk down the drain. Professional breweries use that yeast to ferment the next batch. As a homebrewer, you can repitch your yeast and you can skip starters for high-alcohol monster beers.

If you trust your sanitation procedures completely, you can dump your freshly chilled wort straight into the unwashed primary fermenter. For

Is It an American OR Belgian Blonde?

A simple recipe to demonstrate the complex effect of your yeast choice. The grain bill provides enough traction for yeast antics. All-grain brewers should substitute about 9.5 pounds of pale malt and mash at 152°F.

For 5 gallons at 1.051 OG, 4.0 SRM (Blonde), 15 IBUs

Directions

Follow the standard instructions for the Steeping Grains and Extract Process (page 283).

Malt/Grain/Sugar
6.6 pounds Light Malt Extract Syrup (LME)
0.25 pound Belgian Aromatic Malt
0.25 pound Wheat Malt

Hops
0.25 ounce Magnum (11.5 percent AA) Pellet for 60 minutes
0.25 ounce Styrian Goldings (5.25 percent AA) Pellet for 5 minutes

Yeast
American Ale Yeast (Wyeast 1056 Chico Ale, White Labs WLP001 California Ale, Safale US-05)
Belgian Ale Yeast (Wyeast 1214 Belgian Ale, White Labs WLP550 Belgian Ale)

everyone else, sanitize a few growlers or mason jars and boil some water. Fill the jug with your fermenter sludge and add some of the boiled water. After an hour or so, you're left with a jug of settled gunk and a beige liquid yeast layer. Pour the liquid into a second jar along with a little more water and watch it settle into creamy yeasty goodness. Reuse quickly (within a week) before the yeast dies off!

QUESTION?

Can I use the same yeast over and over again?
Not really. As you reuse the yeast, you carry over any bacteria and mutant yeast that grew in previous batches. Over time, their aromas and flavors become more pronounced. Spotlessly sanitized professional breweries repitch twenty to forty times before grabbing a fresh supply. Homebrewers shouldn't exceed three batches on the same cake.

Hefeweizen Revisited: American **OR** German?

Taste the American version next to the German version for an eye-opening experience. The subtle fruity flavors from the American yeasts are innocuous compared to the bold banana, cloves, and bubble gum of the German yeast.

For 5 gallons at 1.056 OG, 6.3 SRM (Pale Gold), 11 IBUs

Directions

Follow the standard instructions for the Steeping Grains and Extract Process (page 283).

Malt/Grain/Sugar
5 pounds Wheat Beer Dried Malt Extract
1.0 pound German Pilsner Malt
1.5 pounds German Wheat Malt

Hops
0.4 ounce Hallertauer Tradition (6.0 percent AA) for 60 minutes

Yeast
American Wheat Yeast (Wyeast 1010 American Wheat, White Labs WLP320 American Hefeweizen Ale)
German Hefeweizen Yeast (Wyeast 3056 Bavarian Wheat, White Labs WLP300 Hefeweizen Ale)

CHAPTER 7

Ingredients Beyond
the Basic Four

The flavors wrung from the basic four are fantastic, but sometimes you desire something different. Fortunately, brewers had plenty of time and need to experiment before the hegemony of barley, water, hops, and yeast stamped a procrustean frame to beer.

Sugar

Craft brewing's revolution against adjuncts (rice, corn, and so on) put a kibosh on sugar in beer, admirably eliminating corn sugar's use to boost alcohol at the expense of flavor. However, this gave rise to snobbish attitudes toward any use of sugar. Like a swinging pendulum, attitudes are changing.

Sugar's simplicity and fermentability imparts dryness to beer over the more complex, less fermentable barley sugars. Resist the temptation to raid the five-pound bag and instead explore the interesting results offered by less refined sugars.

ALERT!

Older brewers mention that brewing with too much sugar makes your beer taste "cidery." If nothing else, Belgian brews disprove this notion. The current thinking attributes the "extract twang/cidery" flavors to stale extract.

Important Sugar Molecules

Not all sugars are the same, but they are all formed by carbon, hydrogen, and oxygen. Brewers focus on the fermentability and sweetness of sugar types.

Monosaccharides, a single sugar molecule, are the basic building blocks of all carbohydrates from table sugar to pasta. With twenty-four atoms, many natural molecular formations occur. From a brewer's perspective, the best-known monosaccharides—glucose (dextrose), fructose (levulose), and galactose—provide easy chow for yeast. Your finished beer will be almost devoid of them.

Next up the sugar chain are disaccharides, two monosaccharides combined. The most famous sugar is sucrose (table sugar, cane sugar, beet sugar). Virtually every grocery-store-aisle sugar is sucrose. Maltose (malt sugar) unsurprisingly appears in large quantities. Lactose (milk sugar), unfermentable by beer yeast, is used as an adjunct. Cream/milk stouts have a large boil kettle addition of lactose. Tasters perceive a richer mouthfeel, but little sweetness.

As the molecular count rises, fermentability drops. Among trisaccharides, maltotriose, an extension of the maltose molecule, is fermentable. The other common trisaccharide, raffinose, can be attacked by some strains of lager yeast. Beyond these two outliers, yeasts stop fermenting, but wild yeasts and bacteria can destroy longer-chain sugars. Preventing starch in the wort helps prevent infection by denying other microorganisms a noncompetitive food source.

The Beet Versus Cane Debate

Grab a bag of table sugar from your pantry. The white sucrose crystals you hold are the product of endless refinement and bleaching. They started life as either tall, reedy sugar cane or lumpy, super-sweet sugar beets.

For years debate had raged over preference between beet and cane sugar. In most of the United States, particularly the South, cane sugar reigns supreme, while in the Midwest, particularly Michigan (and in Europe), the sugar beet is king. The European beet connection has had brewers insisting on using beet sugar for their Belgian ales. But sucrose is sucrose and the difference between cane and beet is negligible at best.

Avoid scorched sugar and tired arms by letting the boil dissolve your sugar. Add the sugar to a nylon hop bag and tie it to a spoon or stick. Suspend the bag in the middle of the boil and in about 10 minutes, the sugar dissolves.

Types of Sugar

Here are some common sugars for your brewery. To get a feeling for the effect of a sugar on your beer, try brewing the Baby Devil Sugar Bomb Belgian Ale (page 72). Unless otherwise noted, sugar contributes roughly 46 gravity points to a beer. To preserve aroma and flavor, add intense sugars late in the boil, around 15 minutes remaining.

Common Brewing Sugars

- **Beet/Cane table sugar**—The most basic and most refined sugar you'll buy. Adds no flavor or aroma characters to the brew, but dries out and is cheap. Use when you want a gravity boost without sweetness and body.

- **Brown sugar**—Most brown sugar is refined white sugar with varying amounts of molasses added back. To really punch up the flavor and aroma of British beers, look for real brown sugar, richly smelling of raisins and plums. Try muscavado, a very dark unrefined sugar cane brown sugar.

- **Candi sugar**—Bags of Belgian Candi Sugar in your local homebrew store run a pretty penny. To save money, substitute table sugar or Chinese yellow lump sugar, a less refined product tasting of light caramel.

- **Lactose**—Lactose is unfermentable milk sugar. Adds a very light sweetness to the final beer and boosts the beer's final gravity (43 points per pound). For lactose in action see MP's Coffee and Cream Stout (page 81)

- **Piloncillo/Jaggery**—Products of Central America and India respectively, both are unrefined sugars with flavorful impurities. Distinctively packaged in rough, hard cone shapes, they require a grater or a hammer to ready the sugar. Keep an eye out for special jaggery made from date or palm syrup for a different taste.

- **Turbinado sugar**—A less refined cane sugar, the large pale brown crystalline sweetener is known as "Sugar in the Raw" in the United States. Demerara is a paler British version. Tastes like light brown sugar, but with a fruitier aroma.

Additionally here are some brewing syrups you should consider for your home brewery.

Common Brewing Syrups

- **Golden syrup (Invert sugar syrup)**—A British product, this syrup doesn't crystallize. Created from byproducts of the sugar-making process, it is thick and golden with a light caramel and fruity flavor. Invert sugar is, in theory, easier for yeast.

- **Molasses/Treacle**—Molasses is boiled sugar cane juice. There are several grades. For brewing purposes, avoid the sulfured molasses. In darker varieties flavors intensify with less fermentable sugar. Blackstrap, the darkest molasses, is traditional in British old ales and adds unique plum, smoke, and licorice flavors (36 points per pound).
- **Belgian Candi Syrup**—A recent addition to the homebrewer's arsenal is Belgian Candi Syrup, a leftover from rock-candy making. Dark and rich with plum, vanilla, and raisins, a single 1.5-pound bottle can transform a beer from pale to dark. Perfect for dubbels and quads (32 points per pound).

Baby Devil Sugar Bomb Belgian Ale

Baby Devil is your basic Belgian blonde ale with nothing to get in the way of testing sugars. The darker, less refined sugars produce more interesting beers.

Style: Belgian Blond Ale
Brew Type: All Grain
For 5.5 gallons at 1.068, 4.0 SRM, 28.8 IBUs, 7.1 percent ABV
60-minute boil

Directions

Follow the Single-Infusion Brew Process (page 284).

TIP

This recipe starts at a reasonable gravity, but the lack of nutrients in sugar make a starter a good insurance policy.

Malt/Grain/Sugar
4.00 pounds Pale Malt Two-Row
4.00 pounds Pilsner Malt
2.00 pounds Sugar
2.00 pounds Wheat Malt

Extract (for 3.5 pounds of Pale Malt and 3.5 pounds of Pilsner Malt)
2.50 pounds Pale Liquid Malt Extract (LME)
2.50 pounds Lager Liquid Malt Extract (LME)

Hops
0.50 ounce Magnum (14.0 percent AA) Pellet for 60 minutes
0.50 ounce Czech Saaz (3.5 percent AA) Pellet for 1 minute

Other Ingredients
1 tablet Whirlfloc
1 teaspoon Yeast Nutrient

Yeast
WLP550 Belgian Ale

Mash Schedule
Saccharification Rest 150°F 60 minutes

Fruit and Vegetables

Fruit has a long brewing history. Sumerian beers incorporated dates for extra sugar and flavoring. Today's beer aisle shows that fruit continue to be popular. Often, fruit adds a dominant flavor to a bland base beer, such as wheat beer. Other styles use fruit as a background note to enhance character, such as a pale ale with orange pumping up the citrusy hops.

Though not as common, people do also add vegetables. They add pumpkins for "pumpkin" ales (more in the spice section) along with chile peppers, cucumbers, potatoes, corn, and so on. Vegetables don't give much sugar and add a lot of water, something you must account for when using them.

Consider using the peel for veggies like cucumbers since that's where the flavor really resides. Make sure you purchase unwaxed or organic varieties and give a good scrub before using.

What beer styles work with fruit additions? Brewers dose American wheat beers with virtually every fruit. Porters, stouts, and even imperial stouts popularly hide fruit as well. Additions include blueberries, blackberries, raspberries, citrus, and cherries. Other interesting combinations (some by extract only) include bananas, apples, apricots, pineapples, and mango.

Fruit Packaging

Thanks to fruit's universal appeal, growers flood the market with multitudes of fruit and packaging. Each product has different applications and strengths, for example:

- **Fresh fruit**—Fresh is the only way to go with certain fruits, particularly citrus. Most fresh fruits should be juiced to increase access to the sugars. Zest fruits with oil-heavy peels (like citrus), removing the outer peel to capture the oil. To cut down on costs, buy in season from a local farmer's market. Farmers often cut you a deal when buying fruit in brewing quantities.

- **Frozen**—In the brewhouse frozen fruit is often preferable to and cheaper than fresh. Frozen berries work outstandingly well. Freezing creates tiny ice crystals puncturing cell walls and freeing precious juice and sugar. Farmer's market purists: freeze your fresh berries before use. Freezing does not kill off wild yeast and bacteria.
- **Dried**—Dried potent fruits and peels make perfect late additions to the boil. Citrus oils permeate the brew from just a few teaspoons. Other fruits may require substantially more fruit and soaking time.
- **Juice/Purée/Syrups**—Your homebrew store probably carries large cans of fruit purée. Avoid "pie filling" and use purées that are only fruit. Add juice, purée, or syrup to the secondary before packaging.
- **Flavoring extract**—Lurking on the store shelves are small bottles of fruit flavoring. For some impossible fruits, these extracts may be your only way to go. Many extracts carry strongly medicinal flavors, making them suitable for adding flavor to stronger beer that masks the off-flavor.

When purchasing processed fruit like purées, juices, and syrups, buy preservative-free fruit to avoid damaging the yeast. Experiment with amounts of fruit. For fresh and frozen fruit additions, brewers think pounds per gallon of beer.

Getting Fruit in Your Beer

Getting the fruit in your beer largely depends upon form and your fearlessness. Older recipes add juice and fruit in the kettle for a brief sanitizing boil. With adequate sanitation and healthy yeast, you can add the fruit or juice to the fermenter instead. Boil peels and zest to extract oil as possible.

Add juice, purées, and fruit during secondary fermentation. This prevents the vigorous primary fermentation from scrubbing the fruit aroma. Fresh fruit should be frozen or mashed up before adding. Always give fermentation several days before bottling to avoid bottle bombs. (And don't be freaked out by leftover fruit, it's supposed to look like that.)

Invest in a small bottle of liquid pectinase to eliminate haze if you must. The enzyme attacks pectin, a fruit carbohydrate that thickens jams and can cause haze. Many popular brewing fruits, berries especially, are low in pectin.

Fruited fermentations can be explosively violent, even in secondary. Consider using a bucket or a six-gallon carboy for secondary and use a blow-off tube or foil. Put the fermenter in a catch basin and wait a few days.

Flavor extracts are final additions. Before you bottle or keg your beer, draw off a half pint sample and add a measured amount of extract, swirl, and taste. Add small doses of extract until you hit the magic taste. Multiply the amount of extract by the number of half pints in your batch (a five-gallon batch has 80 half pints). Add the extract to the bottling bucket or the keg before racking the beer.

Spices

Brewing with spices was a specialty of older brewers. Before the days of using hops, an herb-and-spice blend called gruit was used to bitter the beer. For millennia, brew-infused herbs and spices were potent medicine and potions. Even today herbalists recommend alcohol tinctures of some remedies.

Herb refers to the leafy green parts of a plant used for seasoning, like mint or basil. Spices are made from seeds, bark, roots, berries, and so on. They include now-common items like cinnamon, ginger, star anise, and nutmeg.

Spicing is a master art in Belgian breweries. There you can expect to find additions of dried fruit peels, chamomile, cinnamon, coriander, and more. Most non-Belgians tend to spice darker and higher-gravity ales. Dubbels, imperial stouts, robust porters, old ales, and quads are all examples of spiced beers.

There are few methods for adding spices and herbs. The first is to boil them. When added in the last few minutes of the boil (ten minutes or fewer remaining), the oils are extracted. Stronger spices, particularly eugenol-bearing spices like nutmeg and clove, remain potent throughout the ferment.

ALERT!

Don't overdo it with your spice additions. New brewers, tempted to add heaps of spices, create undrinkable batches that take ages to mellow. Add spices in small amounts. Strive to hit an elusive spice character.

Sangreal Blood Orange Wheat

Sangreal, the late-medieval name for the Holy Grail, was a pun. In Old French, san greal *means "Holy Grail" while* sang real *means "royal blood." The Da Vinci Code achieved blockbuster status with this same pun.*

Style: Fruit Beer
Brew Type: All Grain
For 5.5 gallons at 1.058, 3.7 SRM, 21.8 IBUs, 6.1 percent ABV
60-minute boil

Directions

1. Follow the Single-Infusion Brew Process (page 284).

2. Add the blood orange juice into the secondary.

TIP

Can't find blood oranges? Substitute super-sweet oranges. Blood oranges are available in the early spring and virtually gone by April.

Malt/Grain/Sugar
5.75 pounds Wheat Malt (American)
4.00 pounds Pale Malt Two-Row
0.50 pound Wheat Malt (German)
0.35 pound Cara-Pils Dextrine Malt

Extract (for 5.25 pounds of Wheat Malt (American) and 3.50 pounds of Pale Malt)
4.50 pounds Wheat Liquid Malt Extract (LME)
2.60 pounds Pale Liquid Malt Extract (LME)

Hops
0.90 ounce Liberty (5.2 percent AA) Pellet for 60 minutes
0.40 ounce Cascade (5.9 percent AA) Pellet for 5 minutes

Other Ingredients
1 tablet Whirlfloc
1 tablespoon Yeast Nutrient
2 Moro Blood Oranges, zested—added for 5 minutes
10 pounds Moro Blood Oranges, juiced

Yeast
WLP001 California Ale

Mash Schedule
Saccharification Rest 153°F 60 minutes

Others add crushed spices directly to the fermenter in hopes of extracting the oils via alcohol. Timing dry spicing can be tricky. An alternative is to create your own tincture by soaking crushed spices in vodka for several weeks. Add this extract to taste at packaging. Another approach replicates the boil character with a spice tea. Boil spices in a small pot of water for ten to fifteen minutes. Cool and strain before use and add like extract.

No matter how you choose to add them, start with fresh spices. You don't know how long that jar of spice has hung out on the store shelf. Stale spices have all the character of dryer lint. Order spices from a reputable spice house to get the best quality for your beer.

Jack O' Pumpkin Amber Ale

Mash the pumpkin with the grain. The exact contribution of pumpkin to the beer's flavor is negligible, but people add it for the romance of it. Used in large enough quantities (and from fresh roasted), you can pick up squash and jalapeño notes.

Style: American Amber Ale
Brew Type: All Grain
For 5.5 gallons at 1.054, 14.3 SRM, 23.1 IBUs, 5.3 percent ABV
60-minute boil

Directions

Follow the Single-Infusion Brew Process (page 284).

TIP

Not all pumpkin ales contain pumpkin. The spices provide the real payoff to the pumpkin pie intent. If you're worried about a stuck mash or just don't want to deal with pumpkin, skip it.

Malt/Grain/Sugar
1.81 pounds Pumpkin (1 large can)
7.00 pounds Pale Malt Two-Row
2.00 pounds Munich Malt
1.00 pound Crystal 120L

Extract (for 6.00 pounds of Pale Malt)
4.25 pounds Pale Liquid Malt Extract (LME)

Hops
1.00 ounce Tettnanger (4.5 percent AA) Pellet for 60 minutes
0.50 ounce Tettnanger (4.5 percent AA) Pellet for 20 minutes

Other Ingredients
1 tablet Whirlfloc
1 tablespoon Yeast Nutrient
¼ teaspoon Cinnamon for 5 minutes
⅛ teaspoon Nutmeg for 5 minutes
⅛ teaspoon Clove for 5 minutes

Yeast
WLP001 California Ale

Mash Schedule
Saccharification Rest 152°F 60 minutes

Coffee and Chocolate

As intertwined as morning and mocha, coffee and chocolate are finding their way into beer. However, dealing with the head-killing oils is a challenge when using coffee or chocolate. Not surprisingly, they mostly appear in porters and stouts, where they intensify roasted malt flavor and head doesn't matter.

QUESTION?

Why add vanilla to a chocolate beer?
Vanillin, the active molecule in vanilla, is a large contributor to the "chocolate" flavor profile. A vanilla bean or extract added to the fermenter will boost the perception of chocolate.

Chocolate

Brewers seeking to add chocolate flavor have numerous strategies to capture it. Cocoa, chocolate's base, is incredibly bitter. If you use chocolate or cocoa with sugar, expect the sweet character to disappear. You can compensate with lactose or mashing hot, leaving residual sweetness, or appreciate a different variety of bitterness. Here are some ways to get chocolate flavor into your beer:

- **Chopped bittersweet chocolate**—Added straight to the boil, chopped bittersweet chocolate adds loads of flavor and fat. Make sure to completely melt and dissolve the chocolate to avoid scorched chocolate solids. Use a couple of ounces per five gallons.
- **Cocoa powder**—Cocoa powder is defatted and can be tossed straight into the boil without scorching. Dose with a couple tablespoons.
- **Chocolate syrup**—The same stuff you use for chocolate milk can be used to chocolatize a beer. Use a half cup in the boil.
- **Chocolate extract syrup**—In this day of artificial flavorings there are a number of chocolate extracts. Designed for Italian soda and coffee, add directly before bottling to add flavor. The lack of fat and color make these perfect for adding chocolate to pale beers, like wheat ale. Use 6 to 8 ounces.

- **Cacao nibs**—Cracked and roasted cacao seeds, nibs are raw chocolate at its finest. They give a potent chocolate flavor over two weeks of secondary aging and don't leech fat. Combine with a vanilla bean to seal the chocolate flavor. Use about 6 ounces for two weeks for maximum flavor and minimum astringency.

Coffee

The African bean that jump-starts the day. The idea of caffeinated beer may be off-putting, but the flavor is well worth the extra jolt. Don't skimp on the fresh coffee that you add as you'll only hurt your beer.

GVC's Imperial Chocolate Porter

Developed over several years, the interplay of the vanilla and cacao nibs with a complex malt bill makes for dauntingly intense beer. Add lactose for a milk chocolate character.

Style: Robust Porter
Brew Type: All Grain
For 5.5 gallons at 1.066, 49.9 SRM, 31.8 IBUs, 6.5 percent ABV
60-minute boil

Directions

Follow the Single-Infusion Brew Process (page 284).

TIP

When using nibs, carefully watch your soaking times and flavor. The nib's complex earthiness quickly turns to harsh ashy tannic flavors that can ruin the enjoyable base beer.

Malt/Grain/Sugar
7.00 pounds Maris Otter Malt
1.40 pounds Brown Malt
1.40 pounds Ashburne Mild Malt
1.20 pounds Crystal 60L
0.60 pound Honey Malt
0.80 pound Crystal 35L
0.20 pound Crystal 120L
1.00 pound Chocolate Malt
0.20 pound Black Patent Malt
0.20 pound Carafa Malt

Extract (for 6.00 pounds of Maris Otter Malt)
4.5 pounds Pale Liquid Malt Extract (LME)

Hops
1.00 ounce Northern Brewer (7.2 percent AA) Pellet for 60 minutes
0.20 ounce Northern Brewer (7.2 percent AA) Pellet for 20 minutes

Other Ingredients
1 tablet Whirlfloc
1 tablespoon Yeast Nutrient
3 Vanilla Beans (in the secondary for 14 days)
6 ounces Cacao Nibs (in the secondary for 14 days)

Yeast
WLP001 California Ale

Mash Schedule
Saccharification Rest 155°F 60 minutes

Here are some ways to get coffee flavor into your beer:

- **Espresso/Pot coffee**—Fresh brewed, cold espresso or auto drip gives a nice jump to a beer. Some brewers run to the café, grabbing 8 to 16 ounces (4 to 8 "shots") of espresso to dump into the beer after fermentation.

- **Ground coffee**—For the hardcore, adding fresh ground coffee is the way to go. Grounds are sturdy stuff, suited for adding to the mash, the boil, or in the fermenter. Give fermenter additions time to settle, unless you like coffee grinds in your pint. Recipes range from a few ounces to a pound.

- **Cold-steeped coffee**—To avoid coffee's harsh acidic flavors, brewers mix a slurry of fine grounds and cold water to soak overnight. The long, slow steep extracts goodness without the edge. Strain and add to the fermenter or bottling.

- **Coffee syrup**—The chocolate syrup manufacturers make coffee-flavored syrup as well. Just like the chocolate syrup, it makes a great last-minute addition.

Spirits: Adding Kick to the Beer

Spirits have more purpose than adding oomph to your beer. A number of interesting flavors can be derived from the bottles. The added alcohol can cut an overly sweet beer or repair a too-weak beer. Alternatively, sweet liquors mask harsh flavors.

A great advantage to using liquor, your addition is sanitary. The cautious use only uncracked bottles and sanitize the outside before adding to the keg, bottling bucket, or fermenter. Here are some spirits you may want to add to your homebrew:

- **Hard alcohol (bourbon, tequila, rum)**—In addition to the burn, each spirit carries a unique flavor profile. The French love adding booze and have several whiskey- and tequila-fueled beers on the market.

- **Fruit liqueurs**—There are two classes of fruit liquors, the eau-de-vie brandy style (all alcohol with no fruit), and the sweet liqueur type. You usually want the sweet schnapps. One batch of GVC's Imperial

MP's Coffee and Cream Stout

Coffee tends to find a home in bigger stouts, where the acidity of the beans is lost in the dense thicket of roasted barley. The lactose adds creaminess, offsetting harsh coffee tones.

Style: Sweet Stout
Brew Type: All Grain
For 5.5 gallons at 1.047, 19.7 SRM, 26.5 IBUs, 4.6 percent ABV
60-minute boil

Directions

1. Follow the Single-Infusion Brew Process (page 284).

2. Grind coffee and add to primary fermenter 1 day before racking to secondary.

TIP

Switch up the coffee addition as you see fit. For instance, add espresso or cold-steeped coffee into the fermenter or squeeze some syrup into a bottle.

Malt/Grain/Sugar
7.00 pounds Gambrinus ESB Malt
0.25 pound Honey Malt
0.75 pound Crystal 90L
0.25 pound Wheat Malt
0.25 pound Roasted Barley
0.75 pound Lactose (during the boil)

Extract (for 6.0 pounds of ESB Malt)
4.5 pounds Pale Liquid Malt Extract (LME)

Hops
1.00 ounce Goldings—E.K. (5.5 percent AA) Whole for 60 minutes
0.25 ounce Fuggle (4.0 percent AA) Whole for 60 minutes

Other Ingredients
1 tablet Whirlfloc
1 tablespoon Yeast Nutrient
0.5 pound Coffee

Yeast
WLP002 English Ale

Mash Schedule
Saccharification Rest 153°F 60 minutes

Chocolate Porter (page 79) was rescued from too long on the nibs by a raspberry schnapps bottle added to the keg. Add blue curaçao to a light beer and you have every Trekker's dream: orange-flavored Romulan ale.

- **Crème liqueurs (cacao, menthe)**—For those times when you want the flavor, but not the hassle of dealing with the ingredient or worries about sanitation, the crème liqueurs rescue you. Use an unopened bottle to ensure the purity of the contents.
- **Coffee liqueur**—A final way of adding a sweet, nonbitter, coffee flavor to your beer. Do a taste test first before adding the coffee liqueur to avoid overpowering the base beer.

QUESTION?

Is it legal to add booze to my beer?
As long as it's not homemade distillate, absolutely. The great freedom of homebrewing is getting away with things the pros can't do for legal reasons. You can even make your own liqueurs at home. Add fruit or spices or flavor extracts from your shop to a neutral bottle of vodka and let sit for a few weeks.

For spirit-infused recipes, see the Gonzo Hemp Poppy Spirit Wine (page 267) and Denny's Bourbon Vanilla Imperial Porter (page 266).

Other Agents

Not everything added to a kettle is meant to add flavor and aroma. Some items are needed for their effect on the beer.

Beer Boosters

Sometime we can all use a little boost up, and your beer is no different. These agents are designed to help you out when your beer falls a little flat.

- **Heading compound**—a liquid or powder that can be added to increase foaming. If your beer lacks the desired fluffy top, this is the stuff for you.

- **Malto-Dextrin**—Lack of body can ruin an otherwise great beer. Dextrins are unfermentable polysaccharides that provide roundness and fullness to the beer.

Clarifying Agents

To major brewers, clarity is king because people don't want to drink cloudy beer. Sometimes, you want to follow suit. You can either invest in a filtering kit or use clarity agents. There are two classes: kettle agents and conditioning agents. Kettle agents are intended for use in the boil and conditioning agents for use in the secondary fermenter or serving vessel.

Kettle Agents

- **Irish moss**—Dried chopped seaweed (carrageen moss), Irish moss causes proteins to clump during a vigorous boil. Rehydrate a half teaspoon for 20 minutes in warm water before adding to the kettle for 15 to 20 minutes.
- **Whirlfloc**—A tablet form of Irish moss, it has enhanced protein clumping. No need to rehydrate; just add a tablet to a batch for 20 minutes.

Conditioning Agents

- **Bentonite**—A clay and silicate mixture that clears yeast.
- **Gelatin**—Dried animal collagen that attracts negatively charged particles, like husk tannin, yeast, and hop.
- **Isinglass**—Made from the swim bladders of sturgeons, isinglass is a weak and gentle clairifier.
- **Polyclar**—A plastic compound used to attract tannins and oxidized malt polysaccharides.
- **Sparkolloid**—A form of diatomaceous earth and silica (fossilized sea life) that is extremely powerful and often works where others haven't.

Yeast Additives

Beer quality directly correlates to yeast health. With the following additives, you send yeast to overwhelming places:

- **Go Ferm**—Specially designed for dried yeast, add Go Ferm to the yeast's rehydration water.
- **Yeast energizer**—Diammonium Phosphate (DAP), dead yeast hulls and vitamins. Energizer is meant to improve the vigor of or restart a stalled fermentation.
- **Yeast nutrient**—Combining DAP, yeast hulls, ureic acid, and zinc, yeast nutrient is added during the boil. The nutrient creates stronger yeast cells capable of more complete fermentations and tackling bigger beers.

CHAPTER 8

Brew Gear

Time to wade through the gear and gadgets designed to make brewing easy and fun. Not every widget on the shelves is worthwhile, and most aren't necessary. In brewing, the guy with most toys doesn't always win the best batch.

General Gear Advice

There's lot of gear out there, but don't think that you need it all. There are brewers banging away on the kitchen stove with a couple of pots and a bucket. Pick and choose the pieces that fit how you brew. Here are a few things to remember.

When it comes to brewing gear, bargain hunting isn't out the window, but cheap gear will frustrate you and break at importune moments. Also don't be attracted to the flashy new toy. Frugal brewers wait for reviews and the do-it-yourself version.

Always have backups. Murphy's Law is mitigated by a supply of alternate solutions. As your brewery grows, little parts—gaskets, clamps, and so on—creep into vital roles. Do yourself a huge favor and keep extras dedicated to the brewery. A little extra outlay up front can save you.

Measuring Gear

Your brew day starts before the fire hits the kettle. Measuring success equals repeating your successes and knowledge of what's happening with your beer.

- **Scales.** Serious bulk-buying brewers buy a digital postal scale for weighing hops and DME. Minimum resolution should be 0.1 ounce, but 0.01 is even better. To weigh a batch's grain or DME, you'll need a bigger packaging scale. Both types are available cheap online.
- **Thermometers.** You have a few choices: the slow reacting, fragile, cheap red alcohol floaters; the finicky and bi-metal dials; and digital sticks or digital probe thermometers. Remember to calibrate your thermometer against a reliable thermometer or boiling water. Recalibrate dial thermometers often and be careful with the fragile digital probes.
- **Hydrometer.** Accurate measuring of your sugar content clues you in to the efficiency of your brewing processes. Verify a new hydrometer's calibration against distilled water before using.

  To read the hydrometer, fill a hydrometer test jar with wort. Give the hydrometer a spin and let it settle before reading the "gravity" number at the surface. Read your sample close to calibration temperature (around 60°F). To read fermented beer, vigorously pour the beer to degas the sample. Bubbles can interfere with your reading.

- **Refractometer.** Hydrometers need a lot of beer to measure gravity. A hand-held refractometer uses a few drops. The device works off density changes to the index of refraction. Refractometers require complicated formulas (or brewing software) to read fermented beer.

Brew-Day Gear

Everything is measured, so it's time to get brewing. No two brewers' setups are the same. Learn from how others create their beer and watch how their equipment impacts the product.

Pots and Kettles

As a beginner, you need a twenty-plus quart for steeping/boiling and another for heating quarts of rinse water. A large soup/lobster pot or enamel canning pot does the job.

As your brewing operations grow, so do your kettle needs. Full-kettle boils of extract or all-grain beers require a boiling kettle of at least 7 gallons in capacity. Buy kettles a few gallons larger than your batch size to boil vigorously. All-grain brewing needs pots for heating sparge water and one for soaking grain.

Many homebrewers use modified kegs as kettles. Some pick up kegs from bars or purchase beer and forfeit their deposit to gain a new pot. The $30 deposit doesn't cover the nearly $200 cost of a new keg. Be kind to your local micro and buy legitimate retired kegs.

Specially built brewpots come with a number of features of varying usefulness. You can rack boiling via a metal siphoning tube, but it is much easier to crack open a valve spigot. Other features include thermometers, sight glass tubs for measuring volume, false bottoms, diverter plates, and more.

Brewers debate between stainless steel or aluminum pots. Stainless steel's toughness and resistance to cleaning chemicals makes it a natural choice, but they are expensive. Large aluminum kettles cost much less, but they react to strong chemicals and some worry about health safety. Brewers report great success with their aluminum kettles when they clean gently.

Mash Paddle/Big Spoon

Never underestimate the power of a big spoon. You need something strong to thoroughly stir thick, sticky heavy mashes and make boiling beer whirlpools. It needs a long handle to keep your fingers from the beer.

To feel like a brewmeister, invest in a stout wood mash paddle and beat the mash into submission. The modern brewer can choose steel, but avoid plastic paddles. They're flimsy and bend while stirring thick mashes.

Coolers

An alternative to big brewing pots are modified coolers. The big, insulated boxes hold preheated water hot for hours and hold thick mashes right on the dot. Many models are easily modified by replacing the preinstalled drain with a standard ball valve. Look online for more instructions.

Burners

Unless you have a professional stove in your kitchen, your range tops out at 12,000 BTUs/hr, inadequate to bring five gallons to a timely vigorous boil. Thanks to fried turkey's popularity, cheap high-BTU propane burners are available. Units range from 30,000 BTUs to rocket-like 200,000 BTUs to power the boil. Pick one with sturdy legs and a base wide enough to accommodate your pots.

ALERT!

Once you move into the world of flame-belching burners, you need to have a fire extinguisher to stop the flames. Make sure it is charged on brew day. Accidents happen fast, so be prepared!

Wort Chillers

Sticking a pot of boiling wort in a sink of ice water quickly becomes impractical and tedious. Several water-powered chilling options can speed up the vital chilling step. Why vital? It produces clearer beer by causing proteins to coagulate into the "cold break." Also, faster cooling preserves fresher hop aroma and flavor. Finally, the faster you cool, the faster the yeast gets to work fermenting, keeping bacteria at bay.

Immersion Chiller

Looking like a still's coil, an immersion chiller sits in the pot of freshly boiled beer. Cold running water wicks away the heat, leaving cool wort behind.

Sanitation is a breeze. Clean the coil of obvious debris and drop into the boil for 15 to 20 minutes. Cover the kettle and run the cold water. Rock the immersion chiller for greater efficiency.

Counterflow Chiller

Take an immersion chiller and run it in a hose and you get a counterflow chiller. Instead of running cold water through hot wort, you run hot wort through a copper pipe surrounded by flowing cold water. The result is a remarkably fast chill from 180°F to 200°F to 70°F to 80°F in 20 to 50 feet. The major downside is cleaning and sanitation. Before every use, you need to run cleaner through, rinse with hot water, and sanitize with a no-rinse sanitizer (Iodophor/Star-San). Once you get the habit, it's a snap.

Plate Chiller

Straight out of the professional brewery are the plate chillers. New to the market, they work like counterflow chillers but use thin layers of metal plates with water and wort on opposite sides. More compact and more efficient than a counterflow, these chillers require diligence to keep clean.

Grain Mill

If you buy in advance of brew days, you'll want a good roller grain mill. Whole grains store longer and preserve their flavor better. A mill allows you to crack malt at the last minute and adjust the grain crush to your needs.

Choose a unit with two rollers and a hopper. Unless you have Popeye arms, buy a mill that you can power with a drill.

Electric Pump

Gravity is great and reliable, but lifting pots of scalding liquid is dangerous. To the rescue is the high-temperature impeller pump. You can pump wort, sparge water, or cleaner all over the brewery. To prevent damage to the pump, always run the input line wide open, restricting the output to control flow.

Fermentation Gear

Now that the mash, boil, and chill are all done, it's time for fermentation. Treated carefully, your basic fermentation gear can last your whole brewing career.

Fermenters

- **Buckets**—The old reliable, buckets are cheap and unbreakable. They scratch easily, leading to high risk of infection. Clean carefully with a soft sponge. Additionally, they are oxygen permeable, unsuitable for long storage. Some buckets come with spigots to eliminate siphoning. Thoroughly clean and sanitize these spigots.
- **Glass carboys**—Glass water bottles, impervious to cleaners and oxygen, they make great fermenters. Use a brush to clean thoroughly. They are fragile to thermal shock and seriously dangerous if dropped. For that reason, care should always be taken when moving a carboy.
- **Better Bottle**—Better Bottles look like the plastic office water bottles. The bottles have special brewing accessories. They also combine the challenges of cleaning a carboy with the care needed for a plastic bucket.
- **Conicals**—Mimicking tanks used by professional brewers, miniature steel conical fermenters are the ultimate fermenters. With a conical,

you can harvest yeast for immediate repitching like the pros. The downsides are their complicated parts and price.

Fermentation Locks

To keep oxygen, bacteria, and flies at bay, you have a few options. They depend either on liquid barriers or the positive pressure of fermentation to keep the beer free of contaminants.

- **Airlocks**—Airlocks use a little water or vodka to prevent gas from seeping in. CO_2 evolved during fermentation escapes by bubbling out.
- **Blow-off tubes**—Vigorous fermentation can spew yeast, gumming up the works, making a mess, and spraying beer everywhere. Fit a piece of tubing over the airlock spigot or jam a 1"-diameter hose into the carboy opening. Drop the tubing in a bucket of sanitizer. The yeast will come crawling out of the pipe.
- **Foil cap**—Incredibly cheap and easy to use. Sanitize a piece of foil and fit tightly over the carboy mouth. Leave a channel for overflow. When the fermentation recedes, remove the foil and cap with an airlock.

Racking Gear

Moving the beer around requires a deft hand with a siphon. To siphon liquid, make sure your source vessel is above your target container.

- **Racking cane**—A long, straight tube with a crook. Made either of inexpensive plastic or impervious metal, a racking cane can be confusing to use at first. Fill the cane and attached hose with sanitizer and hold both ends up. Pinch the tubing and drop the cane into the source vessel. Drop the hose into a pitcher to catch the sanitizer. Switch to the target container and let the beer flow.
- **Auto-siphon**—A racking cane in a manual pump. A few pumps starts the siphon, but the complicated parts make the plastic gizmo prone to breakage.

Yeast

Your yeast needs toys too. These few things will help you get stronger yeast and stronger fermentations.

- **Magnetic stir plate**—This tool consists of a motor spinning a magnet. When combined with a Teflon-coated magnetic bar inside a vessel, it creates a vortex. This adds oxygen and keeps the yeast in suspension. The combination yields five times as much yeast.
- **Aeration/oxygen**—Add oxygen to freshly chilled wort by pumping air or pure oxygen through a diffusion stone to grow strong yeast. The oxygen kits use the little red torch tanks of O_2 found at your local home improvement store.

Bottling Gear

Bottles need washing, sanitizing, drying, and filling, and the brewing world has gear for all those tasks.

- **Bottles**—If you don't want the hassle of cleaning out a bunch of bottles, consider spending a little cash for new bottles from the local supply store. Start clean and keep them clean.
- **Bottle tree**—After washing and sanitizing, you want the bottles to drip dry. You could use your dishwasher, but a bottling tree is a stable place to dry them. Attachments squirt sanitizer into the bottle before you place them down to dry.
- **Bottling bucket**—A great bottling bucket has a spigot to dispense primed beer and a lid to cover the vulnerable beer. Make sure to thoroughly disassemble and clean the spigot before using.
- **Bottling wand**—A simple, hard plastic tube with a spring-loaded tip that you push into the bottle to pour beer.
- **Capper**—To seal the bottle, you'll need a bottle capper. The basic "wing" model is great for light bottling tasks, but if you deal with a large number of bottles or odd bottles, an old-fashioned bench capper is a great upgrade.

Other Gear

Finally, a few last items to round out your gear collection. They may be vital to your brew success depending on your methods.

Aluminum Foil

Aluminum foil is homebrewer's duct tape; endlessly useful in the brewery and cheap insurance against infection. Use regular foil as a sparge diffuser or sanitize it and cover a starter, carboy, or bottling bucket.

The Beer Glass/Pitcher

Even the lowly beer glass requires a bit of thought. Different glass shapes affect beer taste. Serving Belgian-style ales in a pint glass prevents the blooming of their estery, phenolic aromas. A small collection sufficient to cover your needs includes several pint glasses, tall German weizen glasses, British tulip pints, and Belgian chalices. Some obsessed collectors gather hundreds of glasses.

Keep a few glass and plastic pitchers on hand. Reserve the glass pitchers for serving your beer in all its glory. Use the plastic pitchers for moving hot mash liquor and sparge water around. Don't move hot liquids with the glass.

The Brew Box (also called the Toolkit)

With all the bits and bobs that you reach for on brew day, keeping them at hand and organized can save you time and effort. Even a cheap little plastic toolbox festooned with beer stickers is well worth the money.

The Brew Notebook

Unless you have an eidetic memory, a brewer's notebook serves as record keeper and troubleshooting guide. Batch details become muddled over time: "Did I toss in extra hops on this brew, or is this the one that I forgot the sugar?" Start a notebook on your first brew and use it faithfully to record details that otherwise get lost in the haze.

Grain Buckets "Vittle Vaults"

Buying bulk grain can save a pretty penny, or waste it if you're not careful. Malt is susceptible to insect infestation and staling. Proper storage is the key to longevity. Airtight pet food containers make great malt storage. Just make sure to vent them periodically to prevent moisture damage.

Software Calculators

The tedious calculations and number crunching that accompanies calculating grain additions, hop bittering, and strike temps gets old fast. There are now several software packages to choose from. Some are desktop applications like Beersmith, Beer Tools Pro, and Promash, always ready to predict a result or formulate a recipe. Online websites can calculate and store your brews and share them with the world. Each solution covers much of the same basic ground, but they differ in the details, the interface, and the cost. Eventually, software can replace your brew notebook, but be fastidious with data backup.

Vacuum Sealer

The bulk buyer's dream tool comes in handy for those storing or growing hops. Removing as much oxygen as possible along with cold storage will keep your hops fresher longer. Comes in handy when you want to preserve the aroma of specialty grains and spices.

CHAPTER 9

Beyond the Basics: Extract Brewing

The first batch is both the hardest and simplest you'll make. Bubbling pots and tangled hoses mingle with worries about messing up the works, all in the pursuit of a glass of beer. Time to take the next step and try extract brewing.

Dig Deeper into Your Basic Brew

Now that your head is stuffed with ingredients facts, take some time to review your first batch of beer. This basic process forms the skeleton you hang your brews from. As you progress, you'll add a new step or redefine an existing step. Think this way and even all-grain brewing is well within your reach.

All brew levels need good note taking. The brew gods love playing jokes on forgetful brewers. The session of forgotten notes will be the best batch of beer ever. From then on, you'll chase that batch, attempting to recreate its magic.

The Boil

Why boil beer? Wort must be boiled to eliminate natural spoilage creatures such as a lactobacillus and deadly pathogens. Hops need boiling to isomerize and dissolve the alpha acids. Boiling concentrates sugars, generating flavorful caramel and melanoidins. A vigorous boil causes proteins to clump together as "hot break" and drop out of solution. This helps clarify the beer and improves long-term stability. The boil also helps reduce the water's mineral load.

Brewers obsess over the boil strength. Isn't a boil the same no matter what? While temperature is important, the mechanical roiling plays just as big a part. The turbulence mixes the wort, hops, and nutrients, and causes the proteins to clump.

To measure the vigor of their boil, brewers measure "evaporation per hour." Pros aim for a 10 percent volume loss per hour. That means for every five gallons boiled, you boil off a half gallon. Homebrewers acceptably range from 5 to 15 percent.

Your kitchen stove may be adequate for a partial-boil extract batch, but most stoves prove incapable of a full boil. You can split your wort and hops between burners and boil in multiple pots. Alternatively, you can augment the power of your stove with a 1,500-watt electric bucket heater to speed the boil. Most brewers find that turkey fryer burners provide cheap power to push the boil well beyond the 10 percent mark.

The Chill

For your first batch, a mess of cold water, a scoop of ice, and a sink of cold water were all you needed to chill the wort. A wort chiller simplifies life.

The drop from a boil is important for two reasons: sanitation and cold break. Boiling hot wort kills bad guys, but as the wort loses temperature and drops below 140°F, your sanitary safe haven becomes a bacterial playground. A quick drop to a safe temperature gives yeast a headstart over bacteria.

For clarity and stability purposes, a rapid chill causes additional proteins to solidify into "cold break." To augment the clarity, many brewers strain the break from the fresh wort. Worried counterflow chiller users chill their wort; let the cold break settle in one fermenter for several hours before transferring to another fermenter before pitching.

The Pitch

The yeast pitch is always the same. The goal: deliver a mass of healthy yeast. Make a starter or recycle yeast cakes for maximal fermentation firepower. See Chapter 6 for more details. If you can, pitch the slurry with a minimum of extra wort to avoid flavoring the beer.

The Ferment

Your fermentation efforts center on providing a safe and temperate environment for the yeast to work its magic. Lots of yeast, a little oxygen, and careful control over your temperatures will keep the beer on track.

Extract brewers need to carefully balance residual gravity-boosting measures (e.g., cara-pils, crystal malts, malto-dextrin powder) with extract ferments' habits of stalling at higher than desired finishing gravities. If you find your beer's hanging higher than expected, even with copious yeast supplies, modify the recipe and reduce the presence of those malts.

Packaging: Bottling and Beyond

To package you must transfer the beer with a minimum of aeration. Aeration at this point is detrimental because dormant yeast won't consume the oxygen. That leaves a powerful agent loose in your brew to damage the aroma and flavor. Desirable in some styles, like old ale and barleywine, most beers want to avoid tasting and smelling like wet cardboard.

Steeping Grains: Fresh Grain-Fed Beer

While extract is great for knocking out a basic batch of beer, a cooked taste lurks in the background. The extract you're using has already been processed, boiled, and condensed before arriving to you.

With two additional steps, disguising that stale extract pallor comes at the cost of an hour. Examine the recipe for Chico West Coast Pale (page 100). The first difference is the addition of malted grains. These malts need to be crushed with a grain mill like the one at your local shop. They provide fresh grain flavor and character to the extract base.

Steep and Strain: A New Step

Steeping and straining are two steps that add freshness and increase variety. All grain brewing builds directly on this approach, only instead of "steeping and straining," you'll be "mashing and sparging."

Heat three quarts of water to 170°F. Add the crushed malts to the water and stir thoroughly. You want no dry bits of malt and no dough balls. Set a timer for 45 minutes. Meanwhile, heat another three quarts of water to 170°F and wait.

As the grain steeps, starches and sugars leech out of the freshly crushed kernel. Enzymes from the base malt (the two-row here) act upon the starches and slowly convert them to sugar. The roasted, toasted, and long-chain sugars of the specialty malts are dissolved into the mash liquor, as are the colors formed during malting. After forty-five minutes you'll have a lightly sweet, heavily aromatic, dark amber porridge on your hands.

Now onto the next step, the strain. Pour the soup into your main pot, through a fine-mesh strainer or cheesecloth-lined colander. The strainer catches the grain and husk. Don't throw it away! Take the three quarts of clean water and slowly pour it over the grain, allowing it to wash through to the brew pot. When the rinse is complete, remove and discard the grain. Proceed exactly as before for an extract-only batch.

Extract Limitations and Considerations

Challenges aplenty remain for the extract-dependent brewer. You can mitigate some, but remain aware of them as you brew.

- **Color**—The palest extracts can almost match the color of pale malt before the boil. During the boil they darken considerably, making pale styles impossible. The problem worsens because aging extract darkens, making consistent color prediction difficult.
- **Cost**—Malt prices have increased dramatically, but extract still costs. A five-gallon extract batch can easily cost between $20 to $50 where an all-grain batch costs less than half of that.
- **Flavor**—Despite the use of low-temperature methods, extracts caramelize during production. Carmel and oxidative flavors sneak through to the final product.
- **Specialty extracts**—If you want to brew a batch with grain besides barley or wheat, you're out of luck. To use rye or others, you'll have to perform a mini-mash.
- **Nutrition**—Extract has a dearth of nutrition for yeast. Adding yeast nutrient as a source of free amino nitrogen (FAN) is crucial for yeast health, even if you're only brewing low-gravity ales.
- **Residual gravity**—The days of super-sweet extracts are done, but brews often finish sweet. Part of this is nutrition and the rookie tendency to ignore yeast health, but some extracts are still designed for sugar additions.

Pale and Dry Extract Beers

The twin pillars of extract regret: too dark or too sweet beer. Fighting a suboptimal ingredient doesn't stop the desire to push lighter and drier. Recently brewers have reexamined the dogmatic homebrewing approach

Chico West Coast Pale Ale

American Pale Ale is the beer that built the California microbrewer. Caramel rich with a citrusy hop nose, the APA was the antidote to decades of yellow, characterless beers.

Style: American Pale Ale
Brew Type: Extract with Steeped Grains
For 5 gallons at 1.059 OG, 8.4 SRM, 43
    IBUs, 5.9 percent ABV
60-minute boil

Directions

Follow the Steeping Grains and Extract Process (page 283).

TIP

A standard measurement for liquid malt extract (LME) is 6.6 pounds, because a standard can of LME is 3.3 pounds. If you can't find or prefer using dried malt extract, substitute 5.25 pounds of dry for 6.6 pounds liquid.

Malt/Grain/Sugar
1.00 pound American Two-Row Pale Malt
0.50 pound Crystal 60L Malt
0.50 pound Honey Malt
0.50 pound Aromatic Malt

Extract
6.60 pounds Pale Liquid Malt Extract (LME)

Hops
1.0 ounce Perle (8.25 percent AA) Pellet for 60 minutes
0.5 ounce Amarilo (8.9 percent AA) Pellet for 10 minutes
0.5 ounce Cascade (5.75 percent AA) Pellet for 0 minutes

Yeast
American Ale Strain (WLP001, Wyeast 1056, Wyeast 1272, Safale US-05)

Mash Schedule
Steep the malt in 3 quarts of 170°F water for 45 minutes

Kyle's Dry Irish Stout

Stout, the world-famous all-day tipple of the old-fashioned Irish punter, is a forgiving style. Between the espresso and chocolate flavors of the roasted malts and the pitch-black color, tasters will be pressed to discern flaws.

Style: Irish Stout
Brew Type: Extract with Steeped Grains
For 5 gallons at 1.042 OG, 44 SRM, 18 IBUs, 4.2 percent ABV
60-minute boil

Directions

1. Follow the Steeping Grains and Extract Process (page 283).

2. Fermentation should take less than a week. Skip the secondary on the beer and package right away. If you're using kegs, you could conceivably go kettle to tap in as little as 4 days.

TIP

Note that even here, you use pale extract. Doing so makes you less dependent on the extract manufacturer and allows you to pick up more fresh grain character in your beer.

Malt/Grain/Sugar
1.00 pound Crystal 120L
0.75 pound Roasted Barley
0.25 pound Black Patent Malt
0.25 pound Chocolate Malt

Extract
3.5 pounds Pale Dry Malt Extract (DME)

Hops
0.25 ounce Wye Target (10.0 percent AA) Pellet for 60 minutes
0.75 ounce East Kent Goldings (4.75 percent AA) Pellet for 20 minutes

Other Ingredients
2 teaspoons Calcium carbonate, added to the boil

Yeast
Wyeast 1084 Irish Ale

Mash Schedule
Steep the malt in 3 quarts of 170°F water for 45 minutes

of the past eighty years. These new approaches are providing brewers with better pale extract beers.

The full boil is one technique that improves overall quality of your brew regardless of color. Boiling six gallons of wort reduces caramelized sugars and residual gravity, and improves hops bitterness. Fewer caramelized sugars means paler beer. Since yeast can't ferment them, reducing them yields more fermentable, drier beer.

Going Pale

The first rule of going pale is obvious: use the palest extracts. You have several choices on the market. Choose the freshest and palest appropriate extract. Try a new scheme called late extract addition. Normally, you add all the extract when the wort first boils. Late-addition proponents add extract for just the last fifteen minutes to sanitize. Considerably less darkening takes place. Since hops isomerize better with malt, adding a third of the total extract retains hop character.

Dry as a Bone

Can't do a full boil? Push your yeast to make dry beer. Assuming you make starters, your first fix is increasing doses of yeast nutrient. Stronger beers need stronger yeast, and this is doubly true for yeast swimming in nutrient-deficient extract wort.

Nutrient not working? Switch to more attenuative strains. Look for a strain with a high alcohol tolerance and low flocculation characteristics. Neutral American strains like Wyeast 1056, White Labs WLP001, or Safale US-05 can churn through sugars better than many more flavorful strains.

Finally, you may have an extract issue. Try switching a batch's brands with no other changes. If you get better attenuation, switch from your less attenuative extract. With sweet-finishing extracts, add sugar for part of the gravity. The batch will end up with a lower final gravity.

Partial Mash: The Next Step

For little money and space, you can make the next step, the partial mash. You use more grain than in a steeped batch, around five to six pounds

Belgian Summer Fun

The spicy kick of a summertime saison is the farmhouse tipple of Wallonia. The finicky Belgian saison yeasts ferment hot, so start the beer cool (mid-sixties) and let it rise naturally into the eighties. The beer will finish dry and clear of nasty phenols with the desired aroma.

Style: Belgian Saison
Brew Type: All Grain
For 5.5 gallons at 1.062, 3.5 SRM, 34
    IBUs, 6.6 percent ABV
60-minute boil

Directions

Follow the Steeping Grains Late Extract Variant (pages 283-284).

TIP

The late-extract addition method not only creates a paler extract brew, but it also affects your hopping rates. Thanks to the lower gravity in your pot, more alpha acids will be isomerized into solution. Adjust accordingly for delicate beers or your big hop monsters.

Malt/Grain/Sugar
0.75 pound German Wheat Malt
0.50 pound Belgian Pilsner Malt
0.50 pound Vienna Malt
0.25 pound German Acidulated Malt (Sauer Malt)
1.00 pound Sugar

Extract (for 12.00 pounds of Pale Malt)
6.50 pounds Pilsner Liquid Malt Extract (LME)

Hops
0.50 ounce Magnum (14.0 percent AA) Pellet for 60 minutes
1.00 ounce Czech Saaz (3.5 percent AA) Pellet for 5 minutes

Other Ingredients
1 tablet Whirfloc (added at 20 minutes)
0.5 teaspoon Coriander Seed (added at 0 minutes)
0.5 teaspoon Black Pepper (added at 0 minutes)

Yeast
WLP565 Belgian Saison I/Wyeast 3724 Belgian Sasion

Mash Schedule
Steep 160°F 60 minutes

instead of two to three. The additional grain provides fresher flavors matching commercial brews.

Great for brewers stuck in small spaces, the bare-bones partial mash requires a sturdy nylon grain bag and your brew kettle. Your grain capacity depends on the sack. Don't overfill it to avoid interfering with water flow through the bulging mass.

For a little more investment, a small two-gallon cooler holds approximately five pounds of grain and six quarts of water, a miniature all-grain mash tun. Buy a kit for converting the cooler or follow the modifying instructions found online. The valves and other parts from your mini-mash tun can be repurposed for a larger mash tun.

To convert an all-grain recipe for partial mash, use all the specialty grains and as much base malt as you can. To figure out the extract needed to achieve original gravity, follow the Needed Extract for Partial Mash formula in Appendix C.

Heat 1.25 quarts of water per pound of grain to around 13°F above your desired rest temperature (for instance, heat the water around 165°F for a mash at 152°F). Leave the mash for sixty minutes. At the same time heat an equal water portion to 170°F.

For grain bag users, pull the bag and place in a colander. Rinse like steeping grains. Don't squeeze the bag to avoid lipid extraction.

Cooler users should slowly draw a pitcher of wort from the valve and return to the mash. Repeat until the wort runs free of chunks. Slowly run the wort into your boil pot and add the sparge water to the mash.

Once the brew pot comes to the boil, you're back in the familiar world of extract brewing. From here on out, follow your usual steps to achieve beerdom.

CHAPTER 10

Cleaning: Keeping Your Beer Squeaky Clean

The harsh truth lurking behind the myriad decisions made by a brewer is that nothing can ruin batches faster than poor cleaning and sanitation habits. Sound cleaning techniques build the foundation for good brews. Don't fear tedious scrubbing—"beer clean" doesn't have to be a chore.

What Is Beer Clean?

Face it, brewing is a messy business and not just in the kitchen. Look at the rocky fermentation ring around the collar in the fermenter or the lees at the bottom of an unrinsed bottle. Ignoring the mess doesn't help. Not only do mold and other crawlies feed off the mess, but your cleaning tasks get tougher.

Sanitation can only occur when a surface is clear of organic matter, yeast, protein, or dust. Any remaining crud protects harmful creatures. Take extra minutes with your fermenters to guarantee success.

Pre-Boil Clean Versus Post-Boil Clean

Not every step of the brew day requires careful twenty-point cleaning checklists and pre-op-style scrub sessions. The basic rule: Any equipment used before the boil doesn't need a scrupulous cleaning; anything following the boil needs your complete attention.

This is not to say that you can let your pre-boil equipment lay dirty. All-grain brewers can regale you with stories of mash tuns allowed to sit for a few days untouched. The resulting smell scars and creates unusable equipment. Spraying out obvious detritus, inspecting valves, and wiping down surfaces suffices for pre-boil equipment. Allow all the gear to air-dry first to avoid mold.

Remember the boil kills off any bacteria or wild yeasts looking to hitch a ride in your wort. Post-boil the beer begins to cool, entering the danger zone. From now until the beer splashes your glass, everything contacting the wort must be scrubbed and sanitized to prevent spoilage. This includes: the boil kettle, valves, chillers, fermenters, sampling thieves, racking canes, hoses, bottles, and kegs.

Cleaning Tools

There are a number of cleaning tools available, but which ones do you need? You may find a place for the following in your cleaning regimen. And don't be stingy about replacing worn-out cleaning tools—it's not worth ruining your hard work over a $5 tool.

- **Brushes**—The one piece of brewing equipment you absolutely need. The commonly employed brushes are the "L" shaped carboy brush and the straight bottle brush. Bend the carboy brush to better reach the carboy shoulders where the krausen piles on. Suppliers have brushes designed for many tasks, but your best investment is a new toothbrush.

- **Plastic scrub pads**—The ease of buckets comes at a cost. You must be supremely careful not to scratch them. The tiniest scratches can harbor a spoiling army. To keep things clean and scratch free, use soft scrub pads. Gently wipe, don't dig!

- **Sink jet sprayers**—Designed to attach to a faucet, these jet powered beauties blast gunk. Turn on the water and slide a carboy or bottle over the spout. Powerful spray blasts the surface crud. Spraying freshly poured bottles saves you the ache of soaking and scrubbing.

- **Wallpaper trays**—Long hoses and racking canes are challenging to clean and sanitize. It's hard to beat stacked wallpaper paste trays for soaking. Fill about half way with a gallon of solution and drop in your long items. Draw liquid through the hoses for complete contact.

- **Drill brushes**—Looking like a car wash refugee, soft felt noodles are attached to a drill fitting shaft. At high speed they easily slap away anything clinging to the fermenter.

- **Spray bottles**—Plastic spray bottles can be filled with the cleaner or sanitizer of your choice to effectively cover surfaces.

- **Cleaning sprayers**—Combine a cheap pond pump and crimped copper pipe with a bucket of cleaner and you've created an inexpensive home version of a professional Clean In Place (CIP) rig. Stick a carboy or a keg over the pipe; plug in the pump to wash off all the brew detritus.

Cleaning Agents

You can clean gear with a brush and water alone, but better cleaning is possible through chemistry. Don't reach for the squeeze bottle of dish soap! Regular soaps leave a sticky, rinse-resistant residue.

ALERT!

With all chemical solutions, follow basic safety by adding chemicals to water, not the other way around. Adding water to chemicals can superheat the mixture to explode or cause splashes of ultraconcentrated solution.

Commonly Available Cleaners

- **Automatic dishwashing detergent**—In a pinch, the detergent used in your dishwasher can be used. Add 1 tablespoon per gallon of water. Exceeding this may etch glass. A thorough rinse is required to remove any surfactants. Rinse with hot water until the surface no longer feels slick.
- **Bleach**—Regular unscented bleach is a brewing mainstay. It's cheap, widely available, and effective. Throw a couple of tablespoons in a full bucket or carboy and let it sit for hours. Don't let metal sit in prolonged contact with bleach water, to avoid corrosion. Completely rinse and air-dry before use.
- **TSP (Trisodium Phosphate)**—Cheaper than dishwashing detergent and available at hardware stores, hot water and TSP speedily eats brewery funk. Make sure the TSP you buy is food grade.
- **Sodium percarbonate cleaners**—Sodium percarbonate cleaners, like Oxiclean, release hydrogen peroxide (H_2O_2) when mixed with water. The peroxide attacks stains quickly. Buy "crystal-" and fragrance-free versions and rinse well.
- **One-Step**—A cleaner that combines sodium percarbonate with alkaline agents. The One-Step manufacturer claims no rinsing is needed and that prolonged contact time sanitizes your gear. However, One-Step is not an FDA-certified sanitizer.
- **PBW (Powder Brewery Wash)**—PBW from Five Star Chemicals is the strongest of the percarbonate cleaners. PBW solutions dissolve

almost any brewery mess. It has an added advantage of rinsing easily. Mitigate the cost by buying in bulk.

FACT

Caustic (i.e., sodium hydroxide or lye) is the cleaner of choice in professional breweries. Due to the danger, home use is highly discouraged. Caustic solutions chemically burn on contact. This stuff is what's used to unclog drains and clean greasy ovens!

Common threads in the cleaner discussion: hot water and rinsing. Hot water speeds the cleaning reaction. Careful rinsing ensures a clean surface. Let the gear soak just as long as needed, otherwise etching may occur. With powdered detergents, a hard white film can form (a quick soak in a vinegar solution can loosen it).

If you're tempted to use your dishwasher for cleaning, don't! Between drying and clean rinse agents (like Jet Dry) and inconsistent application of cleaner and rinse water, there are too many variables to depend upon the machine to achieve "beer clean."

Sanitation

Sanitation is the act of killing enough "bad" critters from the wort to allow yeast to establish a foothold. As yeast cells multiply, they exhaust nutrients, lower the pH, and produce ethanol that prevents recolonization by good beer foes.

Bacteria and wild yeast hide in the tiniest places and gladly nap behind a spot of dirt or organic material. During the tumultuous churning of racking or fermentation, the protective spot can wash away, exposing the microbes to the yummy, delicious wort. Hence, the initial emphasis on good cleaning practices.

Microbes wouldn't matter if they didn't produce off-flavors and aromas. Your sense of smell is sensitive to low levels of bacterial contamination to safeguard you from bad food. Therefore, bacterial products swamp the pleasant flavors produced by your yeast.

Your brewing job is driving off the bad guys and nurturing your yeast. Don't skimp! You won't notice the effects the first few times, but eventually bugs will roost in your gear. If you develop a house flavor, switch sanitation chemicals and tighten your routine. Professional brewers do this to avoid wasting thousands of dollars of beer.

FACT

The natural antimicrobial effects of boiling, alcohol, low pH, and hops make beer remarkably safe. Dangerous bacteria don't live in beer. No matter how bad your beer may taste, you won't get sick from any wee visitors.

What about Sterilization?

Brewers talk about sanitation, not sterilization. While they both mean eliminating foreign agents from a surface, sanitation allows "adequate" removal. Sterilization requires the complete removal of all bacteria, yeasts, and spores. A sterile object is microbiologically pristine. Why do brewers only practice sanitation? Sterilization of brewing equipment is impractical, prohibitively expensive, and, with good yeast practices, unnecessary.

Sanitation Agents

Unlike cleaning where elbow grease can win, successful sanitation requires the judicious application of chemicals or heat. Sanitation chemicals are safe when used at recommended concentrations. Use too little and proper sanitation won't happen. Use too much and you can hurt your equipment and beer.

ESSENTIAL

Yeast culturing (or "ranching") requires sterilization. Because you're dealing with small quantities of yeast, growing the culture in a sterile environment is critical. Preparing media and other small sterile items is best accomplished with an autoclave or pressure cooker.

Commonly Used Sanitizers

- **Bleach**—The cheap and available option that virtually every brewer uses at the start. A tablespoon per gallon of water sanitizes surfaces after a twenty-minute soak. Rinse with freshly boiled water and dry. The chlorine needs a thorough rinsing and drying to avoid creating chlorophenols. This is a common side effect.
- **Iodophor**—Iodophor combines iodine with coating aids. Used at proper dilution levels, it acts as a "no-rinse" sanitizer after only two minutes of surface contact. Higher concentration levels don't sanitize better and you risk staining any plastic gear and adding an iodine flavor to your beer!
- **Star-San/Sani-Clean**—A suspension of phosphoric acid and other chemicals, this no-rinse sanitizer works in a minute. Star-San foams with little agitation, penetrating cracks to reduce bacterial hiding spots. The foam is perfectly safe in your beer. Many brewers freak out on their first use, but don't fear the foam! Sani-Clean has no foaming agent. It requires more contact time. Keep a small spray bottle of fresh Star-San for quick touchups.
- **Isopropyl Alcohol/Ethanol**—In professional brewing, spray bottles of isopropyl alcohol are used for sanitizing valves before opening and closing. At home, use a concentrated 70 percent solution of alcohol for extra assurance. Before pitching, spray alcohol on starter vessel and carboy mouths.
- **Oven heat**—You can sterilize beer bottles in your oven. Take clean, dry bottles and cap them with foil. Stack them in a cold oven and set thermostat to 340°F. Bake the bottles at temperature for an hour. Shut off the oven and cool the bottles overnight. As long as the foil stays firmly in place, you have a sterile bottle.

Beerstone

After a few brews, your kettles and fermenters start to carry a whitish or brownish coat. You've just encountered calcium oxalate, commonly called beerstone. Hard water, cleaners, and wort proteins combine to form a rough surface. Allowing this stone to build up creates hiding spots for bacteria and reduces kettle efficiency.

Scrub and scrub, you'll remove a fraction of the scale. Some brewers swear by strong cleaner. Even strong solutions still require scrubbing. Attack the problem from the other side of the pH scale and make a weakly acidic solution. Mix citric acid or "Acid 5" with water and soak the vessel for thirty minutes. The beerstone will easily wipe off. Dry your kettles for a few days to passivate the metal.

Cleaning and Sanitizing the Gear Rundown

With equipment and cleaning chemicals in hand, it's time to apply them. Each piece of equipment requires a bit of special care. First, a few general rules:

- When dealing with any strong chemicals, take appropriate precautions. Gloves and glasses are a smart idea!
- Clean everything while it's still fresh. Dried yeast and syrupy malty goo is exponentially harder. Rinse everything immediately after use. They'll be available faster on short notice.

Plastic Buckets

The main downside of the ubiquitous plastic bucket is sensitivity to scratches. Breathe too hard and you create a bacteria-harboring furrow. Handle your cleaning tasks with a soft sponge or a plastic scrubbing pad.

Carboys

Glass carboys are virtually bulletproof as long as you don't press too hard with any metal-tipped brushes. Carboys handle any chemical that you throw at them. For routine cleaning, spray them out to remove major debris. Mix up your favorite hot cleaner and soak overnight. A quick swipe of a carboy brush takes care of anything else.

Save sanitizer solution by filling the carboy halfway. Plug it with a solid stopper and lay it on the side. Roll it to the other side after five minutes for complete sanitation.

Bottles

If you practice good rinsing, your used bottles need a quick spritz. For a cache of dirty bottles fill a big tub with cleaner and soak the bottles. Bleach or ammonia soaking (not together!) takes off stubborn bottle labels.

Rinsed and dried bottles can be sanitized via the oven (see above) or by soaking them in sanitizer. Air dry them on your bottle tree or dishwasher rack (a bottle on each post). When dry, cover with sanitized foil.

Kettles

Kettles are the low-maintenance pieces of the brewhouse. Most sessions they just need a scrubbing. Brush out spigots to avoid mold. When the kettle interiors look brown and grimy, tackle the beerstone. Follow the directions above to restore your kettle's shine.

Stainless steel's corrosion resistance stands up to the strongest chemicals with nary a blemish. Aluminum kettles are cheap and reliable, but strong acids and caustics damage them easily.

Hoses and Racking Canes

All the warnings about cleaning while wet apply in triplicate to your hoses and racking gear. A hose with dried goo is a dead hose. For quick rinsing, get a barb adapter for your sink. Stick a hose on and let the water pressure rip. Pulse the water on and off to dislodge anything stubborn. Soak the canes and hoses in a wallpaper tray and rinse. Twirl and hang to dry hoses.

CHAPTER 11

Fermentation

Beer making finally comes down to managing a great fermentation. Remember, brewers make wort and yeast make beer—but brewers make happy yeast.

A Typical Ferment

Fermentations follow a standard script with the yeast providing the accent and flavor. You manage the successful translation of story to glass. Along the way, there are many pitfalls, but fermentation happens no matter what you do.

Aeration and Oxygenation

The fermentation story begins as the cooled wort transfers to the fermenter. As the beer splashes its way into the vessel, it picks up oxygen. Smart brewers use this opportunity to add more oxygen to the mix. Some aerate the wort mechanically, shaking the fermenter for twenty minutes, using a sanitized whisk or drill-mounted paint mixer to whip air into the wort. Others choose an aquarium pump to push air through a sterile filter and diffusion stone, letting small bubbles rise through the wort. The final choice scraps the pump and attaches the stone to an oxygen tank. This is the last time oxygen is added to the brew. Done right, the yeast grow stronger and more capable of tackling the fermentation task.

Pitching

Pitching yeast isn't a complicated task, but to ensure a successful pitch, make a starter. Follow the All-Purpose Easy Starter (page 63) instructions a day or two before brewing. Starters increase the chances of success. Clean and sanitize the mouth of the starter vessel (or yeast packet) and fermentation vessel before pouring. Use a spray of isopropyl alcohol or Star-San. Pour the yeast and seal up the fermenter. If you're feeling mix happy after the aeration, give it a swirl and walk away.

Phases of Primary Fermentation

Yeast on hitting the wort begins a five-stage fermentation life cycle. They go to work immediately, adjusting to their new environment. During this lag phase, yeast takes in the dissolved oxygen and nutrients, gearing up to convert sugar to ethanol and CO_2. Within a few hours, they enter the accelerating growth phase, a period of reproduction and energy storage.

A few hours after pitching, growth becomes exponential and fermentation apparent. During this time the yeast cells divide to saturate the wort. This exponential phase is when many yeast flavors and aromas are generated. Yeast cells treated to subpar conditions, lack of nutrients, underpitching, or too much heat release stressor chemicals altering the beer's flavor.

Ten hours later, the fermentation hits the decelerating growth phase. The rocky krausen goes mad and alcohol production ramps up. When the airlock blurps crazily, you're here. By this point, you should have your beer at or below fermentation temperature. Fermentation generates enough heat that you can't cool the wort down.

In several days, the messy krausen falls away and the yeast enters the final stage, the stationary phase. By this point no nutrition remains and almost all of the sugar is converted. The yeast and krausen drops and the beer clears. The yeast consumes fermentation byproducts, like buttery diacetyl.

Once the yeast hits the stationary phase, the bulk of fermentation is done. Little activity occurs beyond cleanup work. Less flocculant yeast cells lag behind, consuming additional sugars before giving up the ghost.

With a good starter, you can shorten the lag and accelerating growth phases and jump quickly to the exponential phase. The head start means less energy spent reproducing to reach saturation. The yeast remains less stressed and retains more energy for the ferment ahead.

Autolysis

Some brewers monitor primary fermentation's end with vigilance. The moment the primary is done, they move to secondary to age and clarify. What they hope to avoid is autolysis. Yeast, along with other unicellular creatures, has a built in suicide mechanism. When food runs out, cells go dormant, using their glycogen reserves. Left too long, the cells become damaged. The cell releases digestive enzymes, destroying the cell. The cell's "guts" release into the surrounding beer. The resulting flavor contribution has been described as burnt, rubbery, vegetal, and funky.

Older texts stressed quickly moving the beer to avoid this problem. Conventional wisdom set a week's deadline, but award-winning brewers leave beer in primary for a month with no ill effects when using healthy yeast.

Secondary Fermentation

"Secondary fermentation" is viewed as a magical period. Very little fermentation occurs when you rack the beer to a second smaller vessel to age for several weeks. Transfer-roused yeast may kick off a brief fermentation. New brewers panic seeing "little white islands" appear on their beer. Don't worry. It's just yeast.

To perform a secondary, sanitize a five-gallon carboy and gently siphon the beer from the primary. Glass is preferred because it is impervious to oxygen. The gentle siphon avoids stirring air into the beer.

Allow the beer to age and clarify in the carboy for two to four weeks. Dry hopping is best done in the secondary since, as the ferment is complete, CO_2 won't scrub out the fresh hop aromas. The same goes for flavoring of any sort. Sugary additions, like fruit, require a large six-gallon carboy. Once the yeast are done attacking the new sugar source, rack over to the smaller carboy.

Beer can be held in secondary indefinitely, as long as the airlock is topped up. One brewer's batch of date mead sat in the secondary for nine years before finally being served!

QUESTION?

Is a secondary fermentation absolutely necessary?
No. Many ale styles can go straight from primary to bottling without worry. Dark beers work well since you worry less about clarity. Neutral and flocculant strains of yeast clear in a weeklong primary. Some brewers favor skipping the secondary to avoid the risk of infection and oxidation.

Lagers: Fermenting in the Chill

Lagers love the cold, but fermenting a lager requires more than pitching a lager strain and chucking the fermenter somewhere cold.

The first difference comes with the starter. No matter the gravity of your beer, you'll need a starter. Lagers require 50 percent more yeast for optimal fermentation. Grow your starter in the mid-seventies and chill in the fridge.

You should chill the new wort below 60°F if possible. Once there, pitch the yeast like any other and immediately set in a cold environment to hold the wort at 50°F. If you're using a refrigerator or freezer, set the thermostat 5°F to 8°F below the fermentation temperature. The heat of fermentation puts the beer in the target zone.

You set the thermostat lower because air is a lousy thermal conductor. You can fill a yeast vial with water and stick a waterproof thermostat probe in the vial. This allows the thermostat to get a more accurate reading on liquid temperatures.

Lager primary fermentation takes longer. Primaries of two to three weeks with no krausen are not uncommon. When the beer is ready for transfer to secondary, warm it up for a day. Raise the temp on the fridge to the mid-sixties for twenty-four hours. Reduce to 50°F and wait a day before proceeding. This bump in temperature is called a "diacetyl rest" and allows the yeast to clean up excess diacetyl. Ale yeasts don't require this step thanks to warmer fermentation temperatures.

Rack the beer to secondary, lowering the temperature daily a degree or two until you hit 35°F. Hold the beer before bottling.

Bottles carbonate at normal ale temperatures and before chilling for maximum lifespan.

Techniques for Managing Temperature

After proper yeast management, temperature control brings the biggest boost in beer quality. Even warm fermenting ales need cooler temperatures than the average room temperature.

Fermenting warm does a number of things to the brew. Yeasts produce more esters and fusel alcohols when hot. Fusels are solvent-smelling higher alcohols that lead to nasty headaches. Most yeast produce an overabundance of aromas like diacetyl, sulfur, cooked corn, and so on, while eating too much sugar. It's not a pretty picture.

Hefeweizen strains are the classic example of dramatically changing yeasts. Fermented cool, they generate clove phenols. As they ferment warmer, the clove disappears, replaced by banana and then bubblegum.

Spoilage increases with heat. Traditionally, summer brewing was forbidden for this very reason. Even with an adequate yeast population, spoilage bacteria can leave a mark on your brew.

Monitor the temperature span experienced by the wort. During the course of the fermentation cycle, you want to keep the beer from swinging more than 10°F. Large thermal shifts can shock the yeast cells and cause them to go dormant. Fermenting in an uninsulated garage, for instance, requires a close eye on the needle.

Following are some recommended methods for cooling and heating;

Cooling Methods

- **Evaporative cooling**—The cheapest and easiest-to-implement suggestion. Find a large, shallow pan. Slip a T-shirt over the fermenter and set it down in the pan. Fill the pan with water and wet the T-shirt. As the water evaporates from the shirt, more wicks up from the pan lowering temperatures by a few degrees. Point a fan at the assembly to speed up the effect. Useful for cooling a fermenter in an air conditioned room.

- **Water bath**—Fill a clean trashcan with water and ice to cover the fermenter. Add new ice periodically. Leave a floating thermometer in the bath to check the temperature. To save on ice, freeze water-filled soda bottles. Put two two-litter bottles in the bucket every twelve hours to maintain temperatures.

- **Fermentation chiller**—For craftsmen, look online for the Son of Fermentation Chiller. Using thick polystyrene walls, the SoFC is an ice-powered fermentation chamber. The chiller monitors the temperature in the chamber and blows cold air to keep the temperature down.

- **Refrigerator/Freezer**—Lagers need colder temperatures. An external thermostat-controlled refrigerator or freezer is a powerful fermentation chamber. Set the temperature and your fermenters quietly rock away at the right temperature.

Brewers in northerly climes have the opposite problem. How do you keep the fermenter chugging at 68°F when the wind is howling below 0°F?

Heating Methods
- **Brewbelt**—An electrically heated band the circles a bucket and heats a narrow region of the brew. Cheap and effective.
- **FermenWrap**—A flat-panel heater designed to wrap around a large fermenter. With an external thermostat it can provide heat when needed.
- **Light bulb**—Placed in a refrigerator, an incandescent light bulb keeps a fermenter snug. With a two-stage thermostat, a brewer can set up a year-round fermentation chamber.

Cold-Pitched Ramped Fermentation

Like most homebrewers, you pitch your yeast after letting it come up to room temperature. Based on macrobrewers' practical experience, pitch your yeast straight from the fridge. The wort should be chilled a full 5°F below the target fermentation temperature (for example, a pale ale targeted to ferment at 68°F, should be chilled to 63°F before pitching).

The heat generated by the initial phase of fermentation heats the wort. You can quit wrestling to cool a warmer beer against the increasing fermentation heat.

Starting cool suppresses production of fusel alcohols and other aromas. Doing this guarantees full fermentation of big beers with less harsh aroma. This is great for Belgian brewers.

What to Do If Your Fermentation Stops Fermenting

It happens to all brewers. A chugging fermentation, suddenly stops like it hit a brick wall. Grabbing a sample, you look at the hydrometer wondering if your ferment is done. Sadly, you're stuck with a fermentation that won't finish out. Any number of factors can cause a stuck ferment.

If the gravity is close, you could have reached the alcohol threshold for your yeast strain, mashed too warm, or added too many dextrinous malts. Rouse flocculant yeast strains to resume fermentation. Gently, swirl the vessel to stir the yeast back into solution. Other strains will stop for a week before resuming fermentation. Be patient with those.

If the fermentation has dipped too cold, the yeast may have gone dormant. Bring the fermenter to a warm space, rouse the yeast, and stand back.

Nutrient shortage also causes problems. To correct, boil yeast nutrient or energizer and add to fermenter. Wait a day and watch for signs of fermentation.

Pitching another yeast strain, from a yeast cake or another package, can fix a lot of problems. It's best to take a yeast starter at high krausen for this purpose. Think of it as giving the yeast a running start.

The nuclear option is Beano, the sugar-chomping supplement. Beano contains alpha galactosidase. It attacks complex carbohydrates. It reduces them into fermentation-ready simple sugars. A single crushed Beano tablet added to wort drops the final gravity surprisingly low. Be careful bottling a Beano'd brew! Use hydrometer readings to verify fermentation is complete before bottling.

A Ferment That Never Starts

The only thing scarier than a stuck fermentation is no fermentation. Every new brewer experiences a seemingly dead ferment. "There are no bubbles from the airlock" is the chief diagnostic sign. Before declaring the brew dead, take hydrometer readings and check the lid or stopper. Nine times out of ten the problem turns out to be a loose lid or stopper while the beer chugs away.

No fermentation means you may have pitched a bad pack of yeast or pitched while the beer was hot. Reach for the emergency pack of dry yeast, rehydrate, and pitch. Seal everything up and wait for fermentation to kick off.

High-Gravity Ferments

When it comes to doing a beer above 1.075, everything becomes harder. It wouldn't be fair if there wasn't a price to pay for hitting the high notes.

Like a lager, yeast starters need to be doubled. If you're brewing a lager like the Falconsclaws (page 214), it's even worse. Using a yeast cake from a lower-gravity batch is an economical and prudent way to ferment. Either harvest the yeast cake, or if you're bold, rack the new beer directly onto the cake.

Barley and yeast are pretty simpatico, nutrients-wise. You don't have to worry adding nutrient. For bigger beers, the normally optional nutrient addition becomes mandatory.

The post-chilling oxygen-addition rule goes out the window too. For 1.100+ beers an oxygen addition at twelve hours is recommended. Some brewers use a third addition at twenty-four hours to build super-strong yeast.

Bigger beers cry out for blow-off tubes or foil covers instead of airlocks. Stories abound of brewers making a big, coal-black imperial stout that clogs the airlock, which then shoots off the ceiling. Yeast and jet black beer sprayed over the walls, ceiling, and floor.

High gravities make yeast prone to overproducing esters and fusel alcohols. Don't worsen the situation by neglecting temperature control. Be careful—big beers generate big heat. Be aggressive with your control measures during that critical first twenty-four hours.

Learn to accept higher finishing gravities. You'd normally be upset finishing in the 1.020s, but for a big beer this may be the finish line.

A version of Blackwine IV (page 270) finished in the 1.050s. The combination of hops, ethanol, and coffee resulted in a beer that tasted perfect even at the high gravity. The first edition of Three Floyds' infamous Dark Lord suffered similarly.

Big Bad Barleywine

A big burner barleywine that originally was an extract batch with grains. It went on to win numerous awards. The sweet, burnt-caramel malt character is held in check by the heavy shot of British hops.

Style: English Barleywine
Brew Type: All Grain
For 5.5 gallons at 1.094, 16.4 SRM, 89.0 IBUs, 9.3 percent ABV
60-minute boil

Directions

Follow the Single-Infusion Brew Process (page 284).

TIP

Start first with a bitter, brown, or porter. Use the yeast cake from that batch of beer to ferment this big guy and give it two shots of oxygen to invigorate the yeast.

Malt/Grain/Sugar
16.25 pounds Maris Otter Pale Ale
0.50 pound Crystal 90L
0.50 pound Special B Malt
0.50 pound Biscuit Malt
0.50 pound Turbinado Sugar

Extract (for 15.25 pounds of Maris Otter Malt)
11.5 pounds Pale Liquid Malt Extract (LME)

Hops
2.20 ounces Wye Target (10.6 percent AA) Pellet for 60 minutes
0.50 ounce Goldings—E.K. (5.45 percent AA) Pellet for 20 minutes
1.10 ounces Czech Saaz (5.0 percent AA) Pellet for 0 minutes

Other Ingredients
1 tablet Whirlfloc
1 teaspoon Gypsum
0.50 teaspoon Calcium carbonate
1 tablespoon Yeast Nutrient

Yeast
Wyeast1318 London Ale III

Mash Schedule
Saccharification Rest 150°F 60 minutes

JJ Remix Rye DIPA

An example of recipe sharing, the concept originally came from Josh Jensen. He freely provided his recipe that subsequently was "remixed" into a new, rye-infused Double IPA.

Style: Rye DIPA
Brew Type: All Grain
For 5.5 gallons at 1.084, 6.8 SRM, 151.5
    IBUs, 7.9 percent ABV
120-minute boil

Directions

Follow the Single-Infusion Mash Instructions (page 284) or Partial Mash Profile (page 102).

TIP

Rye has an incredible flavor, but it makes a sticky mash. Rice hulls add lauter insurance. If you're doing a partial mash, definitely use the hulls to supplement all the missing barley hulls.

Malt/Grain/Sugar
12.00 pounds Pale Malt Two-Row
2.00 pounds Rye Malt
1.00 pound Munich Malt
0.50 pound Aromatic Malt
0.50 pound Flaked Rye
0.75 pound Rice Hulls
1.50 pounds Cane Sugar (20 minutes of boil time)

Extract (for 11.0 pounds of Pale Malt)
7.50 pounds Pale Liquid Malt Extract (LME)

Hops
0.50 ounce Chinook (12.0 percent AA) Pellet for 90 minutes
1.00 ounce Columbus (16.7 percent AA) Pellet for 60 minutes
1.00 ounce Columbus (16.7 percent AA) Pellet for 30 minutes
1.00 ounce Horizon (10.0 percent AA) Pellet for 15 minutes
1.00 ounce Columbus (16.7 percent AA) Pellet for 5 minutes
1.00 ounce Warrior (16.0 percent AA) Pellet for 5 minutes
1.00 ounce Cascade (5.2 percent AA) Pellet for 0 minutes
2.00 ounces Amarillo (10.0 percent AA) Whole for Dry Hopping

Other Ingredients
1 tablet Whirlfloc
1 tablespoon Yeast Nutrient

Yeast
WLP001 California Ale

Mash Schedule
Saccharification Rest 154°F 60 minutes

CHAPTER 12

Serving Your Beer

There is nothing like opening the fridge and finding a bottle of your beer waiting: glistening condensation reminding you of the hard work and your upcoming reward. Now is the time to set your beer for a perfect landing.

Bottled Beer

Tour an industrial brewery sometime. The most action-packed part of the day is the whizzing, dangerous bottling line. Bottling beer doesn't have to be that complicated. Bottling involves capturing, instead of releasing, carbon dioxide and dissolving it into the beer. End result, a beer with wonderful crisp CO_2 fizz and frothy suds.

To start, you need a couple cases of clean and sanitized bottles, sugar, and tools including caps, a capper, and a bottling wand. As long as your sanitation is topnotch and you take care with the beer going into the bottles, you'll be on easy street.

Procuring and Preparing Your Bottles

Out of 5.5 gallons, you'll end up with about 5 gallons of beer. That missing half gallon gets left behind in the trub, missed by the racking cane or used for gravity samples. That's why brewing more than 5 gallons per batch is smart.

Choosing the size of your bottles is your first decision. The twelve-ounce longneck is available everywhere. You can buy them new from the store, gather friends and drink a bunch of beer, or nicely ask the local bar for empties. To handle the batch, you need about fifty-four bottles.

ALERT!

If you go the drinking or bar route, avoid screwtop bottles. You can cap a screwtop bottle, but they don't seal consistently.

The downside of the longneck: you have to fill more bottles! Other choices include sixteen-ounce and twenty-two-ounce "bomber" bottles. Proponents argue that you get a fuller glass of beer with less sediment and less work. Evidence suggests that beer ages better in larger volumes thanks to less oxygen exposure.

Two options exist for those who fear caps. The first are twelve-ounce brown PET (plastic) bottles with screw tops. Think stout soda bottles with little white caps. They have low oxygen permeability, but don't use these for long-aging beers.

Swing top bottles, commonly called grolsch bottles, beat the plastics. Coming in a variety of sizes, the stoppers make a satisfying chunk sound when popped. New swing tops cost a pretty penny, but, treated right, they will last. Keep a supply of gaskets on hand and inspect the gaskets before filling.

Planning on entering competitions? Make sure at least a portion of your batch ends up in plain twelve-ounce bottles. Most competitions refuse to accept entries in anything else to anonymize entries.

Priming the Beer for Bubbles

The first bottling step is making sure the bottles are cleaned and sanitized. Follow the instructions in Chapter 10 to ensure that you have safe and ready bottles. Make sure to take apart any bottle wands and bucket spigots and clean and sanitize them completely. This is your last point of contact with the beer before drinking, so don't falter now!

During fermentation, lots of bubbles clinked harmlessly to the void. For the bottle, you provide the yeast with extra food and trap the bubbles. Guides often say add a ¾ cup of sugar, but it's better to weigh your sugar. All priming materials are presented in ounces by weight.

Priming Options
- **Sugar**—The default choice for most brewers. Corn sugar (dextrose) syrup dissolves easily, providing ample fodder for tired yeast. Look at Chapter 7 for different sugar additions.
- **Dry malt extract**—Some brewers believe using DME instead of sugar produces better head and finer carbonation. It may leave a ring around the bottleneck, a possible sign of contamination, and it may take longer to carbonate.

- **Honey**—Brewers attempting to spruce up a beer's aroma can turn to honey. Unlike earlier doses of honey, adding to the bottle retains more honey aroma.
- **Wort**—Breweries that bottle-condition their beer often use unfermented wort to prime the beer. The amount of wort needed is determined by the specific gravity of the wort. You want to add the same amount of gravity from the wort as you do sugar. Germans add actively fermenting wort to the bottle (krausening). In theory, the active beer carbonates faster and clears more postfermentation flaws.
- **Carbonation tablets**—Hard sugar tablet "drops" designed to dissolve in the bottle. Dosage varies by manufacturer, but all go straight in the bottle, which is then capped and shaken. They take longer due to the time it takes to dissolve. Great for a few bottles when kegging.

FACT

Brewers talk about carbonation in terms of volumes of CO_2. What it means is for a given volume of beer, there are X volumes of CO_2 in solution. For instance, one gallon of beer carbonated to 2.5 volumes has 2.5 gallons of dissolved CO_2.

RECOMMENDED CARBONATION LEVEL BY STYLE	
Style	Target CO_2 Level (Volumes)
Ale, default	2.5
American Lager	2.5–3.0
American Pale Ales	2.3–2.6
Barelywine	1.5–2.0
British Browns and Bitters	1.5–2.25
Belgian Ales	2.4–3.5
Dark Lagers	2.2–2.5
Lager, default	2.7
Pale Lagers	2.3–2.8
Saison	3.0–3.5
Stout, Porter	1.5–2.0
Wheat Beers	2.6–4.5

PRIMING NEEDED FOR CARBONATION (ALES, 5 GALLONS)		
Volumes CO$_2$	Sugar (ounces / weight)	DME (ounces / weight)
1.5	1.7	3.4
1.75	2.4	4.75
2.0	3.1	6.1
2.25	3.7	7.4
2.5	4.4	8.8
2.75	5.1	10.1
3.0	5.7	11.5
3.25	6.4	12.8
3.5	7.1	14.1

QUESTION?

Does the priming sugar increase the ABV of my beer?
Yes it does. For a normal (approximately) four-ounce sugar priming in a five-gallon batch, you'll get a bump of about 0.25 percent ABV. The more sugar, the more alcohol and CO$_2$, to a point.

The Final Deed

Dissolve your priming sugar in an equal volume of water. Boil the syrup for at least ten minutes to sterilize. Add the syrup to the sanitized bottling bucket and transfer the beer into the syrup, creating a gentle spiraling action. This will help mix the syrup throughout the beer.

Beers above 8 percent ABV might need a yeast boost. Add a rehydrated pack of dry yeast when the bucket is half full. Some brewers successfully carbonate 11-plus percent ABV beers with the original yeast.

Cover everything with foil. When ready, open the valve or start the siphon to the bottling wand. Press the wand down to fill and remove when full. The wand should leave a perfect headspace. Crimp the cap several times to ensure a seal.

The Waiting Game

Time to exercise patience and restraint. You'll be dying to open that first bottle, but give it a full two weeks to carbonate at 70°F. Take one bottle and chill to check carbonation. Even after two weeks, the beer may still be flat.

Check a bottle every week. If the bubbles still aren't there after a month, you may have to open the bottles up and add a little dry yeast.

Store capped bottles upright for the long term. This keeps the caps from rusting and the yeast sediment resting on the bottom. Keep the bottles cool and out of the light. Stronger beers and meads, bottled properly, can keep for years.

ALERT!

To avoid the dreaded bottle bomb, observe these rules: Bottle your beer only when fully fermented; carefully measure your priming sugar; mix the priming sugar thoroughly to ensure even carbonation.

Kegs: Getting Your Own Draft Beer

Even the happiest brewer faced with a pile of bottles wants to chuck it. Bottling may be the biggest reason people stop brewing. For a little extra cash, you can skip the hassle of bottles for a keg.

The convenience of one container aside, other reasons make the transition worthwhile. You have precise control over carbonation levels and the flexibility to pour a little glass, a big glass, or a pitcher—all yeast free. You even get the thrill of your own tap handles on faucets.

Keg Gear

There's a passel of gear that comes all at once. A simple keg setup runs $100 to $200 without the cost of a fridge or freezer. Look for a setup without a CO_2 tank. In most areas, a local shop can provide you with a tank and fill for a small deposit. When the cylinder runs out, swap the tank for a new one.

The Keg

The homebrewer's keg is the five-gallon Cornelius "Corny" keg. These stainless steel cylinders were used to mix soda syrup, now phased out of service. They are easy to clean and maintain, so get them now before the last used units disappear. Each keg has two posts, one for pushing gas in, the other for taking beer out.

Pepsi and Coke had different fittings. When you buy kegs and parts, pay attention to which style you have: ball lock (Pepsi) or pin lock (Coke). Pick a style and buy the same. Pin-lock kegs tend to be shorter and squatter, an advantage for brewers designing kegerators around short fridges. Ball-lock kegs are more widely adopted among brewers.

Beware the "free" fridge or freezer. The older model units are energy hogs. Readings from a "Kill-a-Watt" meter prove that within six months' time the electric bill exceeds the cost of a newer, more energy-efficient unit.

Commercial sanke kegs are hardier and more difficult to use. Gaining access to the keg innards involves pressure releasing, screw drivers, and a little know-how. Not many brewers have adopted this method.

Other Parts

- **CO_2 tank**—You can buy a new/used aluminum/steel CO_2 tank in two-, five-, and fifteen-pound sizes. You don't need one if you go to places that swap tanks. In fact, you may lose your tank in the rush.
- **Gas regulator**—Choose either a dual- or single-gauge regulator with a cutoff switch. Get a "gauge cage" to prevent your regulator from breaking when the tank falls over.
- **"Cobra" draft lines**—These are your basic serving lines, named for the flattened appearance of the picnic tap. Choose 5 to 7 feet of ³⁄₁₆ inch line for smooth service.
- **Gas/Liquid fittings**—Each side has different adapters to attach to the kegs. They are color coded: gray for gas, black for beer. Ball-lock keg connectors slide on to the post with a pull on a retaining ring. Pin locks twist and lock into place.
- **Refrigerator/Mini-fridge/Chest freezer**—You must have a way to store cold kegs. Choose a refrigerator for ease of access and doorway faucet installation. A mini-fridge converts into a two-keg kegerator for the space conscious. The most versatile option is a chest

freezer. With an external thermostat, you can serve beer from 55°F to 30°F with improved lagering capabilities.

Keg Cleaning

Keg cleaning is the most thankless job assigned to rookie pros. Thankfully, Corny kegs pull apart and clean easier than commercial kegs. Most of the time, a keg can be cleaned and prepped for use in twenty to sixty minutes. If you've purchased unreconditioned kegs, follow the longer breakdown steps.

Typical Keg-Cleaning Steps

1. Rinse the keg immediately. Spray out the beer sludge. Close the keg up and pressurize if you're waiting for several kegs before cleaning. This uses cleaning supplies more efficiently.
2. Fill the keg with a hot cleaning solution. Use a carboy brush to clean the bottom. Hang the lid in the solution with the pressure relief valve cracked open. Wait ten minutes for a relatively clean keg, longer for a grungy one.
3. With the lid on and closed, push the cleaning solution from the first keg to a second rinsed, but dirty keg. Do this with a hose with black liquid fittings on either end, commonly called a jumper hose.
4. Spray out the keg with hot water until the interior is thoroughly rinsed. Place upside down and drip dry for a few minutes.
5. Fill the rinsed keg with sanitizer solution to the brim. Seal and wait several minutes. When done, push the sanitizer out to a clean keg or other holding vessel. Pressurize the sanitized keg and store until needed. Break kegs down completely at least yearly.

The "Complete" Breakdown

1a. Before filling the keg with cleaner, use a deep socket or crescent wrench to unscrew the posts, poppets, and tubes. Leave the long dip tube. Keep each post's parts together. Mix a strong solution of cleaner and soak the fittings. Proceed to Step 2 (above).
2a. Using a dip tube brush, scrub out the beer tube. Let the cleaner in the keg run up the line. Inspect and smell the rubber gaskets (five in all—

keg lid, two outer post rings, and two dip tube rings). Replace any suspect rubber. Rinse off all the parts and reassemble onto the keg before proceeding to Step 3.

Carbonating the Keg

Filling a keg is as simple as racking from fermenter to the keg. Pop the lid, cover with sanitized foil, transfer, and close up. All told, your elapsed kegging time is about five to ten minutes. Compared to the hours of bottling labor, you can see why brewers end up kegging.

But now how do you get the bubbles on board? Force carbonation methods use CO_2 from your tank to put in the bubbles. Pick your target CO_2 volume from the previous Recommended Carbonation Level by Style table (see page 128) and refer to the pressure setting table on page 134 for a pressure setting for your volume and temperature.

Common Carbonation Methods

- **Priming**—Just because you're kegging doesn't mean you can't prime your beer. Many swear by priming for finer carbonation and yeast's oxygen-scavenging qualities. Add the appropriate dose of priming media (see table p. 129) and let set for two weeks before chilling. Carefully move the keg to avoid stirring up sediment.
- **Chill and Wait**—For the patient, set the gas regulator, attach to the chilled keg, and wait for two weeks.
- **Chill and Shake**—To carbonate faster, chill the keg overnight and pick the appropriate regulator setting from the following table. Attach the keg, then lay the keg down sideways. Rock back and forth until the gas stops bubbling, about ten to fifteen minutes. Disconnect the gas and wait an hour. Vent the keg; dial the regulator to 6 to 8 psi and pour.
- **Chill and Slam**—For those times when you need beer now! Take cold beer and crank your regulator to maximum. Attach the gas and roll the keg sideways back and forth for three to five minutes. Disconnect the keg, and settle before venting and serving. Inaccurate, but fast!

PRESSURE SETTINGS TO CARBONATE BEER (PRESSURE AS PSI)							
	Beer Temperature						
	30F	35F	40F	45F	50F	55F	60F
1.5	n/a	n/a	1.4	3.1	4.9	6.8	8.7
1.75	0.4	2.2	4.1	6.1	8.1	10.2	12.3
2.0	2.7	4.7	6.8	9.0	11.3	13.6	15.9
2.25	5.0	7.2	9.6	12.0	14.4	16.9	19.5
2.5	7.2	9.7	12.3	14.9	17.6	20.3	23.1
2.75	9.5	12.2	15.0	17.8	20.7	23.6	26.6
3.0	11.8	14.7	17.7	20.7	23.8	27.00	30.2
3.25	14.0	17.2	20.4	23.6	26.9	30.3	33.8
3.5	16.3	19.6	23.0	26.5	30.1	33.7	37.3

Carbonation (volumes CO_2)

To read the above table, find your volume along the left hand side and the temperature of your beer along the top. Read to the intersection of those two figures and set your regulator to the psi listed.

Short-cut-seeking brewers are tempted by dry ice. It is frozen CO_2, so couldn't you add a chunk to carbonate? There are two problems: First, dry ice is not food safe, it may contain solvents; second, the gas evolves faster than it dissolves in the beer, producing exploding bottles.

Small-Time Beer Service

Kegs are great, but require a commitment of resources. If you want to escape the tyranny of bottles, several options still await you. All of these options serve draft beer in conveniently sized containers. The tradeoffs include a lower startup cost but larger recurring costs compared to a full kegging setup.

Smaller Draft Beer Systems

- **Mini-kegs**—Very popular in Germany, the five-liter mini-keg is enjoying a resurgence here. The plastic-lined steel barrels cost less than $10 a piece and can be used ten times before replacing. Care must be taken not to overprime the kegs or you'll be out a keg and five liters of beer. Spend the money for the better keg tap.

- **Party Pigs**—A 2.25-gallon plastic barrel with attached faucet, you fill the party pig with your primed beer and the manufacturer's special pouch and walk away for two weeks.
- **Tap-a-Draft**—The newest option on the market, the Tap a Draft faucet fits large plastic soda bottles. You can prime the beer as normal or force carbonate via the included CO_2 gas cartridges. The gas canisters primarily pressurize the bottles for service.

QUESTION?

What if my beer keeps foaming every time I pour it?
You probably have an overcarbonated keg of beer. Periodically crack the pressure release valve to vent until the beer settles down. Check your serving line length and size. Serving lines should be ³⁄₁₆" diameter and five to seven feet long to smoothly serve beer driven at 6 to 11 psi.

Beer on the Run

With your draft beer flowing, reasons for leaving the house grow fewer and fewer, but what happens when the party is somewhere else? Schlepping a full keg rig may be overkill, so how to bring beer to share with friends?

- **CO_2 charger**—Based on a design originated for bike tires, these devices inject CO_2 from disposable twelve-gram cartridges when the trigger is pulled. They are perfect for a road trip with kegs. The cartridges quickly add up in price.
- **Carbonator caps**—Specially made screw caps that fit soda bottles. The top is molded to accept a ball-lock gas fitting. To use, fill your sanitized bottle, tighten the lid and inject up to 30 psi. Your beer will hold for a week. Some brewers use them to quickly carbonate a test sample to check flavor. Plans for homemade versions are online.
- **Growler**—Growlers work as well for you as they do for brewpubs. The best are the two-liter German swing-top growlers, capable of keeping beer fresh for a month.

Back to the Bottle

All methods for filling bottles with carbonated beer work best when the beer and sanitized bottles are cold. Carbonation holds in cold solutions, losing less fizz during the transfer process. Your beer should be carbonated just slightly high to compensate for loss.

Ideally, you should see minimal foaming. A little shot of foam at the end is desired to follow the practice of "capping on foam." The industry uses the bubbles to minimize the extra oxygen in the bottle.

Once filled, quickly cap and rinse the bottle. You now have bottled sediment-free beer. Bottle a few extra for testing. After a week, chill one down and crack it open to evaluate carbonation. Use other samples to check for contamination and oxidation.

Bottle-Filling Methods

- **Cobra line with long tube**—The simplest and cheapest solution. Take a clean and sanitized cobra line and jam a piece of tubing over the spout. Place in the bottom of the bottle and dispense slowly before capping.
- **Counter-pressure bottle filler**—Counter-pressure bottle fillers have tubes running through a stopper. The stopper allows the bottle to be pressurized and slowly filled. The most complicated to operate, they preserve the most carbonation.
- **Beer Gun**—The Beer Gun is a one-handed device, as simple as the cobra line solution, but more effective. It eliminates foaming and CO_2 loss with a long line and smooth piping to minimize turbulence.

CHAPTER 13

What Went Wrong?

At some point it'll strike you. You'll reach for your new Über Spiffy Ale and as the beer hits your tongue, horror will cross your face at your problem child. Don't throw it out yet! There may be a solution waiting to spring into action.

Second-Batch Heartbreak

Excited about their first batch, most brewers jump into the second batch. The first batch wasn't hard. Maybe they get a little ambitious or sloppy, and that's when the second-batch heartbreak hits. It's usually a cleaning or sanitation problem, so start by double-checking your gear.

As you continue, you'll hate these moments, but you'll know to pull out all of the stops in an attempt to be a hero. To be successful, you must understand what you smell and taste and their causes. Then you can then formulate a plan of attack.

Off Flavors and Aromas

There are a number of predictable ways for your projects to go off the rails. By tasting and critically evaluating beer, you'll become comfortable in indentifying and diagnosing what caused certain tastes.

The flavors and aromas discussed in the following table are sometimes desirable. For instance, the sharp green apple flavor of acetaldehyde is a component of Budweiser. Buttery diacetyl provides complexity and sweetness to many British ales and traditional pilsners, but would be a flaw in a German hefeweizen.

OFF FLAVORS AND AROMA CAUSES				
Off Flavor	Compound	Root Cause	How to Avoid	Example
Alcoholic	Ethanol	High initial gravity, warm fermentation temperatures and a low terminal gravity.	Ferment the beer cooler and increase residual body via cara-pils, crystal malts, or mashing warming.	Scaldis
Astringent	Tannins/ Alkaline Water/Spices	Alkaline mineral-laden water sources and too finely crushed husks of grains mashed at high pH.	Lighten your water's alkalinity by blending with distilled water. Back off the crush to reduce torn husks.	
Bitter	Isomerized Alpha Acid	Too many hops, use of harsher bittering hops, high sulfate or alkaline water accentuating the bitterness.	Reduce hop charges and switch to lower cohumulone hops. Change water source or reduce sulfate salt additions.	DIPAs (Stone Ruination)

Off Flavor	Compound	Root Cause	How to Avoid	Example
Buttery/ Butterscotch/ Nutty/ Slick feeling	Diacetyl	Produced by yeast and Pediococcus.	Yeast that flocculates early or an early racking preventing the yeast cleaning up the natural byproduct of fermentation.	Shipyard Old Thumper
Cardboard/ Sherry/Musty	Oxidation	Post-pitching aeration of the beer or warm storage.	Reduce the number of times the beer is moved and gently transfer from carboy to bottling bucket or keg. Try oxygen-absorbing caps for bottles.	Any long-aged beer.
Cooked Corn/ Cabbage	Dimethyl Sulfide (DMS)	Contamination by mutated yeast, slow cooling, or inadequate boil to drive off pale malt-supplied precursors.	Better sanitation and chilling practices. More vigorous boil with an open lid to drive off precursor chemicals.	Rolling Rock
Fruity	Esters	Yeast-produced aromas from warm fermentations or inadequate yeast health or population.	Reduce fermentation temperatures. Prepare yeast starters to boost population and health.	
Grassy	N/A	Flavor from some European malts or poorly stored old malt. Also from dry hopping. Can turn "gummy" with more contact time.	Choose fresh malt from trusted sources. Change hops or reduce contact time.	Spaten Helles/ Fresh dry-hopped IPA from a local source.
Green Apple	Acetaldehyde	Produced by yeast during fermentation. Normally cleaned up by healthy yeast. Usually caused by overly flocculant or nutrient-poor yeast or premature racking from primary.	Keep the yeast in contact with the wort longer. Increase yeast health via aeration and nutrients.	Budweiser
Meaty/Yeasty	Autolysis	Caused by the rupturing and breakdown of yeast cells or the overuse of yeast nutrient. Exacerbated by warm storage.	Transfer a beer within two weeks of primary fermentation conclusion. Contact can be extended via cold storage.	
Medicinal/ Band-Aid	Phenols	Wild yeast, chlorinated water, or residual chlorine sanitizer	Improve your sanitation, dechlorinate all brew water, rinse chlorine thoroughly, and air-dry completely or switch to a new sanitizer	Some harder lambics (Cantillon)
Metallic	Iron, Copper	Exposed iron, mild steel, or unoxidized copper in brewing equipment. High metal content in water. Old grain.	Avoid using nonstainless or oxidized aluminum in the brewery. Copper in small quantities is fine. Mix or use only neutral water. Use fresh ingredients	Ciney (from Belgium)

Off Flavor	Compound	Root Cause	How to Avoid	Example
Phenolic	Phenols	Wild yeast, yeast strain	Improve sanitation, choose a different yeast strain if phenols inappropriate for style.	Hefeweizen (Clove is a phenol)
Skunky	Mercaptan	Interaction between isomerized alpha acids and ultraviolet light.	Store beer away from the light in brown bottles or firmly boxed against exposure.	Green bottle lagers
Smoky	Phenols	Wild yeast/bacteria, yeast strain, malt	Improve sanitation to eliminate wild yeast. Choose different yeast strain if smoke is inappropriate. Do not use or reduce use of smoked malt in beer.	Rauchbier
Solvent	Fusel Alcohols	Aroma of acetone and lacquer caused by contamination, warm fermentation, or inadequate yeast health.	Improve sanitation practices. Reduce fermentation temperatures and use starters and aeration to improve yeast count and health.	
Sour	Lactic, Acetic Acid	Bacteria such as Lactobacillus, Pedioccocus, and Acetobacter. Overuse of acid malt or lactic acid for water preparation. Mash or unboiled wort held warm for too long.	Improve sanitation to eliminate bacteria. Reduce the use of acidity while brewing. Don't hold mash or unboiled wort for more than a couple of hours.	Flanders Red Ale (Rodenbach)
Sulfur	Sulfur	Lager yeast fermented too warm or cooled too quickly.	Choose different yeast strains, reduce fermentation temperatures, and control temperature reduction.	
Sweet	Sugar	Inadequate fermentation. Mash bills with high portions of crystal malts, carapils. Mash at high temperatures.	Reduce residual sweetness with improved yeast health and nutrition and longer time in primary. Use more base malts in the bill and mash at a lower temperature.	Malt Liquor
Thin	N/A	Too low a residual gravity due to mashing at too low a temperature or too much sugar in the beer with no compensating proteins.	Mash at higher temperatures or add dextrinous malts or oats to boost the mouthfeel. Reduce the sugar.	

Most, if not all, of the problems off flavors and aromas encountered have easily fixed causes for future batches. With subtle flavors, your best hope is to doctor the beer with strong flavor and aroma to distract the senses. Strong off flavors may mean that you've made a five-gallon batch of slug bait or bean-soaking liquor.

QUESTION?

What is slug bait?
Slugs love beer—it is a naturally green slug killer. When slugs (or snails) attack your garden, dig deep enough to hold a can or bowl and fill with beer. Overnight the slugs will crawl into the beer and have a final sip.

Poor Fermentation

Notice how many off flavors are caused by poor fermentation and yeast health. For the extra cost of DME and nutrient, a starter can skip over a slew of possible problems. Don't disappoint the brew gods, make a starter. Follow the All-Purpose Easy Starter on page 63.

Even with a starter, things can go wrong. Your vial of yeast may be too old, or heat may have weakened it during summer shipping. If you suspect this happened to your pack, start with a cup of starter and give it a few days. Hopefully, any remaining healthy population will replicate and get up to speed in the small starter before hitting a full-sized starter.

Extract-based worts are short of FAN and other nutrients. Yeast cells still need to replicate in the primary. Insufficient nutrient levels hamper reproduction and enzyme production. This is true of inadequate aeration. At lower gravities, this won't be as much of a problem, but higher gravities require aeration.

Another fermentation cause of off flavors is a lack of temperature control. Don't develop the bad habit of thinking your interior closet is cold enough to ferment ales safely. Fermenting too warm, as new brewers do, promotes negative esters and fusels. Conversely, fermenting too cool suppresses desired aromas and flavors, and causes the ferment to stall out and fail to finish. The solutions discussed in Chapter 11 can help keep the temperature in the appropriate range.

Caught early enough, it may be possible to fix a problematic fermentation. Here's how:

Fermentation Fixes

- **Aeration**—Within twenty-four hours of fermentation activity, it is safe to lightly aerate the beer. Make sure there's still enough food for the yeast.
- **Nutrient**—For stalled fermentations, boil a teaspoon or two of yeast nutrient and add to your fermenter. Gently swirl to mix and watch for renewed activity within several hours.
- **Repitching**—The single most used technique for a stalled ferment, repitching can fix more than residual gravity. Off flavors, like acetaldehyde or diacetyl, are consumed by yeast. Active yeast added to the ferment can finish the cleanup.
- **Rousing**—A cheap, effective way to get your yeast back to work. Swirl the carboy or bucket long enough to stir the sediment back up to the surface.
- **Warming**—Another cause of a stalled ferment is the temperature dropping too low, even for a short period of time. Move the fermenter to a warmer location for a day and wait for signs of renewed activity.

Infections

Homebrewers strive for sanitary practices, but fall short most of the time. Open-air transfers expose the wort to dust and pet hair floating by. Steps mitigating these circumstances are easy, but not foolproof. The guiding principle: Beer-loving creepy crawlies don't crawl; they fall on dust into the brew. If you can block easy downward airflow, you're doing well.

One missed cleaning or sanitizing step and a beastie can grab a foothold. For instance, after your last brew session, you left the boil kettle spigot uncleaned. In the few weeks since then, just a tiny amount of mold grew in the nozzle. As your freshly boiled beer flows past, it strips mold with it. With the right conditions in the fermenter, that mold can take hold.

The lack of complete and trustworthy sanitation stresses adding large doses of viable yeast to the brew. The faster fermentation happens, the less chance a contaminant has. When combined with hops' antimicrobial properties, fermented beer has weak, but vital protection.

FACT

Microbiologists work under laminar flow hoods to prevent contamination of their samples. Homebrewers can fake this by working with their yeast under a flame.

Tupelo Weizen Braggot

Braggot is a mead/beer hybrid, normally made with barley as a brown barleywine. When kegged and carbonated, there was a strong odor of diacetyl. This was scrubbed away by returning the keg to room temperature, venting the CO_2, and adding extra yeast for a few weeks.

Style: Mead
Brew Type: All Grain
For 5.5 gallons at 1.120, 3.4 SRM, 27.0 IBUs, 14.0 percent ABV
60-minute boil

Directions

1. Follow the Single-Infusion Brew Process (page 284).

2. Add the honey at the very end of the boil to preserve the aromatics.

Malt/Grain/Sugar
6.0 pounds Wheat Malt
4.0 pounds Pilsner Malt
0.5 pound Cara-Pils Malt
10.00 pounds Tupelo Honey

Extract (for 6 pounds of Wheat Malt and 4 pounds of Pilsner Malt)
8.0 pounds Wheat Liquid Malt Extract (LME)

Hops
2.0 ounces Tettnanger Tettnang (4.3 percent AA) Pellet for 60 minutes

Other Ingredients
1 tablet Whirlfloc
1 tablespoon Yeast Nutrient

Yeast
Red Star Cotes de Blanc White Wine Yeast

Mash Schedule
Saccharification Rest 150°F 60 minutes

TIP

Tupelo honey, with its strong aromas and flavors, is a fantastic mead-making variety. Produced only in North Florida and South Georgia, the honey is well worth the added expense.

Raucous Red West Coast Ale

Take heart, despite the initial failures with this recipe—it turns out to produce great beer when you let it!

Style: American Amber Ale
Brew Type: Extract
For 5.5 gallons at 1.050, 10.6 SRM, 29.3
    IBUs, 4.9 percent ABV
60-minute boil

Directions

Follow the Steeping Grains and Extract Process (page 283).

Malt/Grain/Sugar
0.50 pound CaraMunich 60
0.25 pound CaraWheat
0.25 pound Aromatic Malt
0.25 pound Crystal 120L
0.25 pound Honey Malt

Extract
5.50 pounds Pale Liquid Malt Extract (LME)

Hops
0.80 ounce Glacier (5.8 percent AA) Pellet for 60 minutes
0.60 ounce Palisade (9.4 percent AA) Pellet for 20 minutes
5.50 ounces Amarillo Gold (8.9 percent AA) Pellet for 0 minutes

Other Ingredients
1 tablet Whirlfloc
1 tablespoon Yeast Nutrient
1 tablespoon Gypsum

Yeast
Wyeast 1272 American Ale II

Common Microbiological Contaminants

- **Acetobacter**—Bacteria that produce acetic acid, aka vinegar. Consumes ethanol
- **Brettanomyces**—A wide-ranging class of "wild" yeasts. Produces flavors and aromas from pineapple and tropical fruit to horse sweat and musty blankets.
- **Lactobacillus**—Found on the barley husk, lactobacillus is a common brewery contaminant floating around on milled barley flour. Produces copious amounts of lactic acid.
- **Mold**—Wherever standing water is, so is mold. Mold arrives late in the ferment, usually during a long secondary. To prevent, keep the area mold free and the airlocks filled.
- **Pediococcus**—The single most feared beer spoilage mechanism. Pedio hangs tough once established. Extra diligence fights this diacetyl- and acid-producing organism.

How to Beat a Persistent Infection

Maybe you borrowed a friend's fermenter to brew more beer, or a rabid squirrel dropped a berry in a carboy. No matter the root cause, something has crawled into your equipment. You've scrubbed and sanitized, but time and time again the visitor comes back to ruin your beer.

Taking copious notes helps pinpoint the cause. With good notes, you can determine the infection vector.

Cleaning, Sanitizing, and Killing

Your first great inclination is to clean everything in sight. Here are a few simple rules to follow:

- **Hoses/buckets/stoppers/airlocks**—Thanks to miniscule scratches, plastic is always suspect in a brewery. Start by chucking anything plastic that may have infected a brew or come in contact with one. Continuing batch problems aren't worth the $1.50 to replace an airlock.

- **Tear everything apart**—When an infection appears, tear everything apart and inspect it. The mold example above happened before. Remove hoses from racking canes to clean where they cover up. Pull apart your manifolds, spigots, airlocks, and kegs.
- **Clean twice**—With everything apart, break out the brushes. Soak every part in cleaner and scrub them. Leave everything glistening and wait a week to promote passivation.
- **Change sanitation practices**—Eliminate your usual shortcuts and expose the visitor to a never-before-used sanitizer. A simple change can work wonders in your brewery. Take your metal parts and boil them for ten to fifteen minutes. You can bake and very slowly cool glass items. (Follow the oven sanitation method for bottles.)

Testing to Find the Culprit

Never underestimate the value of intelligence in fighting an enemy too small to see. When a teardown has failed, you need additional data.

The basic detection test you'll use is the "Wort Stability Test." Each step of the brew day, take a sanitized sample and store it. Buy test tubes for easy-to-sanitize storage.

Uncap a sanitary tube, add your sample,152 and cap. Make sure any sampling "thief" is clean and sanitary first. Stick the filled tubes upright some place cool and out of the light. Check every few days for obvious signs of infection. When the beer is ready, sample it and check the tubes if an infection hits. Open the tubes, smell them, and taste them. Any show signs of your infection? If you find one, you'll know the bacteria hit the beer at that stage.

When do you sample the beer? Take samples when: the beer is finished boiling and leaving your pot; the beer is finished chilling; the beer is in the carboy, but not pitched with yeast or oxygen; after pitching; on transfer to secondary; on transfer to bottling or keg. Make sure to label each sample so you'll know their origin. Post-pitching samples should be treated with cyclo-hexamide to kill the yeast.

Tasting is vital to tracking your infection source. At every step of fermentation, take a taste and note any flavors you find.

If the stability tests and taste tests point to a culprit, refocus your attention on that area.

Fixing the Problem Now

An off flavor or aroma doesn't mean the beer is trashed. A deft and clever brewer can adjust the taste of their beer to hide or distract drinkers from a flaw.

When considering approaches, think about the effect of the flaw on the beer. For instance, a brewer had a batch of beer that was lightly astringent with aromas of cooked corn from DMS; to correct and hide it, she added an apricot extract. The sweetness of the apricot aroma played off the sweet corn while the acidic flavor hid the astringency.

Common Post-Fermentation Adulterations

- **Body by powder**—Beers lacking body can be punched up with additions of malto-dextrin powder or lactose for a little sweetness. Boil 4 to 8 ounces in water for fifteen minutes before adding.
- **Color**—If your stout ends up looking more like brown ale, you can turn to a German malt colorant called Sinamar. It can make a blonde beer coal black. Smaller doses add reddish-brown colors.
- **Fruit**—The addition of fruit can cover a multitude of problems, and folks love the flavor. While whole fruit is great, it's not always practical for troubleshooting situations. In addition to the sugarless extract route, sweet fruit liqueurs can provide the needed cover-up.
- **Hops**—Caught early enough, a strong dose of dry hops or hop tea can cut through a sweet beer or provide complimentary spicy or fruity aromas.
- **CO_2 scrubbing**—Some aromas can be scrubbed away or reduced by bubbling CO_2 through the beer. Keg the beer and close the lid. Swap the CO_2 tank fitting for a black liquid fitting. Set the regulator to 5 psi and attach to the liquid post of the keg. Let the gas flow and crack the pressure relief valve. Run the gas for a minute and check the aroma. Repeat as needed.
- **Blending**—The patient can brew a second batch that overemphasizes an opposite character and blend the beers. A beer that's too bitter without balance can be balanced by a second batch pushing malt.

CHAPTER 14

Your First
All-Grain Batch

After a few extract batches, you'll hear the siren call of all-grain brewing. To brew like the big guys! You've already learned the hard stuff. All grain requires a little more gear and patience to produce a panoply of pints.

Why Go All Grain?

Brewing your first batch was a confusing whirl of instructions, equipment, and process, and yet you were successful. Waiting in your fridge is a pint of fresh ale. So why would you want to go and muck it up? Many veteran extract brewers continue making fantastic beers.

Beyond the initial gear investment, all grain is significantly cheaper than extract brewing. Bulk-buying brewers brag about brewing for pennies on the pint. They look for savings everywhere—bulk grain, bulk hops, repitched yeast, and so on.

But the cost savings is ultimately the weakest factor. Instead, focus on control. With all grain, you can brew any strength or color without jumping through hoops or being subject to an extract manufacturer's whims.

Extract brews suffer body issues. On the one hand, extracts finish high, yet they lack satisfying middle-palate richness. With the same malt, you can make full-bodied beers (mashing at 155°F to 160°F) or drier-bodied beers (148°F to 152°F). Even utilizing late addition, extract beers will be darker. The palest pilsner is a sack of pils malt away.

The Simplified View of All-Grain Brewing

In your earlier brews, you steeped a little grain, filtered it, rinsed with hot water, and boiled hops. All grain differs in scale and equipment only.

You start with crushed grain, now with six pounds or more instead of one or two with extract. You "mash" with a few gallons of hot water, the malt enzymes convert starch into sugar, and then you filter the sweet liquid. You rinse with a few more gallons of water and combine all seven gallons of wort in the boil pot waiting for the hops. After the requisite hour boil, you cool things down with a wort chiller and away to the fermenter.

The steps are similar to the earlier partial-mash techniques, just different in scale.

The New Gear

You need a few new pieces of equipment in the form of bigger kettles, a mash tun, and a chiller to get your first batch off the ground.

Hot Liquor Tank (HLT)

Liquor refers to brewing water. To wring from the grain, you'll rinse the grains more thoroughly. The rinse water is kept hot in the HLT. Most brewers use a large (seven-plus-gallon) pot on a burner to provide the sparge liquor; others hold preheated water in coolers.

Mash Tun

The heart and soul of your new brewery operation is the mash tun. It holds masses of barley gruel around 152°F for an hour and then acts like a giant colander draining the sugary liquid away. Ideally, start with a ten-gallon cooler or kettle. The larger volume accommodates enough grain to make strong five-gallon batches.

Bigger Boil Kettle

In the all-grain world, your twenty-quart pot is insufficient. Boil volumes start at six or seven gallons, with room needed for the roiling boil. If you have a metal racking cane (or bend one from copper pipe), you can skip the practical spigot. To add a spigot to an existing pot, drill with a hole saw and install a "weldless" kettle kit.

If you have a couple of large pots, you can split the wort into separate pots to boil instead of buying a large pot and burner.

Wort Chiller

All-grain brewers need to get their large volume of wort down to healthy fermentation temperatures rapidly. Now is the time to invest in an immersion or counter-flow wort chiller. See Chapter 8 for more information.

All Grain on the Cheap

If the potential monetary outlay for all grain is offputting, you can augment a multiple pot boil with a cheap mash rig. Short of equipment that fell off the back of the truck, these are the ways to go when you're short of cash.

Charlie Papazian, author of *The Complete Joy of Homebrewing*, wrote about his basic all-grain setup, the Zap Pap. Take two five-gallon plastic buckets and fit them together. The bottom bucket gets a ⅜-inch hole drilled into the side for a hose with a clamp. The inner bucket gets ⅛-inch holes drilled over the entire bottom. Your mash goes into the inner bucket and the holes filter the wort. Reduce the amount of space between the bucket bottoms by cutting the bottom bucket below the handle ridges.

In Australia, brewers are using a Brew-in-a-Bag (BiaB) system that uses one pot large enough to hold the entire boil volume and a giant brew bag sewn from nylon voile (fine-meshed) fabric. In the kettle they heat all the strike and sparge water, add the bag and fill with the crushed grain. After mashing, they lift the bag and let it drain into the kettle. Look online for more information about building a BiaB setup for less than $10.

ALERT!

For your first all-grain session, bring an experienced all-grain brewer on board to smooth out any jitters. Plan for a longer-than-normal brew session, say eight hours. Eventually, as the process becomes second nature, you can brew a simple beer in four to five hours from kettle ignition.

Designing a Mash Tun

Online research yields countless mash tun designs; most are kettle- or cooler-based with a means to filter the sweet wort.

Think about tun sizing. You want one big enough to do any beer that your heart desires. Choose a tun that's too small and the fun, high-octane beers require extract to achieve. Conversely, choose a too-large tun and suffer unstable rests and shallow grain beds.

Cooler Tuns

Cooler tuns, based on ten-gallon rounds or 40- to 100-quart rectangular coolers, are a breeze to use. Add some hot water to heat the mash tun, toss, add your water and grain, and close for an hour. Many tuns hold temperature perfectly

Add a spigot by punching out the plastic drainage valve and securing a ball valve and bulk head on either side. Some even skip the valve and feed a tight-fitting hose or stopper and pipe through the hole. You can attach any wort-draining rig inside.

The tun's disadvantage is a lack of direct heating. No problem for single-infusion mashes, but to change temperatures you need alternate heating means.

Kettle Tuns

Adding heat is no problem for a mash tun built on a kettle. Just turn on the flame and stir continuously until you're a few degrees under your target. The carryover heat coasts to the right temperature.

Conversely, heat loss is experienced in a kettle. To mitigate the precipitous drop in mash temperature, wrap the kettle with a blanket. Remember to remove it before firing the burner.

To make a kettle tun, you must drill or cut a hole for a valve. With weldless kits, you can screw things together, but for a sturdy, leakproof setup, you'll need experience (or a friend who has experience) with stainless steel welding equipment.

It is imperative that you clean a tun shortly after the brew session. The smell of old mash left stewing in the tun is horrendous and almost impossible to remove from a cooler.

Wort-Draining Apparatuses

Now that you can mash, you need to separate your new wort from the spent grains. In extract brewing you could pour the grain in a fine-mesh strainer, but it's no longer practical. Instead, brewers focus on straining devices at the bottom of the mash tun. These gizmos and the barley husks combine to create escape routes for the precious liquid.

- **False bottom**—A false bottom covers the floor of the tun and the drainage valve. Perforations allow the liquid to flow out of the tun. To prevent scorching on the kettle floor, direct heating is discouraged. When preparing water for mashing, you have to add extra "foundation" water to bring the level to the false bottom.
- **Manifold**—An easy-to-construct alternative is the wort manifold. Built of copper pipes or PVC (for coolers only), manifolds separate wort via a series of drilled holes or slots that face the bottom of the mash tun. The wort flows up into the pipe and out the spigot. Use a ring or rectangular configuration of pipes spaced an inch or so apart to ensure equal drainage from all parts of the mash.
- **Steel braid**—Even easier to construct are stainless steel hose braids which can be found wrapped around rubber water hosing. To create a mash filter, discard the rubber hose, flatten one end, and fold over like a toothpaste tube. With a pair of pliers, crimp the folded end and attach to your spigot. Inserting a length of copper pipe prevents the braid from squashing. With a braid, you must be careful not to damage it by overzealous mash stirring.

ALERT!

When buying a braid, make sure you buy a steel braid. Manufacturers these days are making nylon-braided hoses painted to look like metal.

How Mashing Works

Barley is full of starch. Mashing transforms it into digestible short sugar molecules via the alchemy of enzymes, transforming engines developed during malting. When combined with heat, the water-soluble starches are attacked by the two primary malt enzymes, alpha and beta amylase, which hack and cleave starches into sugar. Other enzymes tackle proteins.

Starch

Starches are chains of glucose molecules. Picture a tree branch, a big one coming off the trunk. Amylose starch is a straight limb with no smaller branches. Amylopectin is a limb with many amylose branches. The crook of the branches makes it impossible for malt enzymes to disassemble starch. The remaining molecules form dextrins and other body-filling molecules.

Malt Enzymes

Mashing provides the perfect working conditions for the production of sugar and reduction of protein, but your mash temperature affects the enzymes. The active temperature range shows where they are most active. They work across the whole spectrum, just not as efficiently. Denaturing (destroying) temperatures aren't light switches. It takes long exposure times to fully deactivate the enzyme population.

Malt Enzymes

- **Alpha Amylase—"The Axe"**—Alpha amylase attacks the amylo-pectin branches, cleaving the bonds and forming long sugars, like maltotriose, maltose, and maltodextrin. A mash favoring alpha amylase produces less fermentable wort with greater residual body and sweetness. Active Temperatures: 155°F to 165°F. Denatures: 168+°F.
- **Beta Amylase—"Pac Man"**—Beta amylase chomps amylose from one end and works down the branch. Each "bite" frees a maltose molecule. A mash maximizing beta activity produces very ferment-able wort and dry beers. Active Temperatures: 130°F to 152°F. Dena-tures: 152+°F.
- **Protease—The Protein Fighter**—Available in limited amounts in malt. Destroys large haze-causing proteins. Can also damage foam-positive proteins if done for too long. Active Temperatures: 115°F to 130°F. Denatures: 140+°F.
- **Peptidase—FAN Producer**—This other proteolytic enzyme boosts the free amino nitrogen (FAN) count in wort. FAN is important for good yeast health. Active Temperatures: 115°F to 130°F. Denatures: 140+°F.

- **Beta Glucanase—Gum Buster**—Glutens are the protein webs that can gum up the mash. This low-temperature enzyme is only necessary with undermodified malts. Active Temperatures: 95°F to 115°F. Denatures: 118+°F.

Be careful with your saccharification rest temperature. Shoot too high and you could leave a mess of unconverted starch. To save the mash, quickly reduce the mash temp with cold water or keep powdered amylase extract on hand.

The Common Rests

When brewers design a mash schedule, they think in terms of "rests," scheduled stops at specific temperatures. Each rest favors certain enzymes for a desired effect.

- **Dough In**—A catchall term for the first step in your mash schedule.
- **Acid Rest**—A low-temperature mash rest that promotes the mash acidification by creating phytic acid. Typical temperature: 90°F to 100°F for thirty minutes.
- **Protein Rest**—The first rest for many Belgian and German beers. Favors the activity of the proteolytic enzymes. Typical temperature: 120°F to 128°F for twenty to thirty minutes.
- **Beta "Intermediate" Rest**—The beta amylase rest favors maltose production. Used when you want a beer to dry out. Typical temperature: 145°F to 149°F for thirty minutes.
- **Saccharification Rest**—The main starch conversion rest. Above 148°F, starch is completely dissolved in the mash liquor. The lower 150s produce balanced wort favoring neither dextrinous wort nor dry wort. Resting at 154°F to 157°F, the mash creates thicker dextrinous wort resulting in rich and sweet beer. Typical temperature: 150°F to 157°F for thirty to sixty minutes.
- **Mash Out**—Heating to mash-out temperatures, in theory, denatures and stops enzymatic activity, freezing the sugar ratio. Some debate

the effectiveness of the step. But as the mash heats up, it becomes looser, helping the lautering process. Typical temperature: 165°F to 170°F for ten to fifteen minutes.

Do I have to use all of these rests to make great beer?
Most beer these days is brewed with highly modified malt, eliminating the acid and protein rests (although brewers using unmalted wheat often use a protein rest). A number of micro and pub breweries have systems only capable of single-infusion mashes, so all you need is a saccharification rest. Some professional breweries even shorten their mash times to as little as twenty to thirty minutes before sparging.

Mash Thickness

The all-grain recipes here use a standard mash ratio of 1.25 quarts of water per pound of malt (for example, for ten pounds of malt in the mash, use 12.5 quarts [3.12 gallons] water in the mash). This standard mash thickness protects the enzymes and favors faster conversion. Mashing with less water yields a thicker mash that converts faster, but produces less fermentable wort. Thinner mashes work more slowly, but smaller sugars comprise more of the final wort.

Heat Additions

There are a number of ways to heat your mash. For any direct heat method, including decoction, you must stir the mash continuously to prevent scorching the sticky mash. Scorched mashes ruin the beer!

- **Infusion**—The simplest method, water infusion is the basis for mashing. When you heat water for the dough in, you're performing an infusion. Calculating the amount of water and temperature of that water to hit a target temperature can be incredibly tricky, but the rule of thumb for dough in is to use 1.25 quarts of water per pound heated 12°F above your desired rest temperature. Other infusions use boiling water to minimize diluting the mash. See Appendix C to calculate infusions.

- **Direct Heating**—Light the fire under the kettle and stir continuously. Check your progress every minute or so. When you're 4°F to 5°F under your target temperature, kill the heat, stir like crazy, and wait five minutes and check again. If you're too warm, add cold water or ice and stir to cool the mash.
- **Decoction**—Back before thermometers, they boiled mash to raise temperatures. Pull one-fourth to one-third of the grain (only a little liquid) to a separate pot. Bring the mixture to a boil and stir for ten to fifteen minutes. Add the boiling mash back to the main pot and stir to distribute. Use this to enhance maltiness.
- **Recirculation**—The mad geniuses of homebrew take their copper immersion chiller and drop it into the HLT. They pump mash liquor through the now submerged coil. The sparge water heats the mash liquor before returning to the mash tun.

With any method other than recirculation, it is vital that you thoroughly stir the mash to eliminate hot pockets and evenly distribute the heat.

Mashing Types

There are several traditional mash methods that vary in laboriousness. Each brewer comes to a place where they have a preference. Each of the mash profiles are listed step by step in Appendix D.

- **Single-infusion mashing**—The simplest and most common mash profile. Infuse the malt into water to achieve a single mash temperature and hold for an hour. After an optional mash out, proceed with the sparge and the rest of your brew day. Most of the recipes in this book use this mash technique.

- **Multistep mashing**—Slightly more complicated, the brewer targets multiple rest temperatures, adding heat to reach the next plateau. What temperatures are used depends upon the composition of the mash and desired beer characteristics. A Belgian brewer would perform a protein rest, followed by a beta rest to promote fermentability, and then a saccharification rest to finish conversion.
- **Decoction mashing**—The old German technique for brewing that relies entirely on decoctions for moving between steps. Requires one, two, or three decoctions to get through the mash program.

Executing the Mash and Sparge

Now that you know the theory and terminology, how about executing an actual mash and sparge? Here is a simple single-infusion mash using the Boat Brake Water Vapor or Pater's Uncle Enkel recipes. The stress on this brew is learning the technique!

Your First All-Grain Brew Day

1. **Water Prep.** Measure out your water. For the Boat Brake Water Vapor recipe, heat 3.25 gallons of strike water to 165°F for the mash (1.25 quarts × 10.5 pounds of grain / 4). For Pater's Uncle Enkel heat roughly 2.25 gallons of strike water to 165°F (1.25 quarts × 7.0 pounds of grain / 4). Heat an additional 7 gallons of water to 170°F for the sparge (adjust the volume once you have a better feel for your system's need, but extra hot water is always welcome on a brew deck).
2. **Dough In.** When your strike water hits temperature, start adding the malt. While rapidly stirring the water, slowly add the crushed malt into the vortex. Mix until all the grain is added. Slowly stir the mash, revealing and crushing any dough balls of malt that you find. Cover the mash tun and wait.
3. **Saccharification Rest.** Wait ten minutes after your last stirring and check the rest temperature. You should be near the target. If not, add hot water to boost the temperature or cold water or ice to cool. Stir and recheck. Don't fret a couple degrees difference. Wait sixty minutes.
4. **Iodine Test.** Confirm that you've successfully converted your starch by putting a small, liquid-only sample on a white plate and adding a drop

of iodine. If the iodine turns purple, wait another ten minutes and try for a cleaner sample. If it stays the same color, you're ready to go.

5. **Vorlauf.** A fancy German word for recirculation. When you partially crack open the valve and pull the initial runnings from the mash, a ton of grain follows with it. As you continue to pull wort and return it gently to the mash, the grain bed and husks will set up and start to produce clear wort. Once the wort runs free of any large particulate matter, move on.

6. **Sparging.** The last unique all-grain step, the sparge is just a bulked-up version of extract grain rinsing. Aim for a sixty-minute sparge, so move slowly. Add enough hot (170°F) water to hold the water level an inch above the grain bed. Once you've gathered five gallons in the boil kettle, stop adding water and let the runoff continue until you have collected 6.5 gallons or so. Alternatively, monitor the gravity of your runoff and stop when the gravity reaches 1.010. Let the mash cool, while bringing your beer to a boil. From here on out, it's exactly the same as a full-boil extract batch.

7. **Chilling.** While the beer is boiling, clean and sanitize your carboys. Make sure to have your chiller ready to go. Immersion chiller users, add your chiller to the boil kettle just after adding the whirlfloc and yeast nutrient. Counterflow chiller users, rinse, clean, and sanitize your chiller prior to use.

ALERT!

Iodine is toxic taken in pure forms and tastes horrible in beer. Don't add any iodine test samples back to the mash!

Following the instructions above, you'll have executed a "fly sparge." There are multiple approaches to sparging. Fly sparging is the method of choice because it maximizes efficiency and is practical on a large scale. Two alternative homebrewing philosophies to explore online are "batch sparging" and its radical cousin "no-sparge brewing."

Boat Weight Water Vapor

California common, traditionally referred to as Steam Beer, is one of the few uniquely American styles of beer. It was created in San Francisco by German immigrants hoping to catch a nugget of the Gold Rush by brewing a warmer lager. If you can't ferment cool, use an American Ale yeast (Wyeast 1056) and make a woody amber ale.

Style: California Common
Brew Type: All Grain
For 5.5 gallons at 1.054, 9.1 SRM, 63.8 IBUs, 5.0 percent ABV
60-minute boil

Directions

Follow the Single-Infusion Brew Process (page 284).

TIP

The dying Anchor Brewery was rescued by Fritz Maytag and revitalized over a decade. By that time, Anchor was the last standing maker of San Francisco's unique Steam Beer. Anchor then trademarked the term "Steam Beer."

Malt/Grain/Sugar
9.50 pounds Pale Malt Two-Row
0.5 pound Crystal 60L
0.5 pound Vienna Malt

Extract (for 8.5 pounds of Pale Malt)
6.00 pounds Pale Liquid Malt Extract (LME)

Hops
1.00 ounce Northern Brewer (9.0 percent AA) Whole for 60 minutes
0.50 ounce Northern Brewer (9.0 percent AA) Whole for 20 minutes
0.50 ounce Northern Brewer (9.0 percent AA) Whole for 5 minutes

Other Ingredients
1 tablet Whirlfloc (for 20 minutes)
1 tablespoon Yeast Nutrient (for 20 minutes)

Yeast
Wyeast 2112 California Lager (Ferment at 60°F)

Mash Schedule
Saccharification Rest 153°F 60 minutes

Pater's Uncle Enkel

Enkel is the old term for a trappist single. Patersbier is the beer a Belgian monk drinks with his daily bread. This is a pale version. Originally brewed to grow yeast for stronger Belgian beers, it's a great tafelbier for your evening meal.

Style: Belgian "Single"
Brew Type: All Grain
For 5.5 gallons at 1.040, 5 SRM, 14 IBUs, 3.7 percent ABV
60-minute boil

Directions

Follow the Single-Infusion Brew Process (page 284).

TIP

To avoid disturbing your set grain bed too much, you need a sparge diffuser. It can be as simple as an upside-down bowl on top of the grain or even better, prodigiously perforated sheets of aluminum foil.

Malt/Grain/Sugar
5.50 pounds Belgian Pale Ale Malt
1.00 pound Flaked Oats
0.50 pound CaraVienne Malt
1.00 pound Turbinado Sugar

Hops
0.50 ounce Styrian Goldings (5.4 percent AA) Pellet for 60 minutes
0.50 ounce Styrian Goldings (5.4 percent AA) Pellet for 15 minutes

Other Ingredients
1 tablet Whirlfloc
1 teaspoon Yeast Nutrient

Yeast
Wyeast 3864 Canadian Belgian Yeast / Wyeast 1214 Belgian Ale / WLP550 Belgian Ale

Mash Schedule
Saccharification Rest 153°F 60 minutes

Efficiency: Not Just for Bean Counters

You'll hear brewers obsess over their "efficiency." They are talking about how much of the available malt sugar they're getting. The higher the percentage, the less sugar left in the grain. Important for production breweries to save money, for homebrewers the difference in efficiency may mean adding a couple more pounds of malt into the mash. Knowing your efficiency makes recipe formulation easier and helps pinpoint problems creeping into your brewing process.

To calculate efficiency, you have to determine how much sugar is available to you. Each malt variety offers sugar inversely proportional to the degree of roasting. This is expressed as Points per Pound per Gallon (PPPPG), or what gravity you would achieve if you mashed a pound of grain and achieved perfect extraction in one gallon of wort.

AVERAGE SUGAR BASED ON MALT VARIETY		
Malt Variety	Average Amount of Sugar (PPPPG)	Sugar Extract (75 percent)
British Maris Otter	1.038	1.029
German Pilsner Malt	1.038	1.029
American Two-Row Pale Malt	1.037	1.028
American Crystal 10L	1.035	1.026
Caramel Pils Malt (Crystal 8L)	1.034	1.026
British Crystal 55L	1.034	1.026
Honey Malt	1.030	1.023
Special B Malt	1.030	1.023
Roasted Barley	1.029	1.022
Black Patent Malt	1.027	1.020

As you can see, barring differences in the base barley, the darker the malt, the less sugar you get out of it. The sugar extract numbers were produced by multiplying the potential gravity points, the decimal digits (for example, 38 gravity points for Maris Otter and Pilsner Malt) by the efficiency:

$$Sugar\ Extract = Potential\ Gravity\ Points \times Efficiency$$

To calculate your efficiency, you need to compare the amount of sugar you produced to the maximum. In a mash of ten pounds of Maris Otter, you should have 380 possible gravity points. As your boil begins, you take a sample: the boil kettle has 6.5 gallons of 1.044 wort. You have collected 286 (44 × 6.5) gravity points. Dividing 286 by 380 yields 0.75 or 75 percent, a pretty standard efficiency. Take the most accurate readings from your boil kettle just after the boil starts.

Percent Efficiency = (Boil Kettle Gravity Point × Volume) / Sum (Potential Gravity Points)

After a couple of batches, you should see consistent results for gravity. If it fluctuates you need to find what's different. Don't fret if you have consistently low efficiency, like 60 to 65 percent. The measure of a beer's worth lies in the glass, not the mash tun.

If you experience a sharp drop in efficiency for a batch, examine the malt crush. A coarse crush is your most likely culprit, since starch has remained locked away in the kernels.

Converting from Extract

Entering the all-grain arena doesn't mean trashing all your great extract recipes. If you used pale extract, you're in luck. If not, there are just a few things to know before you get on the road of re-perfecting your favorite recipe.

With pale extracts, the substitutions are straightforward. See the table below for your basic assumptions. Conversion becomes tricky when you have recipes based on amber or dark malt extracts. For the amber extracts, blend in a healthy dollop of medium crystal malts (35L to 75L) and for darker extracts, add a quarter pound of black patent to the batch.

EXTRACT CONVERSIONS	
Extract Type	**All Grain Substitution (per Pound Extract)**
American Pale DME	1.75 lbs Domestic Two-Row Malt
American Pale LME	1.25 lbs Domestic Two-Row Malt
Belgian LME	1.66 lbs Belgian Pilsner Malt
British DME	1.5 lbs Maris Otter
British LME	1.25 lbs Maris Otter
German LME	1.25 lbs German Pilsner Malt
Wheat Solids (DME)	1 lb Wheat Malt and 0.75 lb Domestic Two-Row (Or German Pilsner for German Wheats)
Wheat LME	0.75 lb Wheat Malt and 0.5 lb Domestic Two-Row (Or German Pilsner)

The table was calculated assuming 75 percent extract efficiency. You may need to adjust the amount based on your system's efficiency. To calculate:

Pounds of Malt = (Gravity Points 1 pound of extract) / ((Gravity Points 1 pound Malt) × System Efficiency)

CHAPTER 15

Joining with and Competing Against Your Fellow Brewers

Tired of spending those long brew days in the kitchen or garage alone? Beer and brewing brings people together for a little fun. Gain a brew buddy and learn from the veterans by finding other brewers in your area.

Your Local Homebrew Club

A homebrew club is a group of dedicated hobbyists eager to share wares, discuss techniques, and trade a few barbs. The collective brewing knowledge and experience accelerates your learning while exposing you to a lot of fun.

Just as no two homebrews or homebrewers are alike, neither are two clubs. Some are dedicated to competitions, others want to party, and yet others emphasize the brew day. If you don't like a club's approach, try another. Some people can't get enough and belong to three or more clubs.

FACT

America's oldest homebrew club is the Maltose Falcons. They were founded in 1974, five years before homebrewing was legal in the United States. Founded by a half dozen brewers, they now boast 250 members at home and in craft breweries. See their 25th anniversary IPA on page 170.

Finding a Club

How do you find a local homebrew club? The first stop is your local store. Smart retailers sponsor clubs and give membership discounts. The shop benefits from a steady stream of loyal customers, while the club benefits from new members. You, the brewer, win the brewing jackpot: an audience that understands your passion.

If your store doesn't sponsor a club, ask if there are any clubs in the area. Check the American Homebrewers Association's (AHA) Club Locator for registered clubs in your state. A simple web search returns a list of nearby clubs' websites. Good club sites list meeting dates and upcoming activities.

If there are enough brewers to sustain a shop, but no club, start one. The AHA publishes a "Start Your Own Club" kit to help you become a Brew Generalissimo. Talk with members of other clubs and scout ideas online to structure your club and activities.

The Meeting

Functioning as a social hour, lecture hall, and tent revival, the membership meeting brings the community together. Meetings have a social period where brewers share samples. Club business and announcements keep the club on track for their next bout of goofiness. An organized education includes tastings of commercial beer along with a presentation by brave brewers.

Located in the middle of nowhere? With no homebrew club around, turn to the Internet. Homebrewing thrives on the Internet as brewers from across the globe trade secrets and jabs. What the online boards lack in direct social contact they make up for in alacrity of their answers. Each website takes on a character and preferred techniques.

Even after reading this book, you're bound to have brewing questions. For generations, brewing's trade secrets were passed from master to apprentice. Clubs have group brew days to teach brewing. Members get to learn and the club gets beer for later events.

Veteran club members invite people to their breweries and walk folks through a brew day. The subject tackled can be anything from the simplest extract batch, your first all-grain brew, or super-complicated projects.

Clubs often arrange discounts on grain and hops. Now you can learn on the cheap. Take advantage of the discount and brew something outrageous.

The American Homebrewers Association

Founded in 1978 by Charlie Papazian, the American Homebrewers Association organizes homebrewers at a national level. Members enjoy a subscription to *Zymurgy* magazine, members' discussion lists, and discounts at affiliated pubs, on books, and for special events, like the Great American Beer Festival (GABF) or the National Homebrewers Conference (NHC).

The NHC is a three-day summer affair that moves from city to city. Each day offers numerous lectures, beer judgings, special tastings, and homebrew gatherings. People from the local area join in the fun as brewers compete in the world's largest homebrew competition. At other points in the year, the AHA sponsors "Teach a Friend to Homebrew" Day, Mead Day, and Big Brew Day, where brewers across the country brew more than 10,000 gallons of beer.

Along with their professional counterpart, the Brewers Association, the AHA lobbies for favorable beer laws and mobilizes the community to fight off impending legislation or aid in legalization efforts.

FACT

The GABF, the giant, Denver-based tasting session, originally started as a part of the NHC. Inspired by the Great British Beer Festival, the original GABF had twenty-two breweries pouring beer for interested homebrewers. Currently more than 46,000 people attend with more than 400 breweries populating the festival floor.

The Competing World

The first homebrew competitions appeared almost with the first homebrew clubs. Each club had a competition, first only for club members, later for any entrant.

Now, every weekend sees multiple competitions from Alaska to Florida. Competitions vary in size from a handful of entries to massive undertakings with more than 5,000 entries. Dedicated volunteers organize and shepherd bottles of homebrew from entrant to judges. Judgings range from a few hours to huge multiday affairs with attendant parties.

Why Enter a Competition?

Maybe you're not harboring any thoughts of being the next undefeated champion of brewing. Why then spend time and money giving your precious beer to complete strangers if you don't desire accolades in return? Because you want the real prize lying on the sheets of paper returned to every entrant: an impartial analysis and critique of each entry.

The Almighty Feedback

While competitions do award medals and ribbons to winning specimens, the pair (minimum) of evaluation sheets can hone your abilities. The

Schutzen European Strong Lager

A strong lager influenced by the pilsner and bock traditions of Bavaria. Too strong for a pilsner and too pale and hoppy for a bock, this is truly a beer that only a homebrewer could love. This recipe, tripled in size, debuted at an all-grain lager brew lesson.

Style: Continental Lager
For 5 gallons at 1.059 OG, 4.5 SRM, 27 IBUs, 6.0 percent ABV
60-minute boil

Directions

1. Follow the Multistep Brew Process profile (pages 284-285).

2. Boil for 60 minutes, adding the hops at specified intervals.

3. Chill as close as possible to 50°F. Pitch with the yeast and ferment for two weeks at 50°F. Rack to secondary and by drop temperature by 1 degree per day until the beer is resting at 35°F. Lager for an additional 2 weeks and package for service.

TIP

Can't lager? Pitch a Kolsch or German Ale strain and ferment cool. The beer will be sweeter and fruitier than the lager version, but just as tasty.

Malt/Grain/Sugar
10.00 pounds German Pilsner Malt
0.25 pound German Melanoidin Malt
0.12 pound German Acidulated (Sauer) Malt

Hops
1.00 ounce Hallertau Hersbrucker (4.5 percent AA) Pellet for 60 minutes
1.33 ounces Hallertau Hersbrucker (4.5 percent AA) Pellet for 60 minutes

Yeast
White Labs WLP 800 Pilsner Lager Yeast

Mash Schedule
Mash In 105°F 30 minutes (Strike at 1.2 quarts / lb—3.1 gallons)
Saccharification Rest 155°F 75 minutes
Mash Out 165°F 15 minutes

Falcons Twenty-Fifth-Anniversary IPA

The winning anniversary project beer is an easy-drinking yet assertively bitter beer that seems almost tame in light of some modern "Hop Bombs."

Style: India Pale Ale
For 5 gallons at 1.070 OG, 10.7 SRM, 59 IBUs, 7.25 percent ABV
60-minute boil

Directions

1. Follow the Single-Infusion Brew Process (page 284).

2. Boil for 60 minutes, adding the hops at specified intervals.

3. Chill to the low end of your yeast's fermentation range. Pitch yeast and ferment for a week, allowing the beer to naturally rise in temperature, but staying below 70°F. Fermentation should take a week and age for another 2 to 3 before packaging for drinking.

TIP

If you're brewing extract (replace the pale malt with 8.4 pounds LME, 6.75 pounds DME), add the First Wort Hops to the boil kettle prior to transferring the steeping liquid to the boil kettle.

Malt/Grain/Sugar
11.50 pounds American Two-Row Pale Malt
1.25 pounds German Munich Malt (Dark/100)
1.25 pounds Crystal 40L Malt
0.50 pound Cara-Pils Dextrine Malt

Hops
0.5 ounce Centennial (7.8 percent AA) Pellet—First Wort Hopped
0.25 ounce Chinook (11.4 percent AA) Pellet for 60 minutes
1.00 ounce Perle (6.5 percent AA) Pellet for 60 minutes
0.5 ounce Centennial (7.8 percent AA) Pellet for 15 minutes
0.5 ounce Crystal (3.8 percent AA) Pellet for 15 minutes
1.00 ounce Cascade (5.6 percent AA) Pellet for 0 minutes

Yeast
American Ale Strain (WLP001, Wyeast 1056, Wyeast 1272, Safale US-05)

Mash Schedule
Mash In / Saccharification Rest 155°F 60 minutes

judges don't know it's your beer before them as they sample it. What they see is entry "#211, American Pale Ale," number five out of twelve in flight.

FACT

Rest assured that your precious ale and lagers aren't falling into the hands of hopeless reprobates. Founded in the mid-1980s by the AHA and the Home Beer Wine Trade Association (HWBTA), the Beer Judge Certification Program (BJCP) oversees amateur beer judges and home-brew competitions. Visit their website at *www.bjcp.org*.

With sharpened pencils they record impressions of aroma, flavor, appearance, mouthfeel, and the overall quality. They'll tell you where your beer excels and where it deviates from style. Most judges are experienced brewers who can offer advice, particularly when they find defects with known causes. Lastly, they award your entry a score. After tasting all the beers in a flight, the judges award prizes.

Don't take a single competition's results as the gospel truth. Judges make mistakes or are less sensitive to certain tastes. Perhaps they got a bad bottle of your brew. To refine a favorite recipe, enter several competitions and aggregate the results. Is there a trend in what the judges are saying? As you read the judge's comments, pour a glass and attempt to find the things they describe.

The Goodies and Accolades

While the feedback is the meat of competing, the accolades are the sweet dessert. It would be a lie to claim that there's no value in awards when brewers have a wall of fame for their accomplishments.

At the very least, winning brewers will receive a ribbon or medal for the wallboard. Competitions that actively seek sponsorships may include a T-shirt with the prize package. First place in a style category may find themselves with a new glass or certificate to a local brewery. The grand prize winner, the best in show, at the bigger competitions often receives equipment.

How to Enter

You've decided that your New Mongolian IPA smokes the competition and want to prove it or maybe there's something off about it and you want the unbiased feedback. How do you get your twelve-ounce bottles before a judge?

QUESTION?

I have a beer with a special ingredient. Does it need to be entered as a specialty?
Can you taste or smell the special ingredient? If so, then yes it's a specialty. If a judge detects an unusual ingredient in a classic category, say coffee in a stout category, they will judge the beer harshly.

Find a list of upcoming competitions on the BJCP website. Choose a good local or regional competition to receive feedback appropriate for your region. Tastes for things like hops can vary by location. Take note of the entry due date, the entry fee, and the competition's website. Most competitions offer online registration to help complete your entry labels.

FACT

For shipping your entry the U.S. Postal Service is out because sending alcohol by mail is a federal offense. The major shipping companies follow alcohol policies of varying strengths. Rather than taking a chance, open an online account with your preferred carrier. Weigh, measure, and pack the box at home. Register the shipment online and print a label, then drop your box off at a retail location for minimal interference.

The final decision you need to make will ultimately affect the feedback you receive. What style do you want your beer judged against? Don't make the mistake of entering what you were trying to brew, enter what you brewed. You may have meant to brew an American pale ale, but if it tastes, looks, and smells like an IPA, enter it as an IPA. The only person who knows that you missed your target is you, and it doesn't matter because you're alone in the brewery.

Fill out the label with your style choice and other information, print it, and prepare to ship the beer just in time for the competition. Before packing the bottles, double-check that they are the right size, clean, and free of distinctive marking and that an appropriate bottle label is rubber banded to the bottle.

What to Expect

With your beer off in strangers' hands you might be nervous about what will happen. Entries gathered to a central location are registered by organizers. At this point, they strip the bottles of any identifying marks and relabel the beer with a number and description.

Before judging day, the beers are chilled and brought to the judging site to settle. On judgment morning, stewards and judges gather for a light breakfast before sitting down at group tables. Score sheets and style guidelines are distributed to the judges while the stewards prepare sampling cups.

To warm up the judging palate, the competition director serves a calibration beer to all the judges. The judges silently grade the beer and compare notes with their judging team. Then stewards bring the appointed beers to the judging teams. First they inspect the bottle for any signs of low fill, infection, or sediment and then listen carefully for a satisfying hiss when opening the bottle. The judges take turns filling cups for the panel. Cup in hand the judge buries his nose in the glass and begins recording his impressions. A quick inspection of the color and clarity is followed by another deep inhale. During this short period, the aroma can completely change. Finally, the judge takes a large sip and records what he tastes, how the beer feels, and how it finishes. The process is repeated again to capture any new impressions. The judge then assigns a score and waits to discuss the results with her fellow panelists. After a short discussion of characters and flaws detected, the scores are checked. If there is rough agreement (plus or minus 7 points), the next beer is brought out. If not, the discussion continues until the judges rework their scores into compliance.

This is repeated until all the beers are judged and the best of show is chosen. The exhausted volunteer competition director then faces the daunting task of recording the results, sorting the score sheets by entrant, preparing the prize packages, and mailing the packages and sheets to the entrants. This last part can take a day, a week, or a month depending on the director's workload.

CHAPTER 16

Recipes from Great Britain and Ireland

The island of Shakespeare, Dylan Thomas, and William Wallace along with jewel-green Ireland maintain a tenuous grasp on beery traditions of yesteryear. Fortunately, for you, your homestead won't be awash in lager lads as long as you learn to brew the island way.

The Island Way

Before 1880, British beers were substantial, averaging 1.060 and reaching the 1.090s. In 1880, William Gladstone pushed new brewery taxes. The Free Mash Tun Act moved away from charging brewers on the amount of malt they used and instead on their gravity. This, combined with the rising needs of the Industrial Revolution, pushed the overall alcohol level down to less than 4 percent on average and created the modern British world of session beers. Ireland, as a part of the UK at the time, experienced the same taxes and transformation of the drinking culture.

A unique British beer tradition is the old-fashioned serving of "Real Ale" pumped from unpressurized casks. Brewers naturally carbonate the beer, much like your bottles of homebrew. The cask is tapped and beer is drawn via a beer engine to the glass. With no extra CO_2 to push the beer or replace the headspace, air is drawn into the cask to mingle and oxidize the beer. Real ale must be served rapidly before it spoils from airborne microbes. The pint reaches the consumer at cellar temperature around 50°F (not warm) and presents wider malt and softer, more floral hop aromas and flavors.

Beware the fake "Real Ale" hand pumps found in a number of "English" pubs in America. Often, even in a brewpub, the beer engines are hooked up to kegs of force-carbonated beer and aren't representative of the true cask beer experience.

By the 1970s British pubs abandoned Real Ale in favor of force-carbonated kegged beer. Disturbed at the change, Brits formed the Campaign for Real Ale (CAMRA) to protect and promote traditional practices. Their consumer campaigns have helped restore flagging pubs and breweries. They run national promotions to encourage the drinking of mild, cider, stout, and porter.

The Joy of the Session Beer

The session ale fuels the classic British pub session. As you trade rounds, the session ale keeps your head in the game and lubricates the conversation and the game of darts. The trick for a brewer lies in making low-alcohol flavorful and refreshing beers.

Some homebrewers don't see the value of brewing lower-gravity ale preferring every beer to come screaming out of the kettles stupendously potent. Sadly, the great session beers of the UK don't travel well, so if you want a mild to sustain you, you'll need to brew your own.

FACT

Adjunct snobs beware! British brewers use a variety of additives and adjuncts to their brews including corn (maize), sugar, molasses, and more. Keep this in mind when designing recipes.

Brown Ales

When you want a drink of toasted malt with a little sweetness, reach for British brown ale. To the hardworking miners, this was their daily quencher. Today brown ales are enjoying a resurgence thanks to their universal approachability. Even those who claim to hate all beer can find something to love in the ale's aroma of light fruit and caramel with a taste of toast and sweet, buttered hazelnuts.

Brown ales get their character from the premium floor-malted pale ale malts such as Maris Otter or Golden Promise. The higher kilning of British malts gives a richer toasted grain than other ale malt or pilsner malts. Crystal (caramel in British terminology) mixes into the equation for increased body, sweetness, and color. Roasted malts polish off the final color. Hop use is minimal, just enough to balance. Brown ales benefit from the fruity British strains to add an ester dimension to the aroma.

CDJK Mild

Mild, once beloved all across Britian, is the subject of an ongoing campaign by CAMRA. After washing down generations of miners' coal dust, the beer has been fading, disparaged as gramps's drink.

Style: Mild Brown Ale
Brew Type: All Grain
For 5.5 gallons at 1.037 OG, 16 SRM, 13 IBUs, 3.2 percent ABV
60-minute boil

Directions

1. Follow the Single-Infusion Brew Process (page 284).

2. Fermentation should take less than a week. Allow the yeast to drop clear (or crash) and package. Carbonate at a lower volume, as mild is not meant to be gassy!

TIP

The Carafa II Special malt is a nontraditional ingredient. From the Weyermann Maltings in Germany, Carafa black malt offers color and crunchy toffee aromas with less harsh roast acidity.

Malt/Grain/Sugar
6.75 pounds Maris Otter Ale Malt
0.50 pound Flaked Oats (Quick Breakfast Oats are fine)
0.25 pound Crystal 150L
0.12 pound Carafa II Special Dehusked Chocolate Malt
0.12 pound Roasted Barley

Extract (sub for 5.75 pounds of Maris Otter)
4.5 pounds Pale Liquid Malt Extract (LME) (Maris Otter preferable)

Hops
0.25 ounce Wye Target (10.6 percent AA) Pellet for 60 minutes
0.12 ounce Challenger (6.5 percent AA) Pellet for 30 minutes

Other Ingredients
1 tablet Whirlfloc (or 1 teaspoon Irish Moss) Added at 20 minutes

Yeast
Wyeast 1275 Thames Valley / White Labs WLP022 Essex Ale

Mash Schedule
Saccharification Rest 152°F 60 minutes

Oat Malt AK Pale Mild

Developed by breweries to capitalize on the newfound pale ale rage sweeping Britian, very few pale milds are left today. Odds are that you've run into one at the pub, such as Boddingtons Pub Ale. Unlike their pale bitter cousins, an AK retains the malt focus of brown ale.

Style: Pale Mild Ale
Brew Type: All Grain
For 5.5 gallons at 1.038 OG, 6 SRM, 13 IBUs, 3.2 percent ABV
60-minute boil

Directions

1. Follow the Single-Infusion Brew Process (page 284).

2. Fermentation should take less than a week. Allow the yeast to drop clear (or crash) and package. Carbonate at a lower volume, as mild is not meant to be gassy!

TIP

The once-common oat malt has fallen on hard times. Only one maltster in the UK continues to produce it, the family owned and operated Thomas Fawcett. Most famously, it's been used to round out stouts. This recipe uses the oat malt's body-developing creaminess and sweetness to boost flavor and mouthfeel. If you can't find oat malt, substitute flaked oats.

Malt/Grain/Sugar
6.00 pounds Maris Otter Ale Malt
1.00 pound Thomas Fawcett Oat Malt
0.50 pound Scottish Crystal 35L
0.50 pound Turbinado "Raw" Sugar
0.25 pound Belgian Aromatic Malt

Extract (for 5 pounds of Maris Otter Malt)
4.0 pounds Pale Liquid Malt Extract (LME) (Maris Otter Preferable)

Hops
0.25 ounce Wye Target (10.4 percent AA) Pellet for 60 minutes
0.12 ounce Challenger (7.1 percent AA) Pellet for 30 minutes

Other Ingredients
1 tablet Whirlfloc (or 1 teaspoon Irish Moss) Added at 20 minutes

Yeast
Wyeast 1275 Thames Valley / Wyeast 1318 London Ale III

Mash Schedule
Saccharification Rest 152°F 60 minutes

Nukey Brown

One famous English brown is often found in American bars. This classic nutty ale of the north is a chewy, creamy, and fruity experience. A little residual sweetness is expected, so don't ferment too warm or mash too low.

Style: Northern Brown Ale
Brew Type: All Grain
For 5.5 gallons at 1.052, 13 SRM, 28 IBUs, 5.1 percent ABV
60-minute boil

Directions

Follow the Single-Infusion Brew Process (page 284).

TIP

Ringwood Ale Yeast is a notorious diacetyl producer. If you don't want to overpower your brew with butter, give the yeast extra time in the primary to clean up.

Malt/Grain/Sugar
9.00 pounds Maris Otter Pale Malt
0.50 pound Crystal 55L
2.00 ounces British Chocolate Malt

Extract (for 9.0 pounds of Pale Malt)
7.00 pounds Pale Liquid Malt Extract (LME)

Hops
0.50 ounce Target (11.0 percent AA) Pellet for 60 minutes
0.50 ounce East Kent Goldings (4.7 percent AA) Pellet for 20 minutes

Other Ingredients
1 tablet Whirlfloc

Yeast
Wyeast 1187 Ringwood Ale / WLP005 British Ale

Mash Schedule
Saccharification Rest 153°F 60 minutes

Bitters/Pale Ales/IPA

Ignore the name "bitter." Sitting at the low end of the bitter–pale ale–India pale ale spectrum, bitters take their name from their fresh hop character. So indelibly woven into pub life was bitter that asking for a pint yielded a glass of the local "ordinary." Stronger versions of the style come in "Best Bitter" and "Extra Special Bitter." Each has a malt backbone sturdy enough to keep hops at bay without reducing drinkability. Bitters contain little more than pale malt, a light dose of crystal, some sugar or maize, and charges of the lovely Fuggles and East Kent Goldings hops.

Pale ales like Bass are more copper and stronger with a brisker hop character. The extra bite comes from the sulfate-rich waters of Burton Upon Trent, Bass's hometown. The reputed hoppiness of English pale ale is tame compared to American versions.

To replicate the hop-boosting water of Burton Upon Trent, most home-brewing shops sell "Burton Water Salts." Read Chapter 5 to learn how to adjust your water.

India Pale Ale (IPA) comes from the time of the British colonization of India. The oft-repeated and historically shaky legend tells of George Hodgson inventing stronger pale ale with more hops capable of surviving the journey to beer-hostile India. The troops would satiate their homesickness with a taste of the civilized world. The legend states that IPA was unknown at home until a ship ran aground in the Thames estuary. Looters grabbed the kegs of brew and grew so fond of the taste that they demanded its sale. Wonderful prattle.

Benton's Bitter

The moniker may be "Ordinary Bitter," but this is a beer with an extraordinary drinkability. You can go about your business after a few pints at 3.2 percent ABV. That's lighter than lite beers and it packs more flavor.

Style: Standard/Ordinary Bitter
Brew Type: All Grain
For 6.0 gallons at 1.037 OG, 9 SRM, 13 IBUs, 3.2 percent ABV
60-minute boil

Directions

Follow the Single-Infusion Brew Process (page 284).

TIP

The White Labs 002 English Ale yeast is a classic bitter strain. It leaves a residual sweetness that offsets larger hopping doses. Esters and diacetyl are noticeable, but not over the top. The yeast also drops clear very quickly.

Malt/Grain/Sugar
7.00 pounds Maris Otter Ale Malt
1.00 pound Crystal 60L

Extract (for 7 pounds of Maris Otter Malt)
5.5 pounds Pale Liquid Malt Extract(LME) (Maris Otter Preferable)

Hops
1.5 ounces Fuggles (5.7 percent AA) Pellet for 60 minutes
0.5 ounce East Kent Goldings (6.1 percent AA) Pellet for 30 minutes

Other Ingredients
0.25 teaspoon Kosher Salt Added at 60 minutes
1 teaspoon Gypsum Added at 60 minutes
1 teaspoon Irish Moss Added at 20 minutes

Yeast
White Labs WLP002 English Ale

Mash Schedule
Saccharification Rest 151°F 60 minutes

Stuffed Extra Special Bitter

Stuffed is chewier with more bite. This is the bitter that you break out for company. See the note above about the use of maize. If you're steeping for extract, don't skip the additional pound of pale malt, it will convert the sugars in the maize.

Style: Extra Special Bitter
Brew Type: All Grain
For 5.5 gallons at 1.059 OG, 13.5 SRM, 45 IBUs, 5.9 percent ABV
60-minute boil

Directions

Follow the Single-Infusion Brew Process (page 284).

TIP

A funny thing about beer style monikers: If a brewery can demonstrate that they alone produce a beer, they can trademark the style name. In the case of ESB, Fuller Smith & Turner (commonly Fullers), trademarked the name "ESB" for their flagship beer.

Malt/Grain/Sugar
10.00 pounds Maris Otter Ale Malt
1.00 pound Crystal 105L
0.50 pound Flaked Maize (Corn)

Extract (for 9 pounds of Maris Otter Malt)
8.0 pounds Pale Liquid Malt Extract (LME) (Maris Otter Preferable)

Hops
0.75 ounce Target (11.0 percent AA) Pellet for 60 minutes
1.50 ounces Challenger (7.5 percent AA) Pellet for 10 minutes
1.0 ounce East Kent Goldings (6.1 percent AA) Pellet—Dry-Hopped

Other Ingredients
1 teaspoon Gypsum Added at 60 minutes
1 teaspoon Irish Moss Added at 20 minutes

Yeast
Wyeast 1968 London ESB / White Labs WLP002 English Ale

Mash Schedule
Saccharification Rest 150°F 60 minutes

Bluebird of Hoppiness British IPA

Smaller than its younger American cousins, the British IPA pushes malt, but retains a crisp dry bite. Up in the Lake District a pub brewery in Coniston makes a wonderful Challenger-only bitter called Bluebird. This is the beefed up version.

Style: English IPA
Brew Type: All Grain
For 5.5 gallons at 1.060, 13 SRM, 51
    IBUs, 6.0 percent ABV
60-minute boil

Directions

Follow the Single-Infusion Brew Process (page 284).

TIP

Swap hops around in this recipe as you feel. A bit of Goldings or Fuggles for the finish would be superb. Coniston makes a version of Bluebird Bitter that uses American Mount Hood in addition to the Challenger.

Malt/Grain/Sugar
10.00 pounds Maris Otter Pale Malt
1.00 pound Crystal 55L
0.50 pound Crystal 75L
0.25 pound Biscuit Malt

Extract (for 9.0 pounds of Pale Malt)
7.00 pounds Pale Liquid Malt Extract (LME)

Hops
1.00 ounce Challenger (8.0 percent AA) Pellet for 60 minutes
1.00 ounce Challenger (8.0 percent AA) Pellet for 20 minutes
1.00 ounce Challenger (8.0 percent AA) Pellet for 0 minutes

Other Ingredients
1 tablet Whirlfloc

Yeast
Wyeast 1275 Thames Valley Ale / WLP023 Burton Ale

Mash Schedule
Saccharification Rest 153°F 60 minutes

Scottish Ales

Unlike the English, the Scottish lacked a hop-growing region. Higher hop costs encouraged malt-oriented styles. Scottish ales settled into weights similar to the Ordinary/Best/Special bitter categories. The Scots use a schilling system of "60/Light," "70/Heavy," or "80/Export," instead of "Ordinary" and so on. The numbers come from the nineteenth-century tax per barrel. Scottish ales are similar to the same weight bitter but with more malt and less hops.

Wee Heavy keeps you warm on the coldest, dankest night. Belhaven produces the most commonly available, but the classic comes from the old manor brewery of Traquair House. Their rich house ale is brewed in a battered open copper kettle before fermenting in an oak vessel.

Alba Gruit Export

This recipe produces a wonderful base Scottish 80/Export with no hops. Instead the recipe depends upon a gruit to deliver the bitterness. Add a quarter pound of peat-smoked malt to emulate the old malt drying fires.

Style: Scottish Export (Specialty)
Brew Type: All Grain
For 5.5 gallons at 1.054 OG, 8 SRM, 0 IBUs, 5.4 percent ABV
120-minute boil

Directions

Follow the Single-Infusion Brew Process (page 284).

TIP

After the Dutch introduced hop-only beer, the British and Scottish stubbornly held on to the gruit ales. Ales were considered distinct from new-fangled hopped "bier."

Malt/Grain/Sugar
10.00 pounds Golden Promise / Maris Otter Ale Malt
0.50 pound Crystal 55L

Extract (for 9 pounds of Maris Otter Malt)
8.0 pounds Pale Liquid Malt Extract (LME) (Maris Otter Preferable)

Hops
None

Other Ingredients
5 grams Marsh Rosemary
1 gram Sweet "Myrca" Gale
14 grams Yarrow
1 tablet Whirlfloc Added at 20 minutes

Yeast
Wyeast 1728 Scottish Ale / White Labs WLP028 Edinburgh Ale

Mash Schedule
Saccharification Rest 154°F 60 minutes

Old Scottish brewers took advantage of abundant local fuel sources to save money on caramel malts. Long boil times created natural "kettle caramels," replacing speciality malts. Even today long boil times are common.

QUESTION?

Can I use Peated Malt for Scottish-style ales?
As a homebrewer, you can, but a Scottish brewer will think you're strange. In Scotland, peat-smoked barley goes to the production of whiskey. Use it to capture the flavor from old malt drying techniques.

Off-Kilter Strong Scotch Ale

A deep, rich beer for cold moor nights. Note the tiny amount of peated malt. The human nose detects smoke phenols very easily. Try this small amount first for a subtle effect before succumbing to the urge to add more.

Style: Scottish Wee Heavy
Brew Type: All Grain
For 5.0 gallons at 1.097, 16.4 SRM, 28 IBUs, 9.6 percent ABV
120-minute boil

Directions

Follow the Single-Infusion Brew Process (page 284).

TIP

For roasted barley, take a measure of pale malt and spread onto a sheet pan. Bake for 15 to 30 minutes in a 350°F oven. Remove from the oven, cool, and store in a paper bag for a couple weeks to mellow.

Malt/Grain/Sugar
10.00 pounds Golden Promise / Maris Otter Ale Malt
2.00 pounds Toasted Pale Malt (See below)
0.67 pound Crystal 80L
0.67 pound Wheat Malt
1.00 ounce Roasted Barley
1.00 ounce Peat Smoked Malt (optional)
3.00 pounds Pale Liquid Malt Extract

Extract (for 9 pounds of Maris Otter Malt)
8.0 pounds Pale Liquid Malt Extract (LME) (Maris Otter Preferable)

Hops
1.0 ounce East Kent Goldings (6.5 percent AA) Pellet for 60 minutes
1.0 ounce East Kent Goldings (6.5 percent AA) Pellet for 45 minutes

Other Ingredients
1 tablet Whirlfloc

Yeast
Wyeast 1728 Scottish Ale / White Labs WLP028 Edinburgh Ale

Mash Schedule
Saccharification Rest 154°F 60 minutes

The Scottish ale yeasts are softly fruity and work well at colder temperatures. They are also hearty and alcohol tolerant, capable of brewing 11 percent and higher ales. The water varies widely, but softer water is preferable to enhance the malt's sweetness.

Porter and Stout

According to legend, English porters (luggage and cargo handlers) drank a nourishing brownish black beer blended from three beers. Harwood Brewery supposedly replicated this experience in a beer called "Entire." Eventually the beer became synonymous with its target working-class audience.

It appears true that porter is eponymous. Porter developed from the dominant brown ales of the day. Designed to age at the brewery, porter's immense and immediate popularity led to the use of nascent industrial techniques to produce and age massive quantities of beer. Porter brewers gave us the hydrometer and spurred the development of pale and black roasted malts. The last British porters were brewed around World War II, and then the style lay moribund until American craft brewers resurrected it.

Stout, the other black beer, was born from porter as a stronger version of the beer. The original name "stout porter" was eventually shortened to stout and thus a new style was born. Over time, as with all British and Irish beer, the gravities dropped to their current levels.

The key ingredients to porters and stouts include black patent malt and pale malt. Some argue that roasted unmalted barley only belongs in stouts, but brewers used both in porters as well as stouts. To reduce roast malt's acidic bite, a boil kettle addition of calcium carbonate (chalk) replicates the naturally carbonated water of London and Dublin.

Gatekeeper Memorial Porter

Brewed in memory of the brewer's loyal canine assistant, this porter contains a staggering mix of grains to produce a beer of complex character.

Style: Robust Porter
Brew Type: All Grain
For 5.5 gallons at 1.067, 46.7 SRM, 31 IBUs, 6.75 percent ABV
60-minute boil

Directions

Follow the Single-Infusion Brew Process (page 284).

TIP

Mild malt is highly kilned pale malt designed to boost body. Think Maris Otter's malty, toasted biscuit and nutty characters turned up higher.

Malt/Grain/Sugar
8.00 pounds Golden Promise / Maris Otter Ale Malt
2.00 pounds Mild Malt
1.00 pound Chocolate Malt
6.00 ounces Crystal 55L
0.25 pound Aromatic Malt
0.25 pound Black Malt
3.00 ounces Crystal 150L
2.00 ounces Biscuit Malt
2.00 ounces Roasted Barley
2.00 ounces Special B Malt
2.00 ounces Special Roast Malt

Extract (for 9 pounds of Maris Otter Malt / Mild Malt)
8.0 pounds Pale Liquid Malt Extract (LME) (Maris Otter Preferable)

Hops
1.0 ounce Fuggle (4.5 percent AA) Pellet for 60 minutes
1.0 ounce Fuggle (4.5 percent AA) Pellet for 30 minutes
1.0 ounce Fuggle (4.5 percent AA) Pellet for 5 minutes

Other Ingredients
1 tablet Whirlfloc

Yeast
Wyeast 1318 London III

Mash Schedule
Saccharification Rest 155°F 60 minutes

Mac's Gone Oat Malt Stout

Scotland's now defunct Maclay Thistle Brewery brewed an oat malt stout. Malted oats replaced a brewer's usual flaked oatmeal. The beer was rich and creamy with a smooth sweet coffee, chocolate flavor.

Style: Oatmeal Stout
Brew Type: All Grain
For 5.5 gallons at 1.052, 43 SRM, 28 IBUs, 5.1 percent ABV
60-minute boil

Directions

Follow the Single-Infusion Brew Process (page 284).

TIP

If you choose to go the flaked oatmeal route, remember to steep with a pound of pale malt to convert the starches in the oatmeal.

Malt/Grain/Sugar
8.00 pounds Maris Otter Ale Malt
1.00 pound Oat Malt (or Flaked Oatmeal)
1.00 pound Crystal 150L
0.75 pound Roasted Barley
4.00 ounces Black Patent Malt

Extract (for 7 pounds of Maris Otter Malt / Mild Malt)
5.5 pounds Pale Liquid Malt Extract (LME) (Maris Otter Preferable)

Hops
0.5 ounce Target (10.0 percent AA) Pellet for 60 minutes
1.0 ounce Fuggle (4.5 percent AA) Pellet for 20 minutes

Other Ingredients
1 tablet Whirlfloc

Yeast
Wyeast 1318 London III

Mash Schedule
Saccharification Rest 153°F 60 minutes

Belgie Guinness Foreign Stout

The Guinness folk have an open "secret." They brew ten to twenty different versions of their iconic stout, each tailored to the local market. In Dublin for export to Belgium, the land of strong beer, they brew Guinness Special Export Stout, an 8-percent hammer of a brew.

Style: Foreign Stout
Brew Type: All Grain
For 5.5 gallons at 1.076, 40 SRM, 34 IBUs, 7.7 percent ABV
90-minute boil

Directions

Follow the Single-Infusion Brew Process (page 284).

TIP

Adding the hops in for ninety minutes boosts the amount of bitterness extracted from the glands. Going beyond ninety-minute boil time, while tempting, produces grassy, vegetal, nasty flavors.

Malt/Grain/Sugar
11.00 pounds Maris Otter Ale Malt
2.00 pounds Flaked Barley
1.00 pound Crystal 60L
0.75 pound Roasted Barley
4.00 ounces Carafa II Special Dehusked Chocolate Malt

Extract (for 10 pounds of Maris Otter Malt)
8.0 pounds Pale Liquid Malt Extract (LME) (Maris Otter Preferable)

Hops
0.88 ounce Target (8.8 percent AA) Pellet for 90 minutes

Other Ingredients
1 tablet Whirlfloc

Yeast
Wyeast 1084 Irish Ale / White Labs WLP004 Irish Ale

Mash Schedule
Saccharification Rest 155°F 60 minutes

Anastasia's Imperial Stout

Is there a sadder case than that of Anastasia Romanov, the executed youngest daughter of the last Russian tsar? The world clung to the possibility of her survival, opening the door to years of women claiming to be Anastasia. Hoist a pint of this rich brew in memory of the romantic legends of the Grand Duchess.

Style: Imperial Stout
Brew Type: All Grain
For 5.5 gallons at 1.088, 42 SRM, 57
    IBUs, 9.0 percent ABV
90-minute boil

Directions

Follow the Single-Infusion Brew Process (page 284).

TIP

Black as a winter night, imperial stout was first brewed by Thrale's Brewery for export to the imperial court of Tsarina Catherine II. This is the bigger, heartier, and more potent version of a stout weighing in at over 9 percent and filled with sweet raisins, dark chocolate, and coffee.

Malt/Grain/Sugar
15.00 pounds Maris Otter Pale Malt
1.00 pound Crystal 150L
0.50 pound Crystal 55L
0.50 pound Roasted Barley
6.0 ounces Black Patent Malt

Extract (for 9.0 pounds of Pale Malt)
7.00 pounds Pale Liquid Malt Extract (LME)

Hops
1.00 ounce Target (11.0 percent AA) Pellet for 90 minutes
2.00 ounces East Kent Goldings (4.8 percent AA) Pellet for 20 minutes

Other Ingredients
1 tablet Whirlfloc
1 teaspoon Yeast Nutrient

Yeast
Wyeast 1084 Irish Ale / WLP004 Irish Ale

Mash Schedule
Saccharification Rest 153°F 90 minutes

Old Ale and Barleywine

Lest you think that Britian's styles are all responsible, low-alcohol ales, from the depths of winter come old ales and barleywines. Take everything you know about other British styles of beer and ramp it. To celebrate the impending yuletide, a brewery anniversary, or the Queen's Jubilee, breweries turn to dense, chewy, caramel-coated toffee ales ranging from 5 percent to an impolite 12 percent ABV. These beers are living proof that British brewers get to let their hair down at least once a year.

Old ales are a sweet tooth's dream. Toffee and roasts mix with oxidative flavors of raisins and sherry. Most styles assiduously avoid oxidation, but with these strong English ales, the oxidative tones add complexity and provide a break from the fruity yeast esters and caramel malt.

Barleywine is the more assertive sibling, made with little more than an obscene amount of pale malt. The mash's thick syrupy first runnings taste like decadent dessert. A liberal hand with the hops keeps the beer from feeling cloying. Over time the hops fade and the barleywine presents the same oxidation characters as old ale. This transformation drives brewers and drinkers to collect "verticals," multiple years, to taste the changes.

To prevent unnecessary hours of boiling to concentrate the wort to the heights needed for barleywine, brewers perform only the bare minimum amount of sparging needed to achieve a normal boil volume. To hike the gravity and promote a drier finish, a dose of sugar or extract is used in the kettle.

Both styles need managed fermentations. Use a large starter or a yeast cake from a previous batch. Run your fermentation cool to express the caramel malt tones instead of estery cherry and apples and to prevent fusel alcohols. These beers can age for years as is attested by the continued quality of the original 1968 batch of Thomas Hardy's Ale.

Old Fuddy Duddy

To produce rich, sweet old ale without a ton of sparging, brewers increase the grain bill and sparge less. What's the cost of a few more pounds of grain? For a few bucks more, you save time and energy. Just remember to only sparge enough to meet your needs (that is, around 6.5 gallons).

Style: Old Ale
Brew Type: All Grain
For 5.0 gallons at 1.080, 16 SRM, 42 IBUs, 8.1 percent ABV
90-minute boil

Directions

Follow the Single-Infusion Brew Process (page 284).

TIP

To ameliorate the expense of a massive brew, pull a "second runnings" beer by sparging the mash again into a second pot. In the case of these recipes, you can produce a nice batch of mild ale.

Malt/Grain/Sugar
23.00 pounds Maris Otter Ale Malt
3.00 pounds Crystal 75L
4.00 ounces Chocolate Malt
4.00 ounces Kiln-Coffee Malt
4.00 ounces Black Patent Malt
8.00 ounces Dark Treacle Molasses (Add during the boil)

Extract (for 20 pounds of Maris Otter Malt)
16.0 pounds Pale Liquid Malt Extract (LME) (Maris Otter Preferable)

Hops
2.0 ounces Target (11.0 percent AA) Pellet for 60 minutes
1.5 ounces Target (11.0 percent AA) Pellet for 15 minutes
2.0 ounces Fuggle (5.0 percent AA) Pellet for 0 minutes

Other Ingredients
1 tablet Whirlfloc

Yeast
Wyeast 1318 London III

Mash Schedule
Saccharification Rest 154°F 60 minutes

Fat Man Barleywine

This is as big as an English-style beer gets. At 11.5 percent, this award-winning barleywine should be enjoyed in serious moderation! With careful packaging it is possible to age this beer for longer than ten years.

Style: English-Style Barleywine
Brew Type: All Grain
For 5.5 gallons at 1.111, 17 SRM, 68 IBUs, 11.5 percent ABV
90-minute boil

Directions

Follow the Single-Infusion Brew Process (page 284).

Malt/Grain/Sugar
17.00 pounds Maris Otter Ale Malt
2.00 pounds Crystal 55L
1.00 pound Biscuit Malt
1.00 pound Dark English Brown Sugar

Extract (for 16 pounds of Maris Otter Malt)
12.5 pounds Pale Liquid Malt Extract (LME) (Maris Otter Preferable)

Hops
1.5 ounces Target (8.8 percent AA) Pellet for 90 minutes
2.0 ounces Fuggle (5.0 percent AA) Whole for 30 minutes
1.0 ounce East Kent Goldings Whole (4.75 percent AA) Whole for 5 minutes

Other Ingredients
1 tablet Whirlfloc

Yeast
Wyeast 1275 Thames Valley

Mash Schedule
Saccharification Rest 150°F 60 minutes

CHAPTER 17

Recipes from Germany and Eastern Europe

Lederhosen, bratwurst, and dirndl-wearing barmaids hefting huge liters of beer—these are the beerlover's image of Germany. You may not have them at home, but you can at least pour a frothy maß of your own.

German Brewing Law and Tradition

Beer has a long tradition in the German region, with written texts dating to 800 B.C.E. The independent kingdoms of German-speaking people all developed varieties suited for their resources.

Monastic brewing traditions rose during the Middle Ages as monasteries brewed for the parishioners. The advent of Protestantism and the state's desire for beer taxes forced cloisters to divest their breweries in favor of secular brewers.

During the 1500s a funny thing happened in the Bavarian and Bohemian beer cellars: Cold-loving yeasts evolved and changed the landscape. These new yeast strains made drier and cleaner-tasting beers. Lagers' chilly nature allowed fermentations at temperatures that kept bugs at bay and preserved the beer.

FACT

Recent genome studies conclusively prove that the two main lager families evolved simultaneously and independently of each other. They analyzed the genome of 100-year-old samples of yeasts to compare the two groups.

Concurrently with the discovery, a new law would shape the nature of beer in the Bavarian region and eventually the whole German state.

Reinheitsgebot: Beer Purity

The Reinheitsgebot, better known as the German Beer Purity Law, forms the foundation of German brewing. The law states that "beer can only be brewed with barley malt, hops, yeast, and water." The law also contains myriad additional rules and exceptions. This little law defines the whole of German beer culture today

The Reinheitsgebot started in the Duchy of Bavaria. In 1516, "white" wheat beers had risen in popularity over brown barley beer. Worried in part about adulteration of beer and largely about the use of wheat for brewing and not baking, Duke Wilhelm IV decreed the law and shut down the wheat breweries. Brewers caught flouting the rules would lose all their beer.

The declining Weisses Brauhaus was acquired in 1872 by Georg Schneider and rechristened as G. Schneider & Sohn. The company aggressively brewed, promoted, and restored weiss beer to popularity.

Facing the pressures of impending war, Bavaria agreed in 1871 to unify with other German states, but only if the rest of Germany adopted the Reinheitsgebot. Agreement was reached, to the horror of the Northern German brewers, who faced elimination of regional styles.

By the end of World War I, more than three-quarters of Germany's beer styles had disappeared. The real pain of the Reinheitsgebot is that it narrowly constricts the world of possible styles. Few of the world's ales are "pure" enough by German standards. Lost to the history is the variety of fruit, herb, spice, smoked, and wheat beers that predated unification.

The modern German beer law allows more "unpure" ingredients than ever. The classic ingredient restriction applies only to lager beers. If you're brewing ales, like hefeweizen, you're allowed all malted grains and sugars.

Is a purity law good? Germany contains numerous breweries focusing on a lager or two. Conservatism runs deep in the breweries. Germans have amazing technical knowledge and unparalleled skill in producing lagers. Experimentation is almost nonexistent in the country. Neighboring Belgium produces a riot of styles, despite being a tenth of the size.

Bavaria and Bohemia

In the past it has been said the Bavarians feel more at home with their neighboring Bohemian Czech cousins than their fellow Germans. Together they've shaped the modern beer landscape.

In 1842, Burger Brauerei recruited Bavarian brewmeister Josef Groll to teach the methods of Bavarian bottom-fermented beer. There in the town of Plzen (Pilsen), 170 miles from Munich, he launched a revolution. Combining the soft water, pale Moravian malt, and Saaz hops, he produced the first pilsner beer. It was an immediate success and spread worldwide, starting with Bavaria. Bavarian brewmasters ran Pilsner Urquell until the 1900s. Others left Germany and brought the new beer style to taps everywhere.

Wheat Beer: Weizen and Beyond

Most Weissbier brewers were forced out of business by the Reinheitsgebot. Only the royal brewery could make wheat beers, which the nobles kept for themselves. When the Duke needed revenue for war debts, laws required every tavern to carry a cask of Weissbier or face closure.

Hefeweizen are cloudy, golden ales brashly perfumed with the scent of cloves, bananas, and bubblegum. The full-bodied, easy-drinking beer tastes slightly sweet and bready. A filtered weizen is known as "Kristallweizen." Dunkelweizen brings dark malt bite and Munich malt complexity to the game. And for those tough days, brewers make the strong, sweet, dark, and spicy Weizenbock.

FACT

The terms *weissbier* ("white beer") and *weizenbier* ("wheat beer") are interchangeable. Traditionally, Bavarians refer to wheat beers as weissbier while the other Germans say weizenbier.

Weizen yeast throws various esters and phenols based on nutrient levels and fermentation temperatures. Malted wheat has plenty of clove precursor ferulic acid freed with a protein rest. Ferment cooler in the low sixties for cloves. To push bubblegum and banana, ferment around 68°F.

Berlin is home to a different wheat beer. Berliner weiss is a low-alcohol, sparkling sour ale. It is intentionally spiked with lactic acid produced by *Lactobacillus debrueckii*. It is served "mit Schuss," or with syrup. The usual choices include raspberry, lemon, or woodruff.

Ball-a-Holic Hefe

*This is a true Bavarian hefeweizen
without any shortcuts. Ferment this one
cool and you'll be rewarded with the
desired clove character from your yeast.
Don't skip the protein rest because
that's where you free the precursors to
the clove. Start to finish, this beer can
be ready in ten days and is best fresh.*

Style: Bavarian Weizen
Brew Type: All Grain
For 5.5 gallons at 1.066, 5.6 SRM, 15
   IBUs, 6.5 percent ABV
60-minute boil

Directions

1. Follow the Decoction Brew Process
   (page 285).

2. For each of the three decoction
   rests, rest the pull at 154°F for 20
   minutes and then boil for 30 minutes
   before returning to the main mash.

TIP

A triple decoction is a lot of work, but
adherents swear by the results. Invite a
brew buddy to help you brew your
decoctions and take turns stirring. You'll
find that the day goes much smoother
that way.

Malt/Grain/Sugar
9.00 pounds Wheat Malt
3.75 pounds Pilsner Malt

Extract (for 8.0 pounds of Wheat Malt and 3.00 pounds of Pilsner Malt)
8.50 pounds Wheat Liquid Malt Extract (LME)

Hops
0.30 ounce Hallertauer (8.6 percent AA) Whole for 60 minutes
0.40 ounce Tettnanger (4.6 percent AA) Whole for 30 minutes
0.50 ounce Czech Saaz (3.8 percent AA) Pellet for 1 minute

Other Ingredients
2.5 tablespoons Yeast Nutrient

Yeast
WLP380 Hefeweizen IV Ale

Mash Schedule
Protein Rest 120°F 50 minutes
Intermediate Rest 140°F 20 minutes
Saccharification Rest 150°F 60 minutes

Trigo Oscuro Dunkelweizen

Maybe all those decoctions aren't needed. This recipe has won scads of awards. Munich malt provides a rich foundation for the wheat sweetness. The small touch of Carafa bumps the color into the right range without any harsh roastiness.

Style: Dunkelweizen
Brew Type: All Grain
For 5.5 gallons at 1.057, 13.5 SRM, 17.3 IBUs, 5.3 percent ABV
90-minute boil

Directions

Follow the Single Infusion Brew Process (page 284).

TIP

A lot of all-grain beers concentrate the gravity with a ninety-minute boil. Long boils create the lip-smacking, earthy kettle caramels.

Malt/Grain/Sugar
6.90 pounds Wheat Malt
3.00 pounds Munich Malt
2.00 pounds Pilsner Malt
0.25 pound Crystal 40L
0.25 pound Special 8 Malt
0.10 pound Carafa Special

Extract (for 6.0 pounds of Wheat Malt and 2.25 pounds of Munich Malt and 1.5 pounds of Pilsner Malt)
6.8 pounds Wheat Liquid Malt Extract (LME)
2.2 pounds Munich Liquid Malt Extract (LME)

Hops
1.00 ounce Hallertau Hersbrucker (4.0 percent AA) Pellet for 60 minutes

Other Ingredients
1 tablespoon Yeast Nutrient

Yeast
WLP300 Hefeweizen Ale

Mash Schedule
Saccharification Rest 152°F 60 minutes

Why Not Berliner Weiss

That boil time is not a typo. You boil briefly to kill undesirables and then add your Lactobacillus cultures. Waiting a day before pitching the yeast gives the Lactobacillus time to produce tangy lactic acid.

Style: Berliner Weiss
Brew Type: All Grain
For 5.5 gallons at 1.039, 2.7 SRM, 3.9
  IBUs, 3.8 percent ABV
20-minute boil

Directions

1. Follow the Single Infusion Brew Process (page 284).

2. After the brief boil, cool the wort and skip oxygenation. Pitch the lactobacillus and wait 24–48 hours before pitching the regular yeast.

TIP

Consider dedicating a set of equipment to sour ales to reduce the chances of cross-contamination. A number of veteran brewers use pin-lock kegs solely for use as sour ale kegs to prevent confusion.

Malt/Grain/Sugar
3.00 pounds Pilsner Malt
4.50 pounds Wheat Malt

Extract (for 2.5 pounds of Pilsner Malt and 4.0 pounds of Wheat Malt)
2.00 pounds Lager Liquid Malt Extract (LME)
3.00 pounds Wheat Liquid Malt Extract (LME)

Hops
1.25 ounces Czech Saaz (3.5 percent AA) Pellet for 10 minutes

Other Ingredients
1 tablespoon Yeast Nutrient

Yeast
Wyeast 5335 Lactobacillus debrueckii / White Labs WLP677 Lactobacillus
Wyeast 1007 German Ale / WLP011 European Ale

Mash Schedule
Saccharification Rest 150°F 60 minutes

Hybrid German Ales

The Reinheitsgebot managed to kill off most German ales. Two odd styles survived. Not really lagers and not really ales, they are considered hybrid ales, fermented cool with ale yeast and lagered for an extended period.

Germany's fourth-largest city, Cologne (Köln) is in the heart of the Rhineland. It is a bustling modern town with a special beer protected by law. The Kölsch Convention of 1986 declared that Kölsch can only be brewed around Cologne. The beer is a pale, straw-colored beer with a crisp white head and a light fruity nose. The beer conveys a light, pleasant sweetness with just a touch of hops.

To be traditional when drinking a Kölsch, you need a special stange (pole) glass. The stange is a tall and thin column that holds 0.2 liters (around 7 ounces).

Altbier, "old beer," is the other ale holdover from the Rhineland. Centered on the state capital, Düsseldorf, the amber-colored Alt stands in contrast to its pale neighbors. Malt stands squarely in the face of an assertive bitter character. Knowledgeable beer lovers time their visits to coincide with the annual tapping of the "Sticke" Alt, a strong variant.

The city of Dortmund provides another old German ale. The extinct Adambier is a strong, malt-forward, and melanoidin-driven German-style barleywine that's fermented cool. The hard water of Dortmund gives the beer a final dry edge.

Der Plumpen Kölsch

Kölsch isn't a very complicated recipe. The trick is in the fermentation. Chill close to 60°F before pitching the yeast and then keep the fermentation temperature down. When you move to secondary, drop the temperature to 50°F and then decrease one degree every day until you're resting at 35°F. Hold there for an additional two weeks before packaging.

Style: Kölsch
Brew Type: All Grain
For 5.5 gallons at 1.052, 3.2 SRM, 17.8 IBUs, 5.1 percent ABV
60-minute boil

Directions

Follow the Multistep Brew Process (pages 284-285).

TIP

The disadvantage to using low alpha acid hops is the wet green grass flavors from all the boiled plant matter. However, with higher alpha hops you won't get the more subtle oil contributions.

Malt/Grain/Sugar
8.50 pounds Pilsner Malt
1.50 pounds Wheat Malt

Extract (for 7.5 pounds of Pilsner Malt)
6.00 pounds Lager Liquid Malt Extract (LME)

Hops
1.00 ounce Hallertau Hersbrucker (2.3 percent AA) Whole for First Wort Hop
0.50 ounce Hallertau Hersbrucker (2.3 percent AA) Whole for 60 minutes
0.50 ounce Tettnanger (4.3 percent AA) Pellet for 20 minutes
0.50 ounce Tettnanger (4.3 percent AA) Pellet for 5 minutes

Other Ingredients
1 tablet Whirlfloc
1 tablespoon Yeast Nutrient

Yeast
WLP029 German Ale/Kolsch Yeast

Mash Schedule
Intermediate Rest 135°F 30 minutes
Saccharification Rest 152°F 60 minutes

Sticke Situation Altbier

If you can't make it to Dortmund in time for the tapping of the sticke, make your own cask. Give this beer a longer lagering period, about two months before serving. That will give the beer plenty of time to mellow out.

Style: Sticke Alt
Brew Type: All Grain
For 5.5 gallons at 1.058, 20.4 SRM, 42 IBUs, 6 percent ABV
90-minute boil

Directions

Follow the Decoction Brew Process (page 285).

TIP

Dortmund water has a lot of minerals. The water salt additions here are designed for average city water, but you should adjust them to your own water supply (see Chapter 5).

Malt/Grain/Sugar
10.50 pounds Munich Malt
1.00 pound German Crystal 90L
2.00 ounces Carafa II Special Dehusked Chocolate Malt

Extract (for 9.5 pounds of Munich Malt)
7.50 pounds Munich Liquid Malt Extract (LME)

Hops
1.00 ounce Perle (8.25 percent AA) Pellet for 60 minutes
1.00 ounce Hallertauer Tradition (6.0 percent AA) Pellet for 15 minutes

Other Ingredients
1 tablet Whirlfloc
1 tablespoon Yeast Nutrient
1 teaspoon Chalk (added to the boil)
½ teaspoon Epsom Salt
1 teaspoon Gypsum (added to the boil)

Yeast
WLP029 German Ale/Kölsch

Mash Schedule
Intermediate Rest 148°F 30 minutes
Saccharification Rest 156°F 30 minutes

Arrogant Sombrero 2.0

Nineteenth-century Adambiers were notoriously strong. Legend tells of a visit by the celebrated drinker Prussian King Frederick William IV. The citizenry of Dortmund proffered a tankard of Adam, which he downed in one go. The king promptly passed out for a day.

Style: Dortmunder Adambier
Brew Type: All Grain
For 5.5 gallons at 1.124, 19.1 SRM, 61.1 IBUs, 11.7 percent ABV
100-minute boil

Directions

Follow the Decoction Brew Process (page 285).

Malt/Grain/Sugar
15.5 pounds Munich Malt
8.5 pounds Maris Otter / Golden Promise
1.75 pounds Rauch Malt
0.25 pound Acidulated Malt
0.12 pound Black Patent Malt

Extract (for 15.0 pounds of Munich Malt and 8.0 pounds of Maris Otter / Golden Promise)
10.50 pounds Munich Liquid Malt Extract (LME)
5.75 pounds Pale Liquid Malt Extract (LME)

Hops
1.00 ounce Hallertauer Hersbrucker (3.9 percent AA) Whole for First Wort Hopping
1.00 ounce Magnum (14.0 percent AA) Pellet for 90 minutes
1.00 ounce Hallertauer Hersbrucker (3.9 percent AA) Whole for 1 minute

Other Ingredients
1 tablet Whirlfloc
1 tablespoon Yeast Nutrient

Yeast
WLP029 German Ale/Kolsch

Mash Schedule
Protein Rest 112°F 30 minutes
Intermediate Rest 125°F 30 minutes
Saccharification Rest 156°F 30 minutes

Pale Lager

Welcome to what the world thinks is "real beer" territory. Combining the new technologies of cheap glassware and pale dried malts, pale golden lagers gained the public's favor globally. Pilsner was invented in 1842, and by World War I pilsner completely dominated the American beer market.

Munich's native pale lager, helles, emphasizes malt character over the hops pushed by the Bohemian or German pilsners. There's a pleasant grainy sweetness that makes this inexpensive brew popular in Munich.

Looking at a recipe for German pils, few differences from pilsner are noticeable. German pils are fermented to a lower final gravity and are more highly carbonated. That combined with the hop-accentuating sulfate water character makes pils less sweet and more aggressive.

Donar's Hammer Pils

Only slightly simpler than the helles recipe, compare this to the Boho the Hobo Pils recipe back in Chapter 5 (page 56). The key difference is that small addition of gypsum. It helps push the hops and drives the beer to an apparently dry finish.

Style: German Pilsner
Brew Type: All Grain
For 5.5 gallons at 1.047, 2.9 SRM, 36.0 IBUs, 4.7 percent ABV
60-minute boil

Directions

Follow the Single-Infusion Brew Process (page 284).

Malt/Grain/Sugar
9.00 pounds Pilsner Malt

Extract (for 9.0 pounds of Pilsner Malt)
7.00 pounds Lager Liquid Malt Extract (LME)

Hops
0.50 ounce Magnum (14.0 percent AA) Pellet for 60 minutes
0.50 ounce Splater Select (5.0 percent AA) Pellet for 15 minutes
0.50 ounce Splater Select (5.0 percent AA) Pellet for 5 minutes

Other Ingredients
1 tablet Whirlfloc
1 tablespoon Yeast Nutrient
1 teaspoon Gypsum

Yeast
Wyeast 2206 Bavarian Lager / WLP 830 German Lager

Mash Schedule
Saccharification Rest 150°F 60 minutes

Walker Helles

On the bigger side of the helles spectrum, this brew hits all the mash marks in an attempt to be faithful to the older style of long mash regimens. The end result is a beer that ends up being crisp even without a lot of hop or carbonation bite.

Style: Munich Helles
Brew Type: All Grain
For 5.5 gallons at 1.057, 3.3 SRM, 22.0 IBUs, 5.7 percent ABV
60-minute boil

Directions

Follow the Multistep Brew Process (pages 284-285).

TIP

Munich's carbonate-rich water marks the primary difference between a helles and a Bohemian pilsner. The water pushes the malt character forward over the hops to make the beer feel sweeter.

Malt/Grain/Sugar
10.50 pounds Pilsner Malt
0.50 pound Cara-Pils Dextrine Malt

Extract (for 9.50 pounds of Pilsner Malt)
8.0 pounds Pilsner Liquid Malt Extract (LME)

Hops
1.12 ounces Hallertauer Mittelfruh (4.2 percent AA) Pellet for 60 minutes
0.50 ounce Hallertauer Mittelfruh (4.2 percent AA) Pellet for 5 minutes

Other Ingredients
1 tablet Whirlfloc
1 tablespoon Yeast Nutrient

Yeast
Wyeast 2206 Bavarian Lager

Mash Schedule
Acid Rest 92°F 15 minutes
Protein Rest 122°F 20 minutes
Intermediate Rest 142°F 40 minutes
Saccharification Rest 152°F 20 minutes
Mashout 164°F

Amber and Dark Lagers

Some darker lagers survived the onslaught of pilsner and helles and continue to tempt drinkers. Munich's carbonate water encouraged the development of the märzen and dunkel lagers. Elsewhere brewers ran with the Bavarian ideas and developed their own twists like the pitch black-schwarzbier.

Märzen Madness

Get ready for the "oom-pah-pah" with this Oktoberfest beer. Accurately capture the spirit of the beer by brewing the batch in March and lager until late September. Gather your friends and give a shout of "O'zapft is!" ("It's tapped"), grab a bratwurst, and have a party.

Style: Märzen/Oktoberfest
Brew Type: All Grain
For 5.5 gallons at 1.058, 9.8 SRM, 23.5 IBUs, 5.7 percent ABV
75-minute boil

Directions

1. Follow the Multistep Brew Process (pages 284-285).

2. Separately collect the first gallon of your runnings and boil vigorously to reduce to a half gallon. Add this caramelized wort back to the rest of the runnings.

3. Ferment at 50°F for two weeks. Raise the temperature to 60°F for 36 hours before returning to 50°F. Rack to secondary and slowly reduce the temperature to 35°F and hold there for a minimum of 4 weeks.

Malt/Grain/Sugar
6.25 pounds Pilsner Malt
3.5 pounds Munich Malt (Light)
1.00 pound Vienna Malt
1.00 pound Crystal 40L

Extract (for 5.75 pounds of Pilsner Malt and 2.75 pounds of Munich Malt)
4.50 pounds Lager Liquid Malt Extract (LME)
1.75 pounds Munich Liquid Malt Extract (LME)

Hops
0.75 ounce Tettnannger Tettnang (4.9 percent AA) Pellet for First Wort Hopping
0.40 ounce Hallertauer (4.4 percent AA) Pellet for 40 minutes
0.40 ounce Hallertauer (4.4 percent AA) Pellet for 20 minutes

Other Ingredients
1 tablet Whirlfloc
1 tablespoon Yeast Nutrient

Yeast
Wyeast 2308 Munich Lager

Mash Schedule
Protein Rest 120°F 30 minutes
Saccharification Rest 153°F 45 minutes

TIP

The Munich lager strain is a notorious diacetyl producer. Scrub the butter with a diacetyl rest, the brief fermentation rest at 60°F. The yeast transforms diacetyl into the flavorless chemical, butanediol.

Märzen is German for March, the last month of brewing before the legally mandated summer hiatus. Developed in the 1840s, the original versions were strong and copper brown. Aged for the summer in the lagering caves, this was the original beer of Oktoberfest.

The Munich dunkel took advantage of the water, piling on darker malts to make a deeply brown beer with toffee, caramel, and nutty flavors. As the style travelled around Germany, it took on different hues. Out of this was born the schwarzbier. The modern schwarzbier is as dark as a porter, but without the acrid roast character. The beer finishes dry after a faint caramel toffee flavor. This is the application for Carafa dehusked malt. It gives color and soft roasted-coffee tones with toffee flavor.

Blackwater Schwarz

As black as any robust porter, Blackwater has a surprisingly light body and clean finish. This smooth beer proves that dark doesn't mean strong, bitter, or acrid.

Style: Schwarzbier
Brew Type: All Grain
For 5.5 gallons at 1.052, 31.6 SRM, 22.6 IBUs, 4.9 percent ABV
90-minute boil

Directions

Follow the Multistep Brew Process (pages 284–285).

TIP

Vienna malt has a different flavor than its cousin Munich malt. Munich is a rich, dark bread in comparison to the toasted cracker flavor of Vienna. Use Vienna when you want a beer that's snappy, but still malty.

Malt/Grain/Sugar
9.00 pounds Vienna Malt
1.00 pound Munich Malt (Dark)
0.50 pound Crystal 60L
0.75 pound Carafa II Dehusked Chocolate Malt

Extract (for 8.00 pounds of Vienna Malt)
5.50 pounds Munich Liquid Malt Extract (LME)

Hops
0.50 ounce Hallertauer Mittelfruh (4.5 percent AA) Pellet for First Wort Hopping
0.50 ounce Tettnanger (4.5 percent AA) Pellet for 60 minutes
0.50 ounce Hallertauer Mittelfruh (4.5 percent AA) Pellet for 20 minutes

Other Ingredients
1 tablet Whirlfloc
1 tablespoon Yeast Nutrient

Yeast
Wyeast 2206 Bavarian Lager / WLP830 German Lager

Mash Schedule
Intermediate Rest 120°F 20 minutes
Saccharification Rest 152°F 60 minutes

Bock

Bock beer may be the only style in the world with a mascot, the billy goat. Bock is German for goat. It is believed to be a corruption of Einbeck, reputed birthplace of the style.

The primary sensation of a bock beer is malt, not sweet caramel flavors, but the deeply satisfying dense, rich toasted flavor of Munich malt. Hops exist to cut the sweetness. The lager yeast and long cold storage ensures a minimum of fruity esters. The finish, while lightly sweet, is not cloying.

In response to the growing popularity of helles and pils beer, modern bock brewers began producing "maibock" or "helles bock," a golden, slightly hoppy, bock-style beer. Still malty and rich tasting, the extra dose of hops snaps the palate to attention.

FACT

The bock tank-cleaning myth may come from an old American brewers' effort to promote bock as a springtime special. Devotees of the style would buy cases of bock during its limited availability to last through the year.

Born out of the monasteries, doppelbocks served as nutrition during Lenten fasts. The beers retained more sugar and nutrients and served as liquid bread for the monks. Ranging from 7 to 10 percent ABV, these beers are intense versions of a bock, bready, rich, and with hints of chocolate, but without any overt roasted coffee notes.

The most fearsome member of the bock family is the eisbock. A brewer mistakenly left a cask of doppelbock outside during a freezing winter night. Dismayed, the brewery staff went to dump the beer, but discovered a core of concentrated rich beer. Thanks to water freezing, the beer lost water, but no ethanol. Whether or not the federal authorities consider freezing a form of distillation (that is, illegal concentration) is contested, but few eisbocks come to the United States.

Bock-Be-Gock

The "chicken bock" is named for the sound made when encountering something challenging. The beer appears to be intimidating, but it's actually a sweetheart.

Style: Traditional Bock
Brew Type: All Grain
For 5.5 gallons at 1.069, 16.7 SRM, 20.2 IBUs, 6.9 percent ABV
60-minute boil

Directions

Follow the Single-Infusion Brew Process (page 284).

TIP

Melanoidin malt tastes like turbocharged Munich malt. It gives brilliant red highlights in addition to contributing dense malt chew.

Malt/Grain/Sugar
6.00 pounds Munich Malt
5.50 pounds Pilsner Malt
1.00 pound Crystal 90L
1.00 pound Munich Malt (dark)
0.25 pound Melanoidin Malt

Extract (for 5.5 pounds of Munich Malt and 5.0 pounds of Pilsner Malt)
4.00 pounds Munich Liquid Malt Extract (LME)
4.00 pounds Lager Liquid Malt Extract (LME)

Hops
0.6 ounce Perle (8.25 percent AA) Pellet for 60 minutes

Other Ingredients
1 tablet Whirlfloc
1 tablespoon Yeast Nutrient

Yeast
WLP833 German Bock

Mash Schedule
Saccharification Rest 150°F 60 minutes

Drogo Doppel Maibock

The Germans may not have a doppel-helles bock, but you can. Named for Saint Drogo, a holy hermit who survived on barley, water, and the Eucharist for forty years.

Style: Maibock/Helles Bock
Brew Type: All Grain
For 5.5 gallons at 1.091, 5.6 SRM, 36.8
    IBUs, 9.1 percent ABV
60-minute boil

Directions

Follow the Single-Infusion Brew Process (page 284).

TIP

Originally sourced from Ayinger brewery, the German bock yeast was traded around the community. What was originally a seasonal yeast got voracious support and became available year round.

Malt/Grain/Sugar
16.00 pounds Pilsner Malt
1.00 pound Munich Malt
0.50 pound Cara-Pils Dextrine Malt
0.12 pound Aromatic Malt

Extract (for 15.00 pounds of Pilsner Malt)
11.50 pounds Lager Liquid Malt Extract (LME)

Hops
1.50 ounces Hallertauer Tradition (6.2 percent AA) Pellet for 60 minutes
0.60 ounce Hallertau Hersbrucker (3.7 percent AA) Pellet for 15 minutes

Other Ingredients
1 tablet Whirlfloc
1 tablespoon Yeast Nutrient

Yeast
WLP833 German Bock

Mash Schedule
Saccharification Rest 152°F 60 minutes

Falkenator Doppelbock/Eisbock

Big, smooth, and dangerous, this is the perfect doppelbock. Follow the "eis'ing" instructions to produce an even stronger and mellower version, Falkenator Eisbock.

Style: Doppelbock/Eisbock
Brew Type: All Grain
For 5.5 gallons at 1.099, 20.5 SRM, 47.5 IBUs, 9.9 percent ABV
150-minute boil

Directions

1. Follow the Multistep Brew Process (pages 284-285).

2. To "eis" the beer, ferment and lager to completion. Rack to a keg and set the keg in a freezer at or below 32°F. After twenty-four hours you should hear slush when you shake the keg. Push the unfrozen beer out of the keg via CO_2 and carbonate to enjoy your new eisbock.

TIP

You can always spot a doppelbock by the name. Starting with the first, Paulaner's Salvator, breweries end a doppelbock's name with "ator." Examples include Optimator, Celebrator and Maximator.

Malt/Grain/Sugar
6.00 pounds Pilsner Malt
1.0 pound Munich 90 Malt
1.0 pound Munich 100 Malt
0.6 pound Honey Malt
0.4 pound Crystal 120L
0.4 pound Crystal 65L
0.3 pound Melanoidin Malt
0.2 pound Carafa II
0.1 pound Acidualted Malt
0.75 pound Pale DME

Extract (for 15.00 pounds of Pilsner Malt)
11.50 pounds Lager Liquid Malt Extract (LME)

Hops
0.75 ounce Magnum (14.8 percent AA) Pellet for 90 minutes
0.50 ounce Tettnager Tettnang (4.9 percent AA) Pellet for 15 minutes

Other Ingredients
1 tablet Whirlfloc
1 tablespoon Yeast Nutrient

Yeast
Wyeast 2206 Bavarian Lager
WLP833 German Bock

Mash Schedule
Protein Rest 122°F 30 minutes
Saccharification Rest 150°F 60 minutes

Strong Lagers

As if the bocks weren't enough, the Germans and their neighbors brew several strong lagers. Among them are brews like the sweet orangey East German EKU 28 or the traditional Swiss (now Austrian) Christmas lager, Samichlaus.

Brewing strong lagers requires even more of a brewer than brewing strong ales. Lager beers already require more yeast cells to start fermentation, 350 billion per 5 gallons of 1.050 OG lager to ale's 175 billion. Bump the gravity up to 1.090 and lagers need 610 billion cells compared to 305 billion. Practically you need a starter batch's yeast cake to successfully ferment the strong lagers.

Black Sea Baltic Porter

This one is a ringer since the recipe was developed by a professional. Regardless, of the pedigree, it is a fantastic, complex Baltic Porter. Looking at the malt bill, it's easy to see why!

Style: Baltic Porter
Brew Type: All Grain
For 5.5 gallons at 1.091, 35.6 SRM, 61.9 IBUs, 9.1 percent ABV
90-minute boil

Directions

Follow the Single-Infusion Brew Process (page 284).

TIP

Proof that not all big beers need long aging times to be winners, this beer won the best of show at a competition six weeks after it was brewed.

Malt/Grain/Sugar
13.00 pounds Pilsner Malt
1.50 pounds Munich Malt (light)
1.50 pounds Munich Malt (dark)
0.50 pound CaraMunich Malt
0.40 pound Chocolate Malt
0.25 pound Crystal 10L
0.25 pound Weyermann Carared
0.10 pound Special B Malt
0.10 pound Weyermann Carafa II
0.50 pound Black Patent Malt
1.00 pound Honey Malt

Extract (for 12.00 pounds of Pilsner Malt)
8.50 pounds Lager Liquid Malt Extract (LME)

Hops
1.50 ounces Czech Bor (6.8 percent AA) Pellet for 90 minutes
0.20 ounce Northern Brewer (7.7 percent AA) Pellet for 60 minutes
0.75 ounce Mount Hood (6.50 percent AA) Pellet for 0 minutes

Other Ingredients
1 tablet Whirlfloc
1 tablespoon Yeast Nutrient
9 mL Lactic Acid

Yeast
Wyeast 2042 Danish Lager/WLP830 German Lager/WLP810 California Lager

Mash Schedule
Saccharification Rest 152°F 60 minutes

The Baltic Porter was a direct market response to Russian Imperial Stout. Despite imperial stout's retreat into the history books, breweries across the Baltics still brew the lager porters that capitalized on the court's favorite beer.

FACT

The world's strongest beer used to be Samichlaus, demonstrating how hardy lager yeasts are. Even still, 14 percent is an incredible benchmark.

Falconsclaws

Inspired by Samichlaus. When Hurlimann, the original Swiss brewery, discontinued the beer, members of the Maltose Falcons took it upon themselves to continue the line.

Style: Doppelbock
Brew Type: All Grain
For 5.5 gallons at 1.148, 31.3 SRM, 28.5 IBUs, 14.1 percent ABV
90-minute boil

Directions

1. Follow the Single-Infusion Brew Process (page 284).

2. Collect only the first 6.5 gallons of runnings. If desired, continue sparging and collect the second runnings for a second batch of beer.

TIP

Samichlaus is brewed yearly on Swiss Christmas (December 6) and aged for a whole year.

Malt/Grain/Sugar
31.50 pounds Pilsner Malt
1.75 pounds Crystal 60L
1.75 pounds Munich Malt
1.00 pounds Vienna Malt
0.50 pound Melanoidin Malt
1.00 pound Belgian Dark Candi Sugar

Extract (for 30.50 pounds of Pilsner Malt)
17.5 pounds Lager Liquid Malt Extract (LME)

Hops
1.90 ounces Syrian Goldings (4.0 percent AA) Pellet for 60 minutes
1.70 ounces Hallertauer Mittelfruh (3.8 percent AA) Pellet for 15 minutes
0.50 ounce Hallertau Hersbrucker (2.3 percent AA) Whole for 2 minutes

Other Ingredients
1 tablet Whirlfloc
1 tablespoon Yeast Nutrient

Yeast
WLP885 Zurich Lager

Mash Schedule
Saccharification Rest 154°F 60 minutes

Rauchbier: Is It Smoky in Here?

The tiny Franconian town of Bamberg retains more than its architecture. The city of 70,000 still has nine breweries that produce distinctive and sometimes challenging rauchbiers.

Historically, most beers have been lightly smoky from the fires used to dry malt. In Bamberg, they never abandoned the tradition of malt flavored by beechwood fires. The two breweries most devoted to the cause, Schlenkerla and Spezial, maintain their own malting operations to generate smoked malt to their specifications.

The most traditional rauchbier offering is a spin off the Munich märzen, although many styles are produced including weizen, helles, and very complex smoked bock beers. The level of smoking can be subtle whiffs to Schlenkerla's smoked ham in a glass flavor.

If you plan on brewing a rauchbier, choose Weyermann's Rauchmalz, a beechwood-smoked malt. Depending on the malt and your tolerance for smoke, you can use it for the whole brew. Keep the hops light to avoid clashing odors.

Bamberg Burner Rauchbier

This will be a wonderfully smoky brew, but not as intense as the hammy Schlenkerla beers of Bamberg.

Style: Rauchbier
Brew Type: All Grain
For 5.0 gallons at 1.054, 19.1 SRM, 44.0 IBUs, 5.3 percent ABV
90-minute boil

Directions

1. Follow the Single-Infusion Brew Process (page 284).

2. Raise the mash to mash out by adding 5 gallons of 190°F water to the mash. Do not sparge to collect your runnings!

Malt/Grain/Sugar
7.50 pounds Munich Malt
6.50 pounds Weyermann Beechwood Smoked Malt
0.25 pound Chocolate Malt

Hops
2.0 ounces Hallertauer (4.5 percent AA) Pellet for 90 minutes
0.25 ounce Tettnanger Tettnang (4.9 percent AA) Pellet for 2 minutes

Other Ingredients
1 tablet Whirlfloc
1 tablespoon Yeast Nutrient

Yeast
WLP920 Old Bavarian Lager Yeast

Mash Schedule
Saccharification Rest 154°F 60 minutes
Mash out 168°F 10 minutes

CHAPTER 18

Recipes from Belgium

Belgium is to beer as America is to barbeque. Everywhere you turn there's another local beer. A country as passionate as Belgium has more styles of beer than any one book could tackle, but here's an overview to get your exploration of beer paradise kicked off.

The Brew-Crazy Country of Belgium

For such a tiny country, Belgium has served as a central crossroads and linchpin for much of European history. From Julius Caesar to Hilter's blitz-krieg, the Belgians have seen army after army march through.

Belgium is divided into two main regions, Flanders in the west and Wallonia in the east. The Flemish and French language barrier marks the beginning of a great cultural divide that covers all spheres, even beer.

The constant invasions and the eternal bickering shaped a people bemused by the world. While they are the capital of the European Union and a diplomatic hub for the world, the Belgians never cease to enjoy their beer and food.

Beer became the central focus of the drinking culture after a hard spirits ban was passed in the wake of World War I. Seizing the chance, brewers met the society's demand for a replacement to Genever. Belgians quickly were awash in a sea of strong ales ranging from 6.5 to 12 percent ABV. The lack of purity laws encouraged experimentation and the incorporation of odd ingredients. Now Belgium is home to the strangest beers.

Although the rise in pilsner and wine has dampened the resolve for a pintje, over 1,200 beers from 150 breweries are available. All this choice packed into a country of 10 million inhabitants.

In Belgium, every brewery and many individual beers has a special glass. Great cafes serve you the proper glass. If no glass is available, they may refuse to serve the beer or present it in a similar glass, but with the logo hidden.

What the Belgians Think of Styles

Peter Brouckaert, Belgian native, former head brewer of Rodenbach and current head brewer of Colorado's New Belgium Brewing disclaims that in Belgium there are no styles. While there are clear style patterns that emerge, Belgian brewers concern themselves with making Blonde, Ambree, or Bruin beers. The flavors, the aromas, and the overall character are more a matter of preference than any desire to brew "dubbel" ale.

This freedom of brewing and labeling makes Belgian beer fascinating and frustrating to explore. The styles discussed by homebrewers are largely concocted by outsiders. They serve as a handy reference and a means to guide your thinking. The Belgians may not rigorously observe styles, but they still exist. Just don't tell them that!

Keys to Successful Belgian-Inspired Brewing

The Belgians obsess primarily over one factor, a beer's "digestibility." How capable you are of drinking another round. If the beer is too sweet and cloying, a common American defect, the beer fares poorly.

To achieve digestibility, substitute a step mash process for the usual single-infusion mashes. Mash low to encourage simple sugar formation and liberally add sugar to boost gravity and undercut remaining malt body.

Belgian brewers only recently began playing wildly with hops. Thanks to the low finishing gravities, bittering hops pop. Keep a light hand with the hops to avoid an overly bitter dry finish. Provide just enough to cut the sweetness of the beer.

Given their typical strength, Belgian beers demand quantities of healthy viable yeast. A large, decanted starter should be your basic tool. Add oxygen and keep your fermentation temperatures under control. Warm ferments lead to unpleasant-smelling beer. Vigorous Belgian strain fermentations consume 80 percent or more of the initial gravity.

Until you play with Brettanomyces or other cultures, Belgian yeasts are like other beer yeasts. Don't worry about Belgian yeast "funk" infecting your other brews.

Lighter Belgian Ales

Not every beer in Belgium is a glorified sobriety-killing monster. The Belgian laws on drunk driving are strict. Every region has their moderate-strength blonde and ambree ales for those longer times at the café. But even these lighter ales are stronger than the British "session" ales or American industrial pilsners.

Artemis Callipygia Witbier

The little town of Hoegaarden (pronounced WHO-garten) claims to be the home of white "wit" bier. In 1965, dairyman-turned-brewer Pierre Celis opened a new brewery to resurrect his town's famous style. Hoegaarden beer has gone on to inspire countless imitators including Coors's Blue Moon series.

Style: Belgian Witbier
Brew Type: All Grain
For 5.0 gallons at 1.046, 3 SRM, 12.9 IBUs, 4.6 percent ABV
60-minute boil

Directions

Follow the Multistep Brew Process (pages 284-285).

TIP

Play with your wit! Add fruit and spices, change up the yeast, and so on. Start light unless you like throwing out overspiced beer.

Malt/Grain/Sugar
4.00 pounds Belgian Pilsner Malt
4.00 pounds Torrified Wheat Berries
0.75 pound Flaked Oats

Extract (for 2.5 pounds of Pilsner Malt and 4 pounds of Wheat)—Late Extract Method
4.00 pounds Wheat Dry Malt Extract (DME)

Hops
0.25 ounce Styrian Goldings (5.25 percent AA) Pellet for 60 minutes
0.25 ounce Czech Saaz (3.5 percent AA) Pellet for 60 minutes
0.25 ounce Styrian Goldings (5.25 percent AA) Pellet for 20 minutes

Other Ingredients
0.25 ounce Bitter Orange Peel (add at 0 minutes)
0.25 ounce Crushed Coriander (add at 0 minutes)

Yeast
WLP400 Belgian Wit Ale

Mash Schedule
Mash In 120F 15 minutes
Saccharification Rest 150°F 60 minutes
Mash Out 168°F 10 minutes

Deknockoff Pale Ale

Belgian pale ales are a staple of the northern segments of the country. In Antwerp, if you're not drinking a pils, you're drinking the local brew, De Konick, a biscuity pale ale with just a hint of fruitiness and spice.

Style: Belgian Pale Ale
Brew Type: All Grain
For 5.5 gallons at 1.051, 13 SRM, 26 IBUs, 4.9 percent ABV
75-minute boil

Directions

Follow the Multistep Brew Process (pages 284-285).

TIP

Both the Wyeast Schelde yeast and White Labs Antwerp yeast are special release strains only available intermittently. If your local doesn't have them, ask if they can special order them or wait for the next release. They really are worth it.

Malt/Grain/Sugar
4.00 pounds Belgian Pale Ale Malt
4.00 pounds Belgian Pilsner Malt
1.25 pounds Vienna Malt
0.50 pound Munich Malt
0.50 pound Special B Malt

Extract (for 7 pounds of Pale Ale and Pilsner Malt)
5.25 pounds Pale Liquid Malt Extract (LME) (Maris Otter Preferable)

Hops
1.15 ounces Czech Saaz (3.4 percent AA) Pellet for 60 minutes
1.15 ounces Czech Saaz (3.4 percent AA) Pellet for 30 minutes
1.00 ounce Czech Saaz (3.4 percent AA) Pellet for 5 minutes

Other Ingredients
1 tablet Whirlfloc

Yeast
Wyeast 3655 Schelde/Wyeast 1214 Belgian Ale/WLP515 Antwerp Ale Yeast/WLP550 Belgian Ale Yeast

Mash Schedule
Intermediate Rest 129°F 20 minutes
Saccharification Rest 150°F 40 minutes

Trappist Ales: Beer of the Monks

In addition to their service to God, the monastic societies of Europe provided bread, cheese, and beer. The best-known continuing monastic brewing tradition is Belgium's collection of Trappist ales. In addition to their secular counterparts, Abbey ales, the Trappist styles are widely sought after and imitated.

The Trappists are an offshoot of the Cistercian Order concerned with simplifying the monastic life. The duties of a Trappist monastery include providing for it, the community, and the Church via manual labor. In America, that means recycling printer cartridges and building coffins. In Belgium and the Netherlands that means bread, cheese, and beer.

The Trappist Breweries

Secular breweries, interested in the handsome prices Trappist beers fetched, licensed the monastery names to pass their Abbey ales off. This was good money for monasteries fighting a dwindling population of monks and crumbling buildings.

To prevent confusion, several monasteries created the International Trappist Association (ITA) to control the use of the special "Authentic Trappist Product Logo." Currently there are only seven breweries in the world as recognized by the ITA. They are Achel, Chimay, Koningshoeven (La Trappe), Orval, Rochefort, Westmalle, and Westvleteren.

Many Trappist and Abbey ales include a number in their names, for example, Westvleteren 12. The numbers indicate the beer's original gravity in the old "Degrees Belgian." To convert to gravity, take the number and divide by 100 and add 1. Our Westvleteren 12 example indicates an 1.120 original gravity. In actuality, Westvleteren 12 starts at 1.081 and finishes at a 1.013, much lower than in the past.

The Beer Styles

Although each abbey offers its own unique lineup of beers, there are a few terms you should know:

- **Enkel**—A "single," it was the lowest-alcohol beer produced.
- **Dubbel**—A strong brown beer with light chocolate and raisin flavors and an alcohol content between 6.5 and 9 percent.
- **Tripel**—A strong golden beer. Strong, crisp, and light with tropical fruit flavors and spicy aromas. They range from 8 percent to a killer 11 percent ABV.
- **Quadrupel (Quad)**—The biggest, maltiest, chewy, ruby-brown beer produced by an abbey. Rich and fruity with a clean if lightly sweet finish. Their punch ranges from 9 to 12 percent ABV.
- **Abt (Abbot)**—Simply a designation for the Abbots beer. This is the strongest beer from the brewery.

Double Bubble Dubbel

Big raisins and chewy caramels abound in this simple dubbel ale. Consider using this as a base for wacky additions.

Style: Belgian Dubbel Ale
Brew Type: All Grain
For 5.5 gallons at 1.071, 19 SRM, 25.5 IBUs, 7.3 percent ABV
90-minute boil

Directions

Follow the Single-Infusion Brew Process (page 284).

Malt/Grain/Sugar
11.50 pounds Belgian Pilsner Malt
1.00 pound Special B Malt
0.50 pound Aromatic Malt
2.00 ounces Carafa II Special Dehusked Chocolate Malt
1.00 pound Dark Sugar (Candi or Turbinado)

Extract (for 10.5 pounds of Pilsner Malt)
8.00 pounds Pilsner Liquid Malt Extract (LME)

Hops
1.75 ounces Styrian Goldings (4.0 percent AA) Pellet for 45 minutes

Other Ingredients
1 tablet Whirfloc (added at 20 minutes)

Yeast
Wyeast 3787 Trappist High Gravity / WLP500 Trappist Ale

Mash Schedule
Saccharification Rest 151°F 90 minutes
Mash Out 168°F 10 minutes

Devil's Holy Water

First brewed by the monks at Westmalle Abbey in the 1930s, the golden tripel took people by surprise. The secret of the style lies in the sparing use of any specialty malts. A well-made example will retain a touch of sweetness balanced by the spicy profile of the yeast and brisk carbonation.

Style: Belgian Tripel
Brew Type: All Grain
For 5.5 gallons at 1.084, 5.1 SRM, 29 IBUs, 9.3 percent ABV
60-minute boil

Directions

Follow the Single-Infusion Brew Process (page 284).

TIP

The differences between tripels and Belgian strong golden ales are subtle, but you should notice that tripels feel softer while most golden ales have a harder edge and hotter burn.

Malt/Grain/Sugar
12.00 pounds Belgian Pilsner Malt
0.50 pound Aromatic Malt
0.50 pound Caramel Pils (C8) Malt
2.00 pounds Sugar

Extract (for 12.0 pounds of Pilsner Malt)
9.50 pounds Pilsner Liquid Malt Extract (LME)

Hops
0.75 ounce Perle (8.25 percent AA) Pellet for 60 minutes
1.50 ounces Styrian Goldings (5.25 percent AA) Pellet for 5 minutes

Other Ingredients

Yeast
1 tablespoon Yeast Nutrient
Wyeast 3787 Trappist High Gravity/WLP530 Abbey Ale Yeast

Mash Schedule
Saccharification Rest 150°F 60 minutes

Belgium Four Ways

Push a dubbel to the firewall to make quad. Prune, plums, raisins, chocolate, and cinnamon with none of the roasted flavors that you usually find in darker beers. Despite the load of sugar, this beer should be rich.

Style: Belgian Quadrupel
Brew Type: All Grain
For 5.5 gallons at 1.097, 24 SRM, 36 IBUs, 10.6 percent ABV
90-minute boil

Directions

Follow the Single-Infusion Brew Process (page 284).

TIP

If there was ever a beer to throw a mix of yeast at, this is the one. Take everything you can find and add it to the mix.

Malt/Grain/Sugar
12.00 pounds Belgian Pilsner Malt
4.50 pounds Munich Malt
1.00 pound Special B
0.25 pound Carafa II Special Dehusked Chocolate Malt
1.00 pound Sugar

Hops
0.75 ounce Perle (8.25 percent AA) Pellet for 60 minutes
1.00 ounce Tettnanger (4.5 percent AA) Pellet for 30 minutes
1.00 ounce Styrian Goldings (5.25 percent AA) Pellet for 15 minutes
1.00 ounce Czech Saaz (3.5 percent AA) Pellet for 0 minutes

Other Ingredients

Yeast
1 tablespoon Yeast Nutrient
Wyeast 3787 Trappist High Gravity/WLP530 Abbey Ale Yeast

Mash Schedule
Saccharification Rest 150°F 60 minutes

Belgian Strong Ales

Where the Trappists' dubbels, tripels, and quads typically have rich bodies and finish sweet, the strong dark and golden ales are lighter and crisper with high carbonation.

To achieve the desired Belgian digestibility, strong ales avoid body boosters. Keeping the gravity up and body down is the job of a sugar addition. Different sugars have different effects on your final beer. You don't have to be beholden to the $5 small bag of rock candi sugar. Read more about sugar in Chapter 7.

Treat the yeast with care. Bad examples are headache machines with loads of fusel alcohols from poor fermentation management. Use healthy viable yeast from a large starter or a yeast cake from primary. Start fermenting cool, in the low sixties, and then allow it to rise to the upper sixties or low seventies.

Transumptum Acerbus Dark Strong Ale

Named for the Catholic test of a candidate for sainthood, this beer was formulated to test the newly available Belgian Dark Candi Syrup. The dark caramelized syrup is what's used by professionals to color their dark beers without large residual sweetness.

Style: Belgian Dark Strong Ale
Brew Type: All Grain
For 5.5 gallons at 1.088, 31.3 SRM, 41 IBUs, 9.7 percent ABV
60-minute boil

Directions

Follow the Single-Infusion Brew Process (page 284).

Malt/Grain/Sugar
14.00 pounds Belgian Pale Malt
1.00 pound Special B Malt
0.25 pound Carafa II Special Dehusked Chocolate Malt
1.50 pounds Belgian Dark Candi Sytup (1 bottle)

Extract (for 12.00 pounds of Pale Malt)
9.00 pounds Pilsner Liquid Malt Extract (LME)

Hops
0.75 ounce Magnum (14.00 percent AA) Pellet for 60 minutes
0.50 ounce Czech Saaz (3.5 percent AA) Pellet for 20 minutes

Other Ingredients
1 tablet Whirfloc (added at 20 minutes)

Yeast
Wyeast 1388 Belgian Strong Ale

Mash Schedule
Saccharification Rest 151°F 60 minutes

Steve French

Steve French proves that a great beer doesn't need a lot of complicated ingredients. If you're brewing extract, follow the Late-Extract Variant (pages 283–284) to ensure a golden color.

Style: Belgian Golden Strong Ale
Brew Type: All Grain
For 5.5 gallons at 1.086, 3.8 SRM, 51 IBUs, 9.3 percent ABV
90-minute boil

Directions

Follow the Single-Infusion Brew Process (page 284).

TIP

Even though Warrior is an American hop, using a high–alpha acid hop for bittering is efficient with little flavor impact.

Malt/Grain/Sugar
12.00 pounds Belgian Pilsner Malt
3.00 pounds Cane Sugar

Extract (for 12.00 pounds of Pilsner Malt)
9.00 pounds Pilsner Liquid Malt Extract (LME)

Hops
0.25 ounce Warrior (5.25 percent AA) Pellet for 90 minutes
1.25 ounces Styrian Goldings (5.25 percent AA) Pellet for 90 minutes
0.75 ounce Tettnanger Tettnang (4.5 percent AA) Pellet for 30 minutes
1.00 ounce Hallertau Hersbrucker (4.75 percent AA) Whole for 0 minutes

Other Ingredients
1 tablet Whirfloc (added at 20 minutes)

Yeast
Wyeast 1388 Belgian Strong Ale

Mash Schedule
Mash In 148°F 30 minutes
Saccharification Rest 158°F 30 minutes
Mash Out 168°F 10 minutes

Belgian Specialty Ales

After enough drinking and exploring the Belgians really do mean to defy style categorization. All that can be done is focused research to find the ingredients that comprise your favorite beer. You will find beers with odd grains, imperial stouts with a Belgian flair, and more. With so much interest, a little Web reading can offer guidance. Many brewers are willing to respond to your questions, but some will only tell you part of the truth.

Haarlem Bokbier

Brewing beer can lead to all sorts of misadventures. This beer was the result of the brewer's desire to explore his family's Dutch roots. Combing through old brewing texts, he uncovered recipes for three different sixteenth-century oat-malt bokbiers from the family homestead.

Style: Belgian Specialty Ale
Brew Type: All Grain
For 5.5 gallons at 1.075, 6.0 SRM, 32 IBUs, 8.1 percent ABV
60-minute boil

Directions

Follow the Multistep Brew Process (pages 284–285).

TIP

Dutch Castle yeast is an intermittently available yeast, but it is the original yeast designed for the beer. Forbidden Fruit, a strong spicy fermenter, serves as an adequate substitute.

Malt/Grain/Sugar
7.50 pounds Oat Malt
4.00 pounds Belgian Pilsner Malt
1.50 pounds Munich Malt
1.50 pounds Rye Malt
1.50 pounds German Wheat Malt

Hops
0.75 ounce Perle (5.7 percent AA) Pellet for 60 minutes
0.50 ounce Hallertau Tradition (6.0 percent AA) Pellet for 40 minutes
0.75 ounce Spalter Select (4.8 percent AA) Pellet for 20 minutes
0.50 ounce Styrian Goldings (4.0 percent AA) Pellet for 5 minutes

Other Ingredients
1 tablet Whirfloc (added at 20 minutes)

Yeast
Wyeast 3822 Dutch Castle/Wyeast 3463 Forbidden Fruit/Wyeast 1388 Belgian Strong Ale

Mash Schedule
Acid Rest 104°F 20 minutes
Protein Rest 122°F 20 minutes
Saccharification Rest 154°F 30 minutes
Mash Out Rest 165°F 10 minutes

Scaliding Amber Quad

Brasserie Dubbison is known around the world for the terrifyingly strong Bush ambree. The 12 percent ABV is softened by a candy caramel sweetness that soothes the burn. Thanks to a fear that you might confuse Dubbison's Bush ambree for the light lager Busch beer, Bush is sold in the United States as Scaldis, the Latin name for the region's Schelde River.

Style: Belgian Specialty
Brew Type: All Grain
For 5.5 gallons at 1.121, 10.0 SRM, 26 IBUs, 13.3 percent ABV
60-minute boil

Directions

Follow the Single-Infusion Brew Process (page 284).

TIP

To provide an obscene quantity of yeast to ferment completely and cleanly, try brewing a batch of Deknockoff (page 220) and using the resulting yeast cake.

Malt/Grain/Sugar
13.25 pounds Belgian Pilsner Malt
6.75 pounds Belgian Pale Ale Malt
0.50 pound CaraMunich Malt
0.25 pound Aromatic Malt
2.00 pounds Sugar

Extract (for 18.00 pounds of Pilsner and Pale Malt)
13.50 pounds Pilsner Liquid Malt Extract (LME)

Hops
1.50 ounces Styrian Goldings (4.1 percent AA) Pellet for 60 minutes
1.00 ounce Styrian Goldings (4.1 percent AA) Pellet for 15 minutes
1.00 ounce Czech Saaz (3.5 percent AA) Pellet for 3 minutes

Other Ingredients
1 tablet Whirfloc (added at 20 minutes)

Yeast
1388 Belgian Strong Ale/WLP570 Belgian Golden Ale

Mash Schedule
Saccharification Rest 149°F 60 minutes

Last Post at Ieper Belgian British Ale

During the fierce trench fighting of World War I, the West Flanders town of Ieper was a key position. The town was held by the British Commonwealth and French against the Germans. To honor the sacrifice of the Commonwealth, the townsfolk built a memorial gate, and every night since 1928, they stop traffic and play the Last Post, *the British equivalent to the American* taps. *This beer honors that sacrifice and the enduring display of gratitude of the town of Ieper.*

Style: Belgian Specialty
Brew Type: All Grain
For 5.5 gallons at 1.089, 13.0 SRM, 49 IBUs, 9.5 percent ABV
60-minute boil

Directions

Follow the Single-Infusion Brew Process (page 284).

TIP

Few Belgian beers rely on a single strain of yeast to ferment the beer. Often the house culture is a mixture of various strains. You can increase the complexity of your brews by pitching multiple yeast cultures.

Malt/Grain/Sugar
14.50 pounds British Pale Ale Malt (Maris Otter)
0.75 pound CaraMunich Malt
0.75 pound Flaked Corn
0.25 pound Cara-Pils Dextrin Malt
0.25 pound Special B Malt
1.00 pound Sugar

Extract (for 12.00 pounds of Pale Malt)
9.00 pounds Pale Liquid Malt Extract (LME)

Hops
1.00 ounce Target (10.6 percent AA) Pellet for 60 minutes
1.00 ounce East Kent Goldings (5.5 percent AA) Pellet for 15 minutes
0.50 ounce Fuggle (5.1 percent AA) Pellet for 3 minutes
0.50 ounce Progress (8.0 percent AA) Pellet for 3 minutes

Other Ingredients
1 tablet Whirfloc (added at 20 minutes)

Yeast
Wyeast 1725 Thames Valley
WLP565 Belgian Saison I

Mash Schedule
Saccharification Rest 151°F 60 minutes

Saison and Farmhouse Ales

The mining and farming communities of Wallonia were home to a number of farmhouse brewing operations. During winter and spring months, the farm staff would turn the harvest into beer. The beer served as refreshment for the field laborers during the hot days working the fields. Today the leading producer, Brasserie Dupont, brews out of a working farmhouse and dairy in the village of Tourpes.

The hallmark of the style, the summer saison (*été* in French) is a dry, spicy, orangish beer with a hop-accented spiced nose. Dry, earthy flavors are propelled by forceful carbonation (3.5-plus volumes).

A new category of "super saisons" has arisen with higher alcohol levels pushing above the 6.5 percent norm of traditional saisons. Dupont brews their Avec Les Bon Voeux de le Brasserie at 9.5 percent with a brisk hoppy bite. A newer saison brewer in Soy, Brasserie Fantome, breaks even further with liberal use of local crops, chocolate, and dandelions.

If you cross the border to France you'll discover a similar farmhouse tradition called bière de garde. Like saisons, these light, grainy beers were brewed and stored for the summer months. This garde period led to the style name. Bière de Gardes tend to rounder malt flavors with low esters and little in the way of hops.

Working with saison yeasts requires contradicting proper fermentation practices for other beer yeasts. The Wyeast Saison and White Labs Saison I strains need to ferment hot in order to achieve the hallmark low terminal gravities. Start fermentation cool, around 65°F, and allow the natural heat generated by the fermentation to raise the temperature into the eighties or even the nineties. It takes a while to get used to, but it works for these strains. If you find your yeast quitting too early, be patient and give it some time. If it still doesn't drop further, pitch a second strain of yeast to finish the job.

JD Saison Été

Glowing orange, a large rocky head restraining the pepper and cinnamon aromas of the saison yeast. For a perfect summer time beer with a kick, make sure to ferment this beer to a low terminal gravity and amp up the carbonation.

Style: Belgian Saison
Brew Type: All Grain
For 5.5 gallons at 1.069, 5.3 SRM, 47 IBUs, 7.5 percent ABV
60-minute boil

Directions

Follow the Single-Infusion Brew Process (page 284).

Malt/Grain/Sugar
8.00 pounds Belgian Pilsner Malt
2.50 pounds German Wheat Malt
2.00 pounds Munich Malt
0.25 pound German Acidulated Malt (Sauer Malt)
1.00 pound Sugar

Extract (for 7.00 pounds of Pilsner Malt)
5.25 pounds Pilsner Liquid Malt Extract (LME)

Hops
0.75 ounce Magnum (14.0 percent AA) Pellet for 60 minutes
2.00 ounces Czech Saaz (3.5 percent AA) Pellet for 5 minutes

Other Ingredients
1 tablet Whirfloc (added at 20 minutes)
0.25 teaspoon Coriander Seed (added at 0 minutes)
0.25 teaspoon Black Pepper (added at 0 minutes)

Yeast
WLP565 Belgian Saison I/Wyeast 3724 Belgian Sasion

Mash Schedule
Saccharification Rest 150°F 60 minutes

Saint Nick's Sleigh Warmer

Even an old hand like jolly old Saint Nick needs help beating back winter's cold. A big, deep, chocolate beer infused with vanilla and cinnamon and a blast of 14-plus percent ABV should do the trick!

Style: Belgian Saison
Brew Type: All Grain
For 5.5 gallons at 1.123, 30.7 SRM, 50 IBUs, 14.3 percent ABV
120-minute boil

Directions

Follow the Single-Infusion Brew Process (page 284).

TIP

Brewing a 14 percent monster requires a lot of extra care. Bring a ton of yeast to the party and be prepared to have patience. This beer might take up to eight months to be ready to drink. The next recipe was originally developed solely to generate enough yeast to tackle the beast.

Malt/Grain/Sugar
19.50 pounds Belgian Pilsner Malt
1.25 pounds Crystal 120L
1.25 pounds Munich Malt
0.75 pound Vienna Malt
0.75 pound German Wheat Malt
0.33 pound Carafa II Special Dehusked Chocolate Malt
1.50 pounds Belgian Dark Candi D2 Syrup

Extract (for 18.50 pounds of Pilsner Malt)
13.5 pounds Pilsner Liquid Malt Extract (LME)

Hops
1.00 ounce Magnum (14.0 percent AA) Pellet for 60 minutes
1.00 ounce Czech Saaz (3.5 percent AA) Pellet for 20 minutes

Other Ingredients
1 tablet Whirfloc (added at 20 minutes)
1 stick Whole Cinnamon (added at 0 minutes)
1 Vanilla Bean, split (added at 0 minutes)

Yeast
WLP565 Belgian Saison I / Wyeast 3724 Belgian Sasion

Mash Schedule
Saccharification Rest 148°F 60 minutes

Springtime in Amarillo

A light, wheaty saison, the grapefruit punch of the Amarillo combines with spicy yeast and sweet wheat to make a fantastic beer. With proper technique and luck this brew can hit the glass in two weeks.

Style: Belgian Saison/IPA
Brew Type: All Grain
For 5.5 gallons at 1.062, 5.0 SRM, 51
    IBUs, 6.6 percent ABV
120-minute boil

Directions

Follow the Single-Infusion Brew Process (page 284).

TIP

Inspired by the variety of Belgian beers, American craft brewers have put their own spin on the beers. And now, the Belgians increasingly brew with American hops and American ideas. Coming in now are a series of Belgian IPAs.

Malt/Grain/Sugar
7.00 pounds Belgian Pilsner Malt
4.00 pounds German Wheat Malt
0.50 pound Aromatic Malt
0.50 pound Sugar

Extract (for 5.0 pounds of Pilsner Malt and 4 pounds of Wheat)—Late Extract Method
7.00 pounds Wheat Dry Malt Extract (DME)

Hops
1.25 ounces Amarillo (8.4 percent AA) Pellet for 60 minutes
0.50 ounce Amarillo (8.4 percent AA) Pellet for 20 minutes
1.00 ounce Amarillo (8.4 percent AA) Pellet for 0 minutes

Other Ingredients
1 tablet Whirfloc (added at 20 minutes)

Yeast
WLP565 Belgian Saison I/Wyeast 3724 Belgian Sasion

Mash Schedule
Saccharification Rest 150°F 60 minutes

Sour Patch Beers

While the Wallonians enjoy their farmhouse ales, the Flemish maintain the old traditions of sour ales. Until, in the wake of Louis Pasteur, brewers started culturing yeast and practicing good sanitation, all beer eventually soured. The old English designations of stale ale and mild ale hinged on when the beer would sour. While the rest of the world has turned away, a couple of soured beer styles still exist in Flanders.

Lambic

Named for the little village of Lembeek, lambic was the working-class sour drink of Flanders for more than 500 years. This oldest continuing style of beer builds on a barley and wheat "turbid" mash with a long, slow boil with aged hops. The resulting wort is pumped into open shallow pans in the attic to cool overnight exposed to bacteria and yeast-laden air. From there the beer is added to "clean" wooden barrels and allowed to ferment for one to three years. A cast of microflora invade the beer, giving lambic its complexity and acidity.

After the long sequestering, a lambic blender mixes batches of older and younger lambic to produce the intense yet smooth gueuze. To make lambic or gueuze more approachable, brewers add fruit. The fruit lambics appear under a variety of names including kriek (sour cherry), framboise (raspberry), and cassis (black currant). Less traditional producers have made sweet versions of lambic-like beers with apples, bananas, peaches, and more.

To explore the world of lambics, start with one of the least traditional and most widely available sweeter lambics from Lindeman's.

The moderate lambics producers, following traditional processes with an eye toward the modern drinker, include Boon, Drie Fonteinen, and Oud Beersel. Finally, when you're ready to tackle the hardest lambics, search for the beers of Cantillon, the last traditional lambic brewer of Brussels.

Flemish Brown and Red Ales

The other brewers of Flanders produce beers that share more characteristics with the old sour porters of Britain than with their lambic cousins. Where the lambics carry deeply funky earthy flavors of wild yeast, the Flemish sour ales taste of oxidized sherry, caramel, red-cherry leather broken by clean acidic character and dominated more by lactic acid than the vinegary acetic acid.

Even here, in a province that comprises half of a country of 12 million, there are divisions over the beer style. In the western part of the province the beers hold a ruby-red or burgundy hue. They finish dry with bright acid and sherry-fruited flavors from aging in old oak barrels. The Eastern province goes for the darker brown ales aged in stainless steel with more bitterness to make up for the less sherry-like tones and to cut through the larger, chewier, brown-sugar malt backbone.

Eee-Zee "Lambic" Sour Ale

This beer is not the same as the much-feared and beloved lambics of the Senne River Valley in Belgium. Where those beers use complicated multistep "turbid" mashes and natural yeast resident in the brewery, this recipe cheats to produce a pseudo-lambic in a fraction of the time. Adding fruit (like a fruit purée) not only adds flavor, but it also adds fuel to drive the bacterial cultures that define the style. Raspberries in particular make a spectacular lambic ale.

Style: Lambic
Brew Type: All Grain
For 5.5 gallons at 1.056, 14.7 SRM, 17 IBUs, 5.5 percent ABV
60-minute boil

Directions

Follow the Single-Infusion Brew Process (page 284).

Malt/Grain/Sugar
5.00 pounds Belgian Pilsner Malt
4.00 pounds Unmalted Wheat
1.00 pound Cara-Pils Malt

Extract (for Wheat and Pilsner Malts)
5.50 pounds Wheat Dried Malt Extract (DME)

Hops
1.00 ounce Any Well-Aged Hops Pellet for 60 minutes

Yeast
Wyeast 3278 Lambic Blend/White Labs WLP 550 Belgian Ale AND WLP 655 Belgian Sour

Mash Schedule
Saccharification Rest 155°F 60 minutes

TIP

Read Jeff Sparrow's *Wild Brews*. The in-depth discussion of traditional and modern practices in the world of Belgian beers offers a complete exploration of the topic and includes practical approaches for the beleaguered homebrewer.

Aichtie's Flemish Red

The balance desired in a Flemish red is a chewy, cherries-rolled-in-brown-sugar, sweet malt character chased away by an assertive acetic and lactic acid (vinegar and tangy milk acid) bite. Don't be worried if this thing makes a mess in your carboys and buckets—it's a good sign.

Style: Flemish Red Ale
Brew Type: All Grain
For 5.5 gallons at 1.056, 14.7 SRM, 17
    IBUs, 5.5 percent ABV
90-minute boil

Directions

Follow the Single-Infusion Brew Process (page 284).

TIP

Exemplified by Brouwerij Rodenbach's "Grand Cru," Flemish red and brown ales differ from their lambic cousins by the balance of acidity to "funk." Where the lambics add the earthy complexity of Brettanomyces and other critters to their acidity, Flemish sour ales aim for an acidic bang to serve as the exclamation to their complex malt characters.

Malt/Grain/Sugar
6.00 pounds Munich Malt
4.25 pounds Belgian Pilsner Malt
0.75 pound Melanoidin Malt
0.33 pound Special B Malt

Extract (for 6.0 pounds of Munich Malt and 4.25 pounds of Pilsner)
8.00 pounds Munich Liquid Malt Extract (LME)

Hops
1.00 ounce Tettnanger (4.0 percent AA) Pellet for 60 minutes

Other Ingredients
1 tablet Whirfloc (added at 20 minutes)

Yeast
Wyeast 3763 Roeselare Ale Blend/White Labs WLP 550 Belgian Ale AND
    WLP 655 Belgian Sour

Mash Schedule
Saccharification Rest 155°F 60 minutes

CHAPTER 19

Recipes from America

Taking a look at your beer shelves, America's melting pot might be a brew pot. With feet planted firmly in the British traditions and the strict German meditations on beer, American brewers have tackled them all and begun to put their own spin on old ideas.

19

The American Brewing Adventure

While the colonists made beer out of everything and anything that they could, (like pumpkins) they brewed in a decidedly British fashion. Porters, browns, and stouts flowed whenever the barley was available.

With the German immigration of the 1800s, the English traditions ceded to the new lager beers. With a growing market of fellow immigrants, the new brewers used new technologies to bring their lagers to new markets and drinkers. American lager brewers were the first to use refrigerated rail cars to move beer from the smaller markets of Milwaukee and St. Louis to big urban centers like Chicago.

American beer became lager beer, pilsners, and bocks with adjuncts added to reduce the haze caused by protein-laden American malting barley.

The initial use of corn and rice adjuncts was motivated by a desire to replicate the flavors of European malts, American barley being too harsh. These days brewers still use adjuncts for lowering protein levels, residual body, and costs. One major rice consumer though pays more for it than their barley.

The first modern microbrewers, finding no appropriately sized brewing equipment, cobbled together breweries with Yankee ingenuity. Many, like Sonoma's New Albion, repurposed old dairy equipment. Lacking lagering capabilities, the new guys pursued ales. Hazy memories of old pub sessions and European trips gave them a sense of direction; the lack of specifics gave their rebellious spirits the freedom to redefine American beer.

On the ingredient front, American barley has improved enormously. The majority of North American barley production focuses on enzyme-loaded malt. Great stuff for making gallons of high-adjunct beer, but lacking the depth found in European malts. Maltsters like Briess push development of more flavorful domestic malt.

While hop growers pursue clones of Continental noble hops or bigger loads of alpha acids, another distinctive thread of hopping has grown to define "American" beer. Centering on the ubiquitous Cascade hop that screams citrus, a class of "C" hops serves as the hub for American-style ale hopping; they include Centennial, Chinook, Columbus, and Crystal. Newer varieties expand these themes and push off in their own direction.

Until the recent change in prices, massive hop additions served as a cheap and easy way to cover up flaws. This is denigrated in some circles as crass, inelegant, and fitting only for hopheads.

QUESTION?

What is a hophead?

In beatnik times, a hophead was a marijuana smoker, but with the advent of boldly hoppy American beers came the person who just can't get enough bite. The hophead seeks out the baddest beers around and laughs where others' faces pucker into oblivion.

The increased popularity of Belgian beer has reached American brew kettles. Since the turn of the millennium, brewers have researched the secrets of Belgium. Recently, they have moved into putting an American stamp on the styles.

Light American Ales and Lagers

American lagers dominate in this country partly due to hot weather. The seemingly unstoppable rise of crisp pilsner beers forced ale brewers to fight back. In response they created one of the few native American beers, the cream ale—a light, corny ale fermented cool to reduce yeast esters and retain a little sweetness to the finish. The major east-coast brand, Genesee Cream Ale, is a long-standing exemplar of the style.

Homebrewers love to banter about how much equine aqueous waste the major brewers add to their products for taste. Most homebrewers won't admit the extreme challenge in brewing an American lager. The beloved ale styles swim in fruity esters, hop aromas, massive flavor, and alcohol that cover up any flaws. The major brewers spend untold sums to prevent stray notes from sneaking into their bland beers. If you, as a homebrewer, can brew a clean and crisp and blandly inoffensive light lager, then you can brew anything. Think of it as a brewer's Everest.

Little Colonel Cream Ale

Little Colonel is the beer for the lazy, sweltering days of summer when grabbing an inner tube for the river is about all you can do. Sit back on the porch and enjoy a cold one.

Style: American Lager
Brew Type: All Grain
For 5.5 gallons at 1.049, 3.0 SRM, 28.9 IBUs, 4.9 percent ABV
60-minute boil

Directions

Follow the Multistep Brew Process (pages 284–285).

TIP

This recipe uses flaked maize to avoid an American cereal mash process. If you want to go more traditional, replace the flaked maize with cornmeal and follow the steps listed for Dougweiser (page 241).

Malt/Grain/Sugar
7.75 pounds Pale Malt Six-Row
2.25 pounds Flaked Corn (Maize)

Extract (for 6.75 pounds of Pale Malt)
4.75 pounds Pale Liquid Malt Extract (LME)

Hops
0.55 ounce Tettnanger Tettnang (4.5 percent AA) Whole for First Wort Hopping
0.55 ounce Cluster (7.0 percent AA) Whole for 60 minutes
0.85 ounce Tettnanger Tettnang (4.5 percent AA) Whole for 15 minutes

Other Ingredients
1 tablet Whirlfloc
1 tablespoon Yeast Nutrient

Yeast
Wyeast 2035 American Lager/Wyeast 1056 (ferment cool)

Mash Schedule
Protein Rest 144°F 30 minutes
Saccharification Rest 158°F 30 minutes
Mash Out 170°F 10 minutes

Dougweiser

Why a clone of macro lagers? This will be the hardest beer you'll ever brew. In addition to the challenging cereal mash, you'll find there is nothing to hide behind. Brewers developed and refined this recipe for a decade before considering it done.

Style: American Standard Pilsner
Brew Type: All Grain
For 5.5 gallons at 1.043, 1.6 SRM, 33.6 IBUs, 4.2 percent ABV
60-minute boil

Directions

1. Infuse the mash with the Two-Row and Cara-Pils with 6.25 quarts of water.

2. In a separate pot, bring the rice to a boil with 3.5 quarts of water. Stir constantly. Be careful, the rice turns into lava-hot porridge. After boiling for 10 minutes, cool to 150°F and stir in the Six-Row. The rice mix should slacken immediately. Let the porridge sit for 15 minutes, then return to boil. Add the porridge to the main mash and stir thoroughly to come up to saccharification.

3. Proceed with a Single-Infusion Brew Process (page 284).

Malt/Grain/Sugar
4.75 pounds Pale Malt Two-Row
2.75 pounds Rice (Long Grain)
1.00 pound Pale Malt Six-Row
0.25 pound Cara-Pils Dextrine Malt

Extract (for 3.75 pounds of Pale Malt Two-Row)
2.50 pounds Pale Liquid Malt Extract (LME)

Hops
0.50 ounce Warrior (15.0 percent AA) Pellet for 60 minutes

Other Ingredients
1 tablet Whirlfloc
1 tablespoon Yeast Nutrient

Yeast
Wyeast 2035 American Lager

Mash Schedule
Protein Rest 135°F
Saccharification Rest 148°F 60 minutes

TIP

The mash process for this beer is the American Cereal Mash. The convoluted boil and rest procedure is intended to gelatinize the rice starches. Gelatinized starch's crystalline structure is blown open, accessible to mash enzymes. If you don't want to go through the extra work, use flaked rice in a single-infusion mash.

Porter and Stout

Looking for a beer that would scream different, many microbrewers decided to go dark with porters and stouts. Crossing style boundaries is a trend in Americans' efforts; the new styles were larger and hoppier than their Old World counterparts.

Craft brewers settled on their own take on the nearly dead style. The brewers' target: a drinkable dry dark beer without a lot of body. The acidic and dry finish is largely due to the insistence on using only dark roasted malts like chocolate malt and black patent malt without body-boosting unmalted barley.

Nick Danger Porter

Named for Firesign Theater's radio gumshoe parody, Nick Danger, Third Eye, this porter is a representative of the larger American porter style. The complicated malt bill with multiple sweet malts curbs the bite of the acidic chocolate and black patent malts.

Style: Porter
Brew Type: All Grain
For 5.5 gallons at 1.072, 33.2 SRM, 49.8 IBUs, 7.0 percent ABV
60-minute boil

Directions

Follow the Single-Infusion Brew Process (page 284).

TIP

Porters require a fine balancing act. You want a rich flavor, but without an overpowering body. For beers pushing the upper bounds of strength, rich bodies guard against the ethanol burn.

Malt/Grain/Sugar
12.00 pounds Pale Malt Two-Row
1.75 pounds Munich Malt
1.00 pound Crystal 60L
1.00 pound Chocolate Malt
0.50 pound Special B Malt
1.00 ounce Black Patent Malt

Extract (for 11.00 pounds of Pale Malt)
8.00 pounds Pale Liquid Malt Extract (LME)

Hops
1.00 ounce Tettnanger Tettnang (3.7 percent AA) Pellet for First Wort Hopping
0.90 ounce Columbus (14.6 percent AA) Whole for 60 minutes
0.70 ounce Cascade (8.1 percent AA) Whole for 10 minutes

Other Ingredients
1 tablet Whirlfloc
1 tablespoon Yeast Nutrient

Yeast
Wyeast 2450

Mash Schedule
Saccharification Rest 155°F 60 minutes

Stouts, on the other hand, use unmalted barley and roasted barley for color and body in addition to the roasted malts. As it turns out in older brewing logs, you see British brewers using unmalted barley in every dark style. Craft brewers tend to shy away from producing Americanized dry session stouts, preferring to stick with the heavier styles, especially the big, jammy, coffee-chocolate hop bomb imperial stouts.

Becky's Bootylicious Cinnamon Porter

Named and developed by a friend for his friend's wife, Becky, who loves both cinnamon and porters, Becky's was originally an extract with steeped grains recipe and so it plays well both ways. The recipe is great even as a straight porter with no cinnamon.

Style: Robust Porter
Brew Type: All Grain
For 5.5 gallons at 1.060, 35.2 SRM, 42.2 IBUs, 4.9 percent ABV
60-minute boil

Directions

Follow the Single-Infusion Brew Process (page 284).

TIP

The recipe calls for "true cinnamon"; what is that? For years, spice merchants have pulled a fast one on Americans substituting the less-expensive cassia. Compared to the profile of true cinnamon, cassia is brash and less refined.

Malt/Grain/Sugar
13.50 pounds Pale Malt Two-Row
0.75 pound Black Patent Malt
0.50 pound Crystal 55/60
0.25 pound Chocolate Malt

Extract (for 12.50 pounds of Pale Malt)
7.50 pounds Pale Liquid Malt Extract (LME)

Hops
0.50 ounce Columbus (16.7 percent AA) Pellet for 60 minutes
0.25 ounce Centennial (8.0 percent AA) Pellet for 60 minutes
0.25 ounce Wilamette (4.1 percent AA) Pellet for 60 minutes
1.00 ounce Nugget (13.0 percent AA) Whole for 0 minutes

Other Ingredients
1 tablet Whirlfloc
1 tablespoon Yeast Nutrient
0.25 gram Ceylon "True Cinnamon" (Added at 0 minutes in the boil)

Yeast
Wyeast 1272 American Ale II

Mash Schedule
Saccharification Rest 156°F 45 minutes

American Dream Stout

The late, lamented New Albion Brewing was responsible for introducing American brewers to homegrown stout. American Dream follows the basic guidelines American brewers follow for their stouts: a generous portion of black roasted barley and a big, bright, piney hop character to add bite.

Style: American Stout
Brew Type: All Grain
For 5.5 gallons at 1.055, 43.7 SRM, 31.8 IBUs, 5.4 percent ABV
90-minute boil

Directions

Follow the Single-Infusion Brew Process (page 284).

TIP

In keeping with other American styles, the domestic version increases strength over the British/Irish classics. Most of this impetus comes from the flaw cover-up provided by increased strength and flavor and a desire to stand separately from the typical perception of American beer.

Malt/Grain/Sugar
9.00 pounds Pale Malt Two-Row
1.50 pounds Roasted Barley
0.75 pound Crystal 75L
0.50 pound Honey Malt

Extract (for 8.00 pounds of Pale Malt)
6.00 pounds Pale Liquid Malt Extract (LME)

Hops
0.25 ounce Columbus (15.0 percent AA) Pellet for 60 minutes
1.00 ounce Centennial (10.5 percent AA) Pellet for 20 minutes
0.50 ounce Columbus (15.0 percent AA) Whole for 0 minutes

Other Ingredients
1 tablet Whirlfloc
1 tablespoon Yeast Nutrient

Yeast
Wyeast 1056 American Ale / WLP001 California Ale

Mash Schedule
Saccharification Rest 152°F 60 minutes

Old Rasty

North Coast Brewing's Old Rasputin drinks dangerously well for a 9 percent ABV beer. It should come with warning labels. The old Toms hashed out the recipe for this beer over a number of sessions and came up with this recipe that tastes the same.

Style: Russian Imperial Stout
Brew Type: All Grain
For 5.5 gallons at 1.095, 54.7 SRM, 96.9 IBUs, 8.8 percent ABV
90-minute boil

Directions

Follow the Single-Infusion Brew Process (page 284).

TIP

Tom insists on the use of dark candi sugar in the recipe, claiming that anything else tastes wrong. Whether or not this is true for you is all a matter of taste.

Malt/Grain/Sugar
15.00 pounds Maris Otter Malt
1.00 pound Crystal 65L
0.80 pound Crystal 55L
0.60 pound Roasted Barley
0.50 pound Black Patent Malt
0.50 pound Victory Malt
1.00 pound Dark Candi Sugar

Extract (for 14.00 pounds of Maris Otter Malt)
10.00 pounds Pale Liquid Malt Extract (LME)

Hops
3.40 ounces Cluster (6.7 percent AA) Pellet for 90 minutes
0.25 ounce Centennial (9.0 percent AA) Pellet for 15 minutes
0.40 ounce Northern Brewer (7.7 percent AA) Pellet for 15 minutes
1.10 ounces Liberty (5.2 percent AA) Pellet for 0 minutes

Other Ingredients
1 tablet Whirlfloc
1 tablespoon Yeast Nutrient

Yeast
Wyeast 1028 London Ale

Mash Schedule
Saccharification Rest 155°F 90 minutes

Brown, Amber, and Red

Following other practices, American craft brewers took British brown ales up in alcohol and bite. Where the British versions focus on nutty and biscuity malt tones, the American browns lead with sweet caramel and acidic roast bite. A number of American browns are closer in color and temperament to a hoppy brown porter.

Texas Warrior Brown

The American brown ale had a different name for awhile among Texans. The Dixie Cup Homebrew Competition was supposedly the first competition to separately judge American brown ale. This recipe is named in honor of those Texans and a good excuse to use the potent grapefruit Amarillo hops.

Style: American Brown Ale
Brew Type: All Grain
For 5.5 gallons at 1.057, 18.4 SRM, 68.0 IBUs, 5.7 percent ABV
90-minute boil

Directions

Follow the Single-Infusion Brew Process (page 284).

TIP

Want to go spicy Tex-Mex style on your beer? Add 1 to 3 habanero chile peppers to the beer in secondary and "dry pepper" for several weeks. Give a periodic taste and rack away when the heat is perfect. Be vigilant, this can happen fast!

Malt/Grain/Sugar
6.00 pounds Pale Malt Two-Row
4.50 pounds Maris Otter Malt
0.50 pound Chocolate Malt
0.25 pound Crystal 55/60
0.25 pound Crystal 60

Extract (for 5.00 pounds of Pale Malt Two-Row and for 3.50 pounds of Maris Otter Malt)
7.00 pounds Pale Liquid Malt Extract (LME)

Hops
0.25 ounce Palisade (9.4 percent AA) Pellet—First Wort Hopped
0.25 ounce Amarillo (10.0 percent AA) Pellet—First Wort Hopped
0.50 ounce Warrior (17.4 percent AA) Pellet for 90 minutes
0.25 ounce Palisade (9.4 percent AA) Pellet for 1 minute
0.25 ounce Amarillo (10.0 percent AA) Pellet for 1 minute
1.00 ounce Amarillo (10.0 percent AA) Whole for 0 minutes

Other Ingredients
1 tablet Whirlfloc
1 tablespoon Yeast Nutrient

Yeast
Wyeast 1056 American Ale

Mash Schedule
Saccharification Rest 152°F 60 minutes

There are no widespread American ordinary bitter counterparts, but Scottish ales and British ESBs morphed into hybrid amber- and red-type ales. Bigger and more caramel sweet, early reds and ambers had large doses of crystal malt with just enough hops to balance. While crystal is still a defining trait and needed for those ruby red hues, the trend is to use less and boost the body in other ways.

Evil Twin

San Diego's Alesmith brews a much sought-after fall classic, Evil Dead Red. A blood-red malty beer with tons of juicy citrus and pine hop bite to keep you interested. This recipe is much loved for good reason. For extra "pow," dry-hop with more Amarillo and Centennial.

Style: American Red
Brew Type: All Grain
For 5.5 gallons at 1.067, 19.9 SRM, 25.8 IBUs, 6.6 percent ABV
60-minute boil

Directions

Follow the Single-Infusion Brew Process (page 284).

TIP

A beer with all late hop additions like this one is less efficient at adding bitterness, but great at loading the glass with big hop flavor and aroma. Chill this beer as quickly as possible to preserve that fresh hop aroma.

Malt/Grain/Sugar
11.00 pounds Maris Otter Malt
1.00 pound Crystal 40L
1.00 pound Munich Malt
0.50 pound Victory Malt
0.50 pound Special B Malt
0.25 pound Chocolate Malt

Extract (for 10.00 pounds of Maris Otter Malt)
7.00 pounds Pale Liquid Malt Extract (LME)

Hops
0.50 ounce Amarillo (7.0 percent AA) Pellet for 20 minutes
0.50 ounce Centennial (10.0 percent AA) Pellet for 20 minutes
1.00 ounce Amarillo (7.0 percent AA) Pellet for 10 minutes
1.00 ounce Centennial (10.0 percent AA) Pellet for 10 minutes
1.00 ounce Amarillo (7.0 percent AA) Pellet for 0 minutes
1.00 ounce Centennial (10.0 percent AA) Pellet for 0 minutes

Other Ingredients
1 tablet Whirlfloc
1 tablespoon Yeast Nutrient

Yeast
Wyeast 1056 American Ale/WLP001 California Ale / US-05

Mash Schedule
Saccharification Rest 154°F 60 minutes

Pale Ale

Pale ales, the style that killed porter in Britain, became the hallmark of the American microbrewery scene. Bright and bracing with a chewy malt structure, these ales gave most American drinkers their first real hoppy sensation.

Today the APA comes in all shapes and sizes from the crisp, light, bitter extra pale ales to the ever-creeping dividing line between an APA and an IPA. Each of them shares a focus on the comfortable hop experience. They supply enough bitterness to wake you up, but with enough malt and body to keep the palate from tiring before the next sip. APAs pack more hop bite than British pale ales.

From here on out is the chance to really let those "C" hops shine. The pale ales, the IPAs, DIPAs, and barleywines push brassy American hops more than any other style.

Gumball Thoughts Wheat Pale Ale

Inspired by Three Floyds and their brightly hoppy Gumball Head wheat ale, Gumball Thoughts is the bigger, meaner cousin of that great beer. It borders on being a wheat IPA with the juicy Amarillo mixing with the sweet, bready wheat character.

Style: American Wheat
Brew Type: All Grain
For 5.5 gallons at 1.062, 5.9 SRM, 52.8 IBUs, 6.1 percent ABV
60-minute boil

Directions

Follow the Single-Infusion Brew Process (page 284).

Malt/Grain/Sugar
7.50 pounds Wheat Malt
5.00 pounds Pale Malt Two-Row
0.75 pound CaraVienne Malt

Extract (for 7.0 pounds of Wheat Malt and 4.50 pounds of Pale Malt)
7.50 pounds Wheat Liquid Malt Extract (LME)

Hops
0.75 ounce Amarillo (9.4 percent AA) Pellet for 60 minutes
0.75 ounce Amarillo (9.4 percent AA) Pellet for 30 minutes
0.75 ounce Amarillo (9.4 percent AA) Pellet for 15 minutes
1.50 ounces Amarillo (9.4 percent AA) Pellet for 0 minutes

Other Ingredients
1 tablespoon Yeast Nutrient

Yeast
Wyeast 1056/WLP001 California Ale/Safale US-05 American Ale

Mash Schedule
Saccharification Rest 152°F 60 minutes

Brutal Bittered

Rogue has a funny habit of forgetting style conventions when creating new beers, but their American "bitter" ale, Brutal Bitter, is a hit no matter what you call it. To make this beer, Rogue dominates the Crystal hop market.

Style: American Pale Ale
Brew Type: All Grain
For 5.5 gallons at 1.062, 5.5 SRM, 61.3 IBUs, 6.1 percent ABV
60-minute boil

Directions

Follow the Single-Infusion Brew Process (page 284).

TIP

Rogue Brewing has a long history of supporting homebrewers. Try their unique "Pacman" yeast; buy a couple of bottles of lighter Rogue beers and build up the yeast from the bottle bottom.

Malt/Grain/Sugar
10.50 pounds Pale Malt Two-Row
0.75 pound Cara-Pils Dextrin Malt
0.70 pound CaraVienne Malt
0.70 pound Wheat Malt

Extract (for 9.50 pounds of Pale Malt)
7.00 pounds Pale Liquid Malt Extract (LME)

Hops
1.25 ounces Newport (11.1 percent AA) Pellet for 60 minutes
0.75 ounce Crystal (3.1 percent AA) Pellet for 15 minutes
0.75 ounce Crystal (3.1 percent AA) Pellet for 0 minutes
1.10 ounces Crystal (3.1 percent AA) Whole for Dry Hopping

Other Ingredients
1 tablet Whirlfloc
1 tablespoon Yeast Nutrient

Yeast
Wyeast Pacman (Seasonal/Wyeast 1272 American Ale II)

Mash Schedule
Saccharification Rest 152°F 110 minutes

Summer Bloody Summer Ale

The name comes from an incident that cost a brewer his finger tip. Don't ever touch the belt of jammed malt mill unless you like sudden surprises! A testament to perseverance, both brewers stuck with the brew, one singlehandedly.

Style: American Specialty Pale Ale
Brew Type: All Grain
For 5.5 gallons at 1.049, 4.7 SRM, 20.9 IBUs, 4.9 percent ABV
60-minute boil

Directions

Follow the Multistep Brew Process (pages 284-285).

TIP

The beer isn't very bitter, but the hop character is surprisingly potent. This is a poster child for knowing what you brewed, not what your recipe claims.

Malt/Grain/Sugar
8.25 pounds Pale Malt Two-Row
0.40 pound Cara-Pils Dextrine Malt
0.40 pound Belgian 8L
0.40 pound Aromatic Malt

Extract (for 7.25 pounds of Pale Malt)
5.50 pounds Pale Liquid Malt Extract (LME)

Hops
1.0 ounce Crystal (3.25 percent AA) Whole for 60 minutes
1.0 ounce Ultra (2.75 percent AA) Whole for 30 minutes
0.50 ounce Cascade (5.75 percent AA) Whole for 5 minutes

Other Ingredients
1 tablet Whirlfloc
1 tablespoon Yeast Nutrient

Yeast
Wyeast 2565 Kolsch

Mash Schedule
Intermediate Rest 120°F 30 minutes
Saccharification Rest 150°F 60 minutes

IPA/DIPA

IPA is the default drink of many a craft brewer and homebrewer. Something about that biscuit malt toasted crust playing off a juicy grapefruit gets to people. Several variations exist on the IPA; some rock big caramel with a hefty chew to the base. Others strip the beer clean of malt interference. The BUGU ratio of an IPA should hover right around 1:1, decidedly more bitter than the British version.

Next in the chain of hophead enthusiasm is the double "imperial" IPA (DIPA). The obnoxious bop of hops is matched only in strength. The design philosophy behind awarding-winning DIPAs borrows from the Belgians. To enhance the bite without tossing in ever-growing hop charges, the gravity is boosted and body cut with sugar.

Designed to confound a drinker's expectations, the new Black IPA appears pitch black thanks to a brewer's ruse. Using small amounts of a natural colorant called sinamar or late-addition chocolate malt (particular Carafa malt), the beer looks like a stout, but with the body and bite of an IPA.

Bombay Bomber IPA

A light copper IPA that has a mineral-driven crispness. The gypsum acidifies the mash (from the calcium) and the sulfates promote a brisker hop character.

Style: American India Pale Ale
Brew Type: All Grain
For 5.5 gallons at 1.060, 7.3 SRM, 53.8 IBUs, 5.9 percent ABV
60-minute boil

Directions

Follow the Single-Infusion Brew Process (page 284).

TIP

Sometimes a little industrial espionage is in order. A local microbrewery brews a much loved beer. One day, fiendish homebrewers noticed unattended notes and seized the opportunity to learn its secrets.

Malt/Grain/Sugar
10.00 pounds Pale Malt Two-Row
1.00 pound Carastan Malt
0.50 pound Munich Malt

Extract (for 9.00 pounds of Pale Malt)
7.00 pounds Pale Liquid Malt Extract (LME)

Hops
0.50 ounce Chinook (13.0 percent AA) Whole for 60 minutes
0.50 ounce Goldings—E.K. (4.75 percent AA) Whole for 60 minutes
0.50 ounce Fuggle (5.0 percent AA) Whole for 60 minutes
0.25 ounce Northern Brewer (9.0 percent AA) Whole for 60 minutes
1.33 ounces Chinook (13.0 percent AA) Whole for 0 minutes

Other Ingredients
1 tablet Whirlfloc
1 tablespoon Yeast Nutrient
2 tablespoons Gypsum

Yeast
Wyeast 1056/WLP001 California Ale/US-05 Safale American Ale

Mash Schedule
Saccharification Rest 154°F 60 minutes

Double Down Double IPA

Originally brewed for the 2004 AHA National Homebrewer's Conference, Double Down DIPA proved to be an instant hit. Not the bitterest DIPA by far, the beer packs a huge hop flavor and aroma along with a bite. Enhance the bite, subbing a pound of sugar for 1.75 pounds of Maris Otter.

Style: Double India Pale Ale
Brew Type: All Grain
For 5.5 gallons at 1.083, 8.6 SRM, 99.9 IBUs, 8.2 percent ABV
90-minute boil

Directions

Follow the Single-Infusion Brew Process (page 284).

TIP

Unlike other large beers, a DIPA should be drunk within weeks. You want to enjoy the quickly fading aroma. The flavor and bittering hang around a lot longer, but a well-aged DIPA tastes more and more like a barleywine as time slips by. Batches of this beer go on tap within five to six weeks.

Malt/Grain/Sugar
7.75 pounds Pale Malt Two-Row
8.00 pounds Maris Otter
0.50 pound Crystal 55L
0.50 pound Wheat Malt
0.25 pound Munich Malt
0.10 pound Biscuit Malt

Extract (for 7.25 pounds of Pale Malt and 7.5 pounds of Maris Otter)
10.50 pounds Pale Liquid Malt Extract (LME)

Hops
0.70 ounce Centennial (9.1 percent AA) Pellet for First Wort Hopping
0.80 ounce Cascade (5.4 percent AA) Pellet for First Wort Hopping
0.50 ounce Warrior (15.6 percent AA) Pellet for 60 minutes
0.10 ounce Chinook (12.1 percent AA) Pellet for 60 minutes
0.60 ounce Amarillo (8.9 percent AA) Pellet for 30 minutes
0.60 ounce Cascade (5.9 percent AA) Pellet for 30 minutes
0.50 ounce Simcoe (13.7 percent AA) Pellet for 15 minutes
0.70 ounce Cascade (5.9 percent AA) Pellet for 0 minutes
0.90 ounce Cascade (7.3 percent AA) Whole for Dry Hopping

Other Ingredients
1 tablet Whirlfloc
1 tablespoon Yeast Nutrient
1.5 tablespoons Gypsum

Yeast
WLP001 California Ale/Wyeast 1056/US-05

Mash Schedule
Saccharification Rest 151°F 90 minutes

Black Perle DIPA

This beer pours midnight stout black, but it has the body and punch of a DIPA.

Style: Double India Pale Ale
Brew Type: All Grain
For 5.5 gallons at 1.109, 58.4 SRM, 266.2 IBUs, 11.0 percent ABV
90-minute boil

Directions

Follow the Single-Infusion Brew Process (page 284).

TIP

For a beer with this many hop additions it helps to break out your handy scale and weigh the additions in advance. Add each minute addition (90, 60, 55, and so on) into a separate labeled paper cup or bowl. Use the cups to keep your additions straight!

Malt/Grain/Sugar
22.00 pounds Pale Malt Two-Row
1.50 pounds Biscuit Malt
1.50 pounds Cara-Pils Dextrine Malt
1.00 pound Special B Malt
0.75 pound Carafa Chocolate Malt
0.75 pound Chocolate Malt
0.50 pound Crystal 150L
0.25 pound Black Patent Malt

Extract (for 21.0 pounds of Pale Malt)
15.50 pounds Pale Liquid Malt Extract (LME)

Hops
2.00 ounces Chinook (14.3 percent AA) Whole for 90 minutes
1.00 ounce Perle (13.0 percent AA) Pellet for 90 minutes
0.15 ounce Cascade (6.8 percent AA) Whole for 60 minutes
0.15 ounce Chinook (14.3 percent AA) Whole for 60 minutes
0.15 ounce Cascade (6.8 percent AA) Whole for 55 minutes
0.15 ounce Chinook (14.3 percent AA) Whole for 55 minutes
0.16 ounce Cascade (6.8 percent AA) Whole for 50 minutes
0.16 ounce Chinook (14.3 percent AA) Whole for 50 minutes
0.17 ounce Cascade (6.8 percent AA) Whole for 45 minutes
0.17 ounce Chinook (14.3 percent AA) Whole for 45 minutes
0.20 ounce Cascade (6.8 percent AA) Whole for 40 minutes
0.20 ounce Chinook (14.3 percent AA) Whole for 40 minutes
0.24 ounce Cascade (6.8 percent AA) Whole for 35 minutes
0.24 ounce Chinook (14.3 percent AA) Whole for 35 minutes
0.30 ounce Cascade (6.8 percent AA) Whole for 30 minutes
0.30 ounce Chinook (14.3 percent AA) Whole for 30 minutes
0.37 ounce Cascade (6.8 percent AA) Whole for 25 minutes
0.37 ounce Chinook (14.3 percent AA) Whole for 25 minutes
0.45 ounce Cascade (6.8 percent AA) Whole for 20 minutes
0.45 ounce Chinook (14.3 percent AA) Whole for 20 minutes
0.56 ounce Cascade (6.8 percent AA) Whole for 15 minutes
0.56 ounce Chinook (14.3 percent AA) Whole for 15 minutes
0.75 ounce Cascade (6.8 percent AA) Whole for 10 minutes
0.75 ounce Chinook (14.3 percent AA) Whole for 10 minutes
1.00 ounce Chinook (14.3 percent AA) Whole for 5 minutes

Other Ingredients
1 tablet Whirlfloc
1 tablespoon Yeast Nutrient

Yeast
WLP001 California Ale Yeast

Mash Schedule
Saccharification Rest 152°F 60 minutes

Barleywine

Prior to the DIPA's popularity, barleywine ruled the hop roost. Brewed for winter release, these stand between 8.5 percent ABV on the low side to 15 percent on the high side. Barleywines have rich malt bodies redolent of caramels, wine, fruit, and hops to punch through the sweetness

Fresh barleywines have such strong hop characters that collectors try one bottle per year, cellaring the rest for at least six months. Barleywines benefit from the time to meld and mellow.

FACT

Anchor Brewing rolled out their mellow Old Foghorn barleywine in 1975. Serving as an inspiration for later barleywine brewers, they also set a legal precedent followed to this day. The Bureau of Alcohol, Tobacco, and Firearms balked at approving the term "Barley Wine" for fear that customers would confuse it for table wine. But they had no problems with the term barleywine-style ale, reflected on labels to this day.

Due to the amount of malt and boil time needed to reach barleywine strength, specialty malts aren't critical to achieve the colors and flavors associated with the style. As with other strong beers, the best approach to a complete and fast fermentation is to pitch with yeast fresh from a smaller batch of beer. A common tactic: brew a strong APA or IPA first and use the resulting cake to drive the barleywine.

Old Smokey Barleywine

Every competition this recipe has been entered in has yielded a medal for the brewer. Sometimes it even wins the whole shebang, like the time it won the national Masters Championship of Amateur Brewing.

Style: American-Style Barleywine
Brew Type: All Grain
For 5.5 gallons at 1.134, 21.8 SRM, 87.7 IBUs, 12.7 percent ABV
120-minute boil

Directions

Follow the Multistep Brew Process (pages 284-285).

TIP

This is another homebrewer's missed target special. The original intent was to replicate Sierra Nevada's Celebration Ale, but the brewer swung for the fences and went large. The end result was a genius barleywine.

Malt/Grain/Sugar
22.00 pounds Pilsner Malt
1.00 pound Crystal 90L
1.00 pound Crystal 30L
0.25 pound Special B Malt
0.13 pound Chocolate Malt
1.40 pounds Light Dry Malt Extract (DME)
1.00 pound Corn Sugar

Extract (for 21.00 pounds of Pilsner Malt)
13.75 pounds Lager Liquid Malt Extract (LME)

Hops
0.80 ounce Chinook (6.6 percent AA) Pellet for 120 minutes
1.00 ounce Northern Brewer (8.0 percent AA) Pellet for 120 minutes
1.00 ounce Centennial (10.6 percent AA) Pellet for 120 minutes
0.20 ounce Cascade (7.0 percent AA) Pellet for 120 minutes
2.00 ounces Centennial (10.5 percent AA) Whole for 0 minutes
1.00 ounce Cascade (7.00 percent AA) Pellet for 0 minutes
1.00 ounce Goldings—E.K. (4.75 percent AA) Pellet for 0 minutes

Other Ingredients
1 tablet Whirlfloc
1 tablespoon Yeast Nutrient

Yeast
Wyeast 1056 American Ale

Mash Schedule
Intermediate Rest 132°F 30 minutes
Saccharification Rest 151°F 60 minutes

Experiments: Recipes from the Laboratory

Bored already? Would another pale ale make you cry tears of frustration? Well, your brewery already looks a bit like a laboratory—so why not treat it like one? Put the experimentation back in fermentation.

20

Making History

There are a number of pitfalls to consider when going from historical beers to present taste. How sweet were the beers? Texts indicate that beer was typically underattenuated. How do you translate archaic measurements and estimate hop bitterness? Do you throw in a portion of smoked malt to replicate the malt-drying fires? Do you allow the beer to sour or serve it fresh? Don't worry about getting it right though. Just like with Latin pronunciation, no one really knows what the flavor was like.

FACT

Scan sites on the Internet for old brewing texts. In addition to eBay, sites like BeerBooks.com gather old volumes for sale and make reprints of exceedingly rare key texts. A few modern breweries like Anchor Brewing and Kirin have published papers about their attempts to brew "old school."

Smoke 'Em If You Got 'Em

Compared to the rest of the animal kingdom, human beings have a terrible sense of smell. Smoke is one thing humans are extremely sensitive to. Scientists and perfumers talk about detection thresholds for different compounds. For many aromatic compounds they discuss thresholds in "parts per million." For smoke phenols, the discussion turns to "parts per billion."

Over the course of human history, most of our beer has been smoky, an unavoidable consequence of malt drying. With a switch to cleaner fuels and isolated drying kilns, beer went smokeless.

Who says the Germans rauch brewers get to have all the fun? You can take advantage of their beechwood-smoked rauchmalz or the Scottish peat smoked. A producer in California makes alder wood–, cherry wood–, and maple wood–smoked malts. At home you can dampen malt in a pan and cold smoke it for several hours until dry and then let it sit for two weeks before using. The damp malt will grab the smoke particles better and the airing out allows any nasty phenols to out gas before they end up in your beer.

Gilgamash Sumerian Beer

You'll need two sessions to brew. One to bake the Sumerian PowerBar equivalent, the hard date bread called bappir. The second day is brew day. Be prepared to drink this beer quick! Since the beer isn't boiled or hopped, the lactobacillus will activate immediately. Baked correctly and stored dry, bappir can last more than six months.

Style: Historical Beer
Brew Type: All Grain
For 5.5 gallons at 1.044, 11 SRM, 0 IBUs, 3.5 percent ABV
0-minute boil

Directions

1. Grind all the bappir barley into flour in a flour mill or your food processor. Chop dates and process with a little water to make date paste. Mix all the bappir ingredients together and then knead until the dough holds together and is less sticky.

2. Form the dough into 1"-thick round discs (approximately 8) and bake for 35 minutes at 375°F on a pizza stone. Cool the loaves completely and then bake for another 15 to 20 minutes at 350°F to complete drying. Store until brew day.

3. Mash the beer barley with 3.5 gallons of water and then crumble the bappir into the soupy mash and stir. A pound of rice hulls might be handy to make the eventual runoff easier.

4. Sparge and collect 5.5 gallons of hot wort and place directly into your fermenter. Allow to cool over night before adding the yeast. Serve cool, cloudy, and flat after fermentation. Try serving it in bowls with straws like the ancient Sumerians.

Malt/Grain/Sugar
6.00 pounds Pale Ale Malt
6.00 pounds Bappir Bread (see below)

Bappir Ingredients
6.00 pounds Pale Ale Malt
3.00 pounds Zahidi Dates
1.00 pound Flaked Barley
0.50 pound Special B Malt
0.25 pound Carafa II Special Dehusked Chocolate Malt
4 large Radishes, grated
3.0 teaspoons Yellow Mustard Seeds, ground
4.0 teaspoons Coriander Seeds, ground
4.0 teaspoons Anise Seeds, ground
3.5 quarts Water

Yeast
US-05 American Ale Yeast

Mash Schedule
Saccharification Rest 150°F 60 minutes

TIP

Not all historical beers need to be this weird. Look online and you can find diverse projects out there including original London porters and George Washington's or Thomas Jefferson's beer recipes.

Got Wood?

Roll out the barrel and we'll have a barrel of fun. That line made more sense back in the pre-metal keg days. Sadly, the days of coopers feverishly maintaining wooden beer casks have passed. But you can join brewing's fast-growing trend and put the romance of wood back into beer with barrel aging. Strong beers like barleywine and imperial stout are aged in used bourbon or other barrels for an added depth provided by a shot of sandalwood, cinnamon, vanilla, and whiskey.

Cherrywood Smoked Mild

Here is a low-alcohol mild, the smoke adds another dimension to intrigue you. Use a smaller dose (1 pound) of rauchmalz if you can't get cherry wood malt.

Style: English Mild
Brew Type: All Grain
For 5.5 gallons at 1.038, 15 SRM, 13 IBUs, 3.6 percent ABV
60-minute boil

Directions

Follow the Single-Infusion Brew Process (page 284).

Malt/Grain/Sugar
3.50 pounds British Maris Otter Malt
3.50 pounds Cherrywood Smoked Malt
0.50 pound British Crystal 75L Malt
0.50 pound Munich Malt
0.25 pound Carafa II Special Dehusked Chocolate Malt

Hops
0.25 ounce Target (10.6 percent AA) Pellet for 60 minutes
0.12 ounce Challenger (6.5 percent AA) Pellet for 30 minutes

Other Ingredients
1 tablet Whirlfloc

Yeast
Wyeast 1275 Thames Valley/WLP 001 California Ale

Mash Schedule
Saccharification Rest 152°F 60 minutes
Mash Out 168°F 10 minutes

Schmitty's Smoked Porter

What better way to demonstrate the strength of peat-smoked malt than comparing Schmitty's porter to the smoked mild. Here just three ounces (less than a quarter of a pound) gives a very strong smoky aroma and flavor. If you're a big smoke fan, feel free to bump the amount used, but give serious thought before crossing the half-pound threshold.

Style: Porter
Brew Type: All Grain
For 5.5 gallons at 1.056, 23 SRM, 33 IBUs, 5.5 percent ABV
60-minute boil

Directions

Follow the Single-Infusion Brew Process (page 284).

TIP

The admonishments regarding overdoing the smoke in your beer come from smoke's hardiness and resistance to aging out. Peated malt is used in Scotland for whiskey distilling. Scotches are famous for their dense and heady peat-smoke aromas. All of that smoke character survives the distillation process and aging for years in barrels.

Malt/Grain/Sugar
11.00 pounds Domestic Two-Row Pale Malt
0.75 pound Cara-Pils Dextrine Malt
0.75 pound CaraWheat
0.50 pound Chocolate Malt
0.33 pound Honey Malt
3.00 ounces Peat Smoked Malt

Extract (for 10.0 pounds of Pale Malt)
7.50 pounds Pale Liquid Malt Extract (LME)

Hops
0.75 ounce Perle (7.8 percent AA) Pellet for 60 minutes
0.75 ounce East Kent Goldings (3.7 percent AA) Pellet for 30 minutes
0.33 ounce Fuggle (4.7 percent AA) Pellet for 15 minutes

Other Ingredients
1 tablet Whirlfloc
2 teaspoons Calcium Carbonate (to boil kettle)

Yeast
Wyeast 1318 London Ale III

Mash Schedule
Saccharification Rest 153°F 60 minutes
Mash Out 168°F 10 minutes

Unless you're working with a massive system or a club of brewers, a full-sized barrel (fifty to sixty gallons) requires more work than your average brewer can manage. Don't consider your dreams of barrel aging dashed though. You can take a white oak chair leg, whittled to fit into a carboy, and seal tight and char it with a blowtorch.

QUESTION?

Why do so many brewers use bourbon barrels?
By federal law all spirits labeled bourbon must be aged for two or more years in new, unused, charred white oak barrels. Bourbon distillers sell off their used barrels regularly to Scotch distillers who have no such restriction. Their cheap price, alcohol-sanitized wood, and flavor encouraged experimentation.

Available on the market are several oak products designed to aid vintners with exhausted oak barrels. Soak your oak in your spirit of choice or steam them for fifteen minutes prior to use. If you can find them, choose "oak beans" over "oak chips," and under no circumstances should you use "oak powder." The cube's ratio of surface area to core has more layers of toasted flavor and behaves more like a barrel stave than the more shredded options. Like real barrels, the chips and cubes have levels of toasting to them. For beer-aging purposes, stick with the medium toast to avoid overpowering the flavor.

You have several source countries for your oak. Typical options include:

- **American**—Bold, aggressive oak character with a pleasant vanilla aroma and assertive tannic twang.
- **French**—Softer oak than the American. Leads with spicy oak characters, sandalwood, cinnamon, all spice, and hints of sweet caramel to round out the wood.
- **Hungarian**—Huge vanilla notes with strong coffee and dark chocolate notes. It is the least aggressive of the oaks.

Soak the beans for as long as you can before adding them to the secondary for flavoring. Two weeks of soaking is a good minimum. Some brewers plan far ahead and have beans soaking for more than five years in bourbon and other spirits.

Even though beer was fermented and stored in wooden vessels it wasn't flavored by the wood at all. The wood character in fermentation tanks would quickly be leeched out and washed away or they, like the oak casks that predate kegs, were lined with a pitch or wax coating that prevented the wood from imparting its character to the beer. In some cases, the brewery's pitch recipe lent additional flavor to the draft beer.

Add your oak to secondary and age to taste, at least two weeks. With beans, brewers have the best results at two weeks with about two ounces of beans, minus their soaking liquid. More complex characters can be leeched by aging for a month or more at cold (under 50°F) temperatures. Chips require both less weight (approximately one ounce) and time (as short as three days) to oak a beer, but the complexity suffers.

Kitchen-Sink Brewing

A pre-twentieth-century brewer had more options to create frosty suds for his customers. Anything was game for the boil kettle. Every source of starch ended up in the kettle. This wasn't always for the best. During the Napoleonic Wars, British brewers lowered the alcohol on their porters to avoid excess taxes. To keep the desired "kick" they reportedly added agents like tar, lead, and sulfuric acid. Of course, this is rightfully outlawed these days.

An old brewer's maxim says, "If it has starch, it can mash." Whether it's an odd form of sugar, old corn tortillas, potato flakes, or chocolate cake, there's little that can't ferment. To preserve head retention you must de-fat unusual brew additions. For example, the chocolate birthday cake was defrosted and boiled briefly. The butterfat was skimmed from the top of the cool slurry.

Other crazy ideas gleaned from fellow homebrewers include: rye bread, pretzels, apple pie, cucumbers, peanut butter, Jolly Ranchers, Mountain Dew soda, Red Zinger tea, ginger snap cookies, ad infinitum.

KIPA—Bourbon Barrel IPA

This big IPA plays on the legends told about the creation of IPA. Although most certainly mythical, the idea of a strong beer sloshing across the waves makes a good story. The beer is kept a little sweet to soften the oak tannins.

Style: American IPA
Brew Type: All Grain
For 5.5 gallons at 1.070, 11 SRM, 79
    IBUs, 7.2 percent ABV
60-minute boil

Directions

1. Follow the Single-Infusion Brew Process (page 284).

2. Add oak (without bourbon) and dry hops to the secondary and rack beer from primary. Age for 2 weeks at the upper sixties or 4 weeks in the forties.

TIP

Don't like bourbon? Want to give the beer a more British angle? Soak your cubes in rum or scotch. Don't use the fancy expensive stuff for these purposes. The bourbon used in this recipe was a bottle of $8 Ten High.

Malt/Grain/Sugar
6.00 pounds Domestic Two-Row Pale Malt
6.00 pounds British Maris Otter Malt
1.0 pound British Crystal 55L
0.50 pound Biscuit Malt
0.50 pound Honey Malt

Extract (for 10.0 pounds of Pale Malt)
7.50 pounds Pale Liquid Malt Extract (LME)

Hops
0.50 ounce Cascade (8.3 percent AA) Whole—First Wort Hop
0.25 ounce Chinook (10.4 percent AA) Pellet for 45 minutes
1.00 ounce Amarillo (8.9 percent AA) Pellet for 30 minutes
1.00 ounce Crystal (4.0 percent AA) Pellet for 15 minutes
1.00 ounce Warrior (15.6 percent AA) Pellet for 15 minutes
0.50 ounce Cascade (8.3 percent AA) Whole for 2 minutes
1.00 ounce Cascade (8.3 percent AA) Whole—Dry-Hop for 2 weeks

Other Ingredients
1 tablet Whirlfloc
2 teaspoons Gypsum (to boil kettle)
2 ounces Medium Toast American Oak (soaked in Bourbon for minimum 2 weeks)

Yeast
Wyeast 1056 Chico Ale/WLP001 California Ale/US-05 American Ale

Mash Schedule
Saccharification Rest 153°F 60 minutes
Mash Out 168°F 10 minutes

Kentucky Gulch Tripel

Brewers usually pair their oak with darker beers. Kentucky Gulch is a pale tripel. Use well-soaked beans to add less raw oak taste and more spicy wood and vanilla to match the spicy yeast.

Style: Tripel
Brew Type: All Grain
For 5.5 gallons at 1.086, 5.2 SRM, 19
    IBUs, 9.4 percent ABV
60-minute boil

Directions

1. Follow the Multistep Brew Process (pages 284-285).

2. Add oak (without bourbon) to the secondary and rack beer from primary. Age for 4 weeks in the forties to encourage more subtle extraction and aid clarity.

TIP

When pairing oak, look at what you want to counterpoint the malt profile. Well-aged oak carries less tannic bite and works better in drier beers like a tripel.

Malt/Grain/Sugar
14.00 pounds Pilsner Malt
0.25 pound Aromatic Malt
0.25 pound Caramel Pils (Crystal 8L)

Extract (for 13.0 pounds of Pilsner Malt)
10.00 pounds Pale Liquid Malt Extract (LME)

Hops
0.30 ounce Magnum (14.0 percent AA) Pellet for 60 minutes
0.50 ounce Tettnanger Tettnang (4.3 percent AA) Pellet for 15 minutes
0.50 ounce Czech Saaz (3.8 percent AA) Pellet for 5 minutes

Other Ingredients
1 tablet Whirlfloc
2 ounces Medium Toast French Oak (soaked in Bourbon for minimum 4 weeks)

Yeast
Wyeast 3787 Trappist High Gravity/WLP500 Trappist Ale

Mash Schedule
Protein Rest 120°F 30 minutes
Saccharification Rest 150°F 90 minutes

Denny's Bourbon Vanilla Imperial Porter

People love this recipe. The interplay of the vanilla bean and the bourbon makes this an electrifying dessert beer. So good and famous that Wyeast reproduced his favorite yeast.

Style: Porter
Brew Type: All Grain
For 5.0 gallons at 1.086, 45 SRM, 31 IBUs, 8.8 percent ABV
60-minute boil

Directions

1. Follow the Single-Infusion Brew Process (page 284).

2. Split vanilla beans, scrape out the caviar, and add with the chopped beans to the secondary. Allow to soak for 5 to 14 days.

3. At bottling, add the bourbon to the bottling bucket along with the beer and priming sugar. Allow to age for at least 2 months in the bottle.

TIP

In this recipe, the bourbon is a flavoring, so go top shelf. Cheap booze will kill the flavor you're working hard for.

Malt/Grain/Sugar
11.00 pounds Domestic Two-Row Pale Malt
2.50 pounds Munich Malt
1.50 pounds British Brown Malt
1.25 pounds Chocolate Malt
1.00 pound Crystal 120L
0.50 pound Crystal 40L

Extract (for 10.0 pounds of Pale Malt)
7.50 pounds Pale Liquid Malt Extract (LME)

Hops
0.65 ounce Magnum (15.0 percent AA) Whole for 60 minutes
0.40 ounce East Kent Goldings (6.0 percent AA) Whole for 10 minutes

Other Ingredients
1 tablet Whirlfloc
2 whole Vanilla Beans (for secondary)
350 ml Bourbon (or to taste, for bottling)

Yeast
Wyeast 2450 Denny's Favorite/Wyeast 1056 Chico Ale

Mash Schedule
Saccharification Rest 155°F 60 minutes

Gonzo Hemp Poppy Spirit Wine

The ultimate example of surprising yourself. This beer was thrown together at the last minute after the suicide of Hunter S. Thompson. It is a running joke on the drugs Hunter was known for consuming from the "acid" malt to the "Coke" at the knockout. Turned out to be an amazingly well-balanced beer.

Style: Barleywine
Brew Type: All Grain
For 5.5 gallons at 1.104, 14 SRM, 94
    IBUs, 11.8 percent ABV
90-minute boil

Directions

1. Follow the Single-Infusion Brew Process (page 284).

2. While the beer is mashing, combine the tequila, bourbon, and Coke in a glass and soak the shiitake mushrooms in it. Just before adding the amarillo, squeeze the mushrooms dry, collecting the liquid and add with the remaining bourbon/tequila/Coke mixture.

Malt/Grain/Sugar
10.00 pounds Domestic Two-Row Pale Malt
9.25 pounds Maris Otter Pale Malt
1.00 pound Crystal 40L
6.00 ounces Biscuit Malt
6.00 ounces Melanoidin Malt
0.25 pound Special B Malt
2.00 ounces Acidualted Malt
1.00 pound Dark Sugar (Add during the boil)

Extract (for 18.0 pounds of Pale Malt)
12.50 pounds Pale Liquid Malt Extract (LME)

Hops
0.15 ounce Summit (18.1 percent AA) Pellet for 60 minutes
1.00 ounce Warrior (16.1 percent AA) Pellet for 60 minutes
1.50 ounces Centennial (7.5 percent AA) Pellet for 30 minutes
1.25 ounces Palisade (9.3 percent AA) Pellet for 10 minutes
2.00 ounces Amarillo (8.3 percent AA) Pellet for 0 minutes

Other Ingredients
1 tablet Whirlfloc
1 tablespoon Yeast Nutrient
2 tablespoons Hemp Seeds, Crushed (Add at 5 minutes)
1 teaspoon Poppy Seed (Add at 5 minutes)
3 Dried Shiitake Mushrooms
1.5 ounces Bourbon
1.5 ounces Tequila
1.5 ounces Coca-Cola

Yeast
Wyeast 1272 American Ale II

Mash Schedule
Saccharification Rest 150°F 90 minutes

Imperial Anything

Americans have the reputation of going outsized: bigger cars, bigger houses, and bigger everything. As witnessed by the number of imperial beers, the brewing scene is no different. Traditional brewers argue that imperial brewers are sacrificing the subtle beauty of brew for the sake of an outsized flavor hit. Where's the skill in throwing a bunch of stuff at the wall and seeing what sticks?

There is truth to that argument, but there's still skill needed to create a drinkable beer that clearly expresses its origins. Simply scaling up all the

Falling Man Wheat Wine

What happens when you push a boring, staid hoppy American wheat beer too far? You end up with a pale beer of sweet wheat and a mean kick to the teeth.

Style: Strong Wheat Ale
Brew Type: All Grain
For 5.5 gallons at 1.085, 5 SRM, 65 IBUs, 9.0 percent ABV
60-minute boil

Directions

Follow the Single-Infusion Brew Process (page 284).

TIP

The hopping schedule for this beer is designed to play a trick on the drinker. It's packed with low-cohumulone bittering and Hallertau-derived hops typical of a wheat ale until that tricky finish with the grapefruit pow of the amarillo.

Malt/Grain/Sugar
8.00 pounds Malted Wheat
7.00 pounds Domestic Two-Row Pale Malt
0.25 pound CaraVienne Malt
1.00 pound Turbinado Sugar (Add during the boil)

Extract (for 8.0 pounds of Wheat Malt and 6 pounds of Pale Malt)
10.50 pounds Wheat Liquid Malt Extract (LME)

Hops
1.00 ounce Santiam (6.8 percent AA) Pellet—First Wort Hopped
0.25 ounce Warrior (17.1 percent AA) Pellet for 60 minutes
0.75 ounce Palisade (9.4 percent AA) Pellet for 30 minutes
1.00 ounce Glacier (5.8 percent AA) Pellet for 15 minutes
1.00 ounce Amarillo (9.4 percent AA) Pellet for 5 minutes
0.50 ounce Glacier (5.8 percent AA) Pellet—Dry-Hop
0.50 ounce Amarillo (9.4 percent AA) Pellet—Dry-Hop

Other Ingredients
1 tablet Whirlfloc
1 tablespoon Yeast Nutrient

Yeast
Wyeast 1056 Chico Ale/WLP001 California Ale/US-05 American Ale

Mash Schedule
Saccharification Rest 152°F 60 minutes

ingredients to push the gravity and IBUs doesn't do it. Even in these imperial beers you want a sense of balance and that desire for another pint.

Style purists get agitated by the term "imperial." They argue that it only makes sense for Russian Imperial Stout since the style was brewed for an imperial court. They joked about the willingness to imperialize anything by loudly proclaiming their wait for an imperial mild. Stone Brewing obliged them in 2004 with the release of their Stone 8th Anniversary Ale, an imperialized version of Lee's Mild.

Abby Imperial UK IPA

IPA imperialization is not just for Americans. Here we get an organic hippy spin on a British IPA that harkens back to the day when beers were stronger.

Style: British Imperial IPA
Brew Type: All Grain
For 6.0 gallons at 1.090, 18 SRM, 80 IBUs, 9.6 percent ABV
120-minute boil

Directions

Follow the Single-Infusion Brew Process (page 284).

TIP

The sugar additions in this recipe is designed to yield a beer with a lower finishing gravity. This is critical to a successful imperial beer.

Malt/Grain/Sugar
17.00 pounds Maris Otter Malt
2.00 pounds British Crystal 40L
2.00 pounds Dark Brown Sugar (Add during the boil)

Extract (for 16.0 pounds of Pale Malt)
12.50 pounds Pale Liquid Malt Extract (LME)

Hops
4.25 ounces Spalt (4.5 percent AA) Pellet for 60 minutes
1.50 ounces Organic Hallertaur (8.00 percent AA) Whole for 15 minutes
1.00 ounce East Kent Goldings (4.7 percent AA) Whole for 5 minutes
0.50 ounce Organic Hallertaur (8.00 percent AA) Whole for 1 minute

Other Ingredients
1 tablet Whirlfloc
1 tablespoon Yeast Nutrient

Yeast
Wyeast 1056 Chico Ale/WLP001 California Ale/US-05 American Ale

Mash Schedule
Saccharification Rest 153°F 90 minutes

The Land of the Extremely Strong Beer

With most brewers happy to imperialize their beers to a potent 10 to 12 percent ABV, you might think that's the end of the story. After all, beer yeasts weren't supposed to survive more than 13 percent alcohol. Both Boston Beer Company (also called Sam Adams) and Delaware's Dogfish Head Brewing set out to prove the common wisdom wrong. In their arms race to the summit, they shattered old records. By the turn of the millennium both Sam Adams's Utopias and Dogfish Head's World Wide Stout were over 20 percent. The current champion, Utopias, weighs in at more than 25 percent ABV!

Blackwine IV

This thick, rich, and stupidly potent beer carries clear lines of influence both to Dogfish Head's World Wide Stout and San Diego's Alesmith Speedway Stout, an espresso-infused 12-percent ABV stout.

Style: Mega Beer
Brew Type: All Grain
For 5.5 gallons at 1.162, 80 SRM, 117 IBUs, 18.0 percent ABV
180-minute boil

Directions

1. Follow the Single-Infusion Brew Process (page 284).

2. Take the first gallon of runoff and mix in one pound of sugar. Boil until the total volume is approximately a half gallon. Add back to the runoff. Mix the remaining pound of sugar into the runoff before the boil begins.

Malt/Grain/Sugar
12.00 pounds Domestic Two-Row Pale Malt
12.00 pounds Maris Otter Pale Malt
2.25 pounds Roasted Barley
1.00 pound Flaked Barley
1.00 pound Flaked Oats
0.75 pound Chocolate Malt
0.75 pound Crystal 90L Malt
0.25 pound Acidulated Malt
2.00 pounds Muscovado Sugar (see instructions for use)

Hops
0.50 ounce Northern Brewer (6.2 percent AA) Pellet—First Wort Hopped
0.50 ounce Mt Hood (5.4 percent AA) Pellet—First Wort Hopped
1.00 ounce Eroica (12.00 percent AA) Pellet for 90 minutes
1.00 ounce Chinook (15.90 percent AA) Pellet for 90 minutes
0.50 ounce Northern Brewer (6.2 percent AA) Pellet for 30 minutes
0.50 ounce Eroica (12.00 percent AA) Pellet for 5 minutes
0.50 ounce Mt Hood (5.4 percent AA) Pellet for 5 minutes
2.0 ounces Mt Hood (4.3 percent AA) Whole for 0 minutes

Other Ingredients
1 tablet Whirlfloc
1 tablespoon Yeast Nutrient
2 cups Organic Ground Coffee (added to the mash)

Yeast
Wyeast 1272 American Ale II—1 gallon+ Starter or Yeast Cake

Mash Schedule
Saccharification Rest 152°F 60 minutes

The beer is served flat from a glass bottle shaped to resemble a copper brewing kettle. Jim Koch of Sam Adams credits his "ninja yeast" for the potentcy.

Brewing to these heights requires patience, enough yeast to ferment the world, and a shade of luck. Making them amazingly approachable and drinkable requires a deal with the devil. Multiple sugar additions and rounds of oxygenation to acclimatize the yeast to higher and higher concentrations of ethanol make the task more labor intensive, but it can yield great results.

Frankenale

Frankenale is the Utopias to the Blackwine's World Wide Stout and came about via a brewer's vacation. Worried that his yeast would be bored during his vacation, he threw every sugar in the kitchen into the carboy and let it ride. The end result was a beer of epically stupid proportions that compares favorably to Sam Adams's product.

Style: Mega Beer
Brew Type: Partial Mash
For 5.0 gallons at 1.203, 17 SRM, 382 IBUs, 23.0 percent ABV
90-minute boil

Directions

1. Follow the Single-Infusion Brew Process (page 284).

2. All of the sugars are added slowly over the course of a few weeks. Whenever the fermentation appears to be slowing, boil the sugar in just enough water to dissolve for 15 minutes and add to the carboy. Swirl to mix. Eventually the yeast will cry uncle; hit with rehydrated wine yeast and sit back. This will take around a year to approach drinkable.

Malt/Grain/Sugar
13.50 pounds Pale Liquid Malt Extract
4.50 pounds Domestic Two-Row Pale Malt
0.75 pound Cara-Pils Dextrine Malt
0.50 pound Flaked Barley
2.00 pounds Corn Sugar (see instructions for use)
2.00 pounds Brown Sugar (see instructions for use)
2.00 pounds Honey (see instructions for use)
1.50 pounds Turbinado Sugar (see instructions for use)
1.00 pound Cane Sugar (see instructions for use)

Hops
13.50 ounces Bullion (9.0 percent AA) Pellet for 90 minutes
1.50 ounces Fuggle (5.1 percent AA) Pellet for 15 minutes
1.50 ounces Cascade (5.4 percent AA) Pellet for 2 minutes

Other Ingredients
1 tablet Whirlfloc
1 tablespoon Yeast Nutrient

Yeast
Wyeast 1056 Chico Ale/WLP001 California Ale/US-05—1 gallon+ Starter or Yeast Cake
Red Star Premier Cuvee (to finish)

Mash Schedule
Saccharification Rest 152°F 60 minutes

TIP

There is a practical limit to the IBUs you can cram into beer, and the higher you go, in gravity and bitterness, the less you can stuff in solution. The calculations don't compensate for this, so when you see an IBU listing above 80, be a little suspicious.

Brutal Brewing

Champagne—the tiny bubbles go straight to your head. Over the years many brewers have tried to capture or capitalize on those famous little bubbles. Miller High Life, for instance, used to arrive in mini bottles touting it as "The Champagne of Beers." Since the turn of the millennium, a pair of Belgian brewers have moved beyond the rhetoric and created bottled beers using the traditional labor intensive "Méthode Champenoise." Both Bosteel's DeuS and Landtsheer's Malheur Brut are incredibly finely carbonated beers reminiscent of champagne despite their barley natures.

The goal of the method is to produce a highly carbonated drink with fine bubbles and superb clarity with no yeast. This is accomplished by bottling the beer in champagne bottles with a large dose of sugar syrup and capping the bottle. It is left to sit undisturbed for a month before being laid on its side. Slowly, over the course of a month or two, the bottle is brought to rest on its cap. Each day as the bottle is elevated slighty it is given a sharp twist to knock yeast off the bottle.

After settling for a month on the cap, the bottles are chilled and then frozen and disgorged. The chilled bottles are set cap first in a vat of acetone and dry ice. Within a minute the −40°C/F mixture freezes an ice plug in the neck that traps all the yeast. The bottle is then aimed away and opened. In a second, the ice plug shoots out and the bottle is refilled lightly with some extra beer or spiced sugar syrup. A cork is placed into the neck and a wire cage is screwed on. Voila! You have champagne beer. Do a Web search and you'll find more information online to further demonstrate the process.

The level of effort involved with one of these project beers demands partners, but don't be intimidated. There's a reason that the Belgian professionals can charge $20 to $40 for a bottle of champagne beer after all.

Brut du Faucon

This is the pale champagne beer (the Brut of the Falcon) that kicked things off. Pushy carbonation drives the spices to burst on your palate and in your nose. The lavender proves an unexpected flavor, while the ginger offers a peppery sweetness that distracts from how little sugar remains.

Style: Champagne Beer
Brew Type: All Grain
For 5.5 gallons at 1.085, 5 SRM, 22 IBUs, 12.0 percent ABV
60-minute boil

Directions

1. Follow the Single-Infusion Brew Process (page 284).

2. Make the priming sugar by bringing 1 cup of water to the boil, add the sugar, stir to dissolve, and return to the boil. Add the spices and boil for 15 minutes before straining through a coffee filter.

3. Follow the bottling instructions in text.

TIP

The usual Belgian quest for a dry finish is even more important in this beer. With so much priming sugar coming on board, you must have a perfectly dry beer to start in order to avoid unexpected extra carbonation or a super-sweet taste.

Malt/Grain/Sugar
13.00 pounds Pilsner Malt
0.25 pound Caramel Pils
0.25 pound Aromatic Malt
2.00 pounds Light Sugar

Hops
1.00 ounce Styrian Goldings (5.25 percent AA) Pellet for 60 minutes
0.50 ounce Czech Saaz (3.50 percent AA) Pellet for 20 minutes

Other Ingredients
1 tablet Whirlfloc
1 tablespoon Yeast Nutrient
0.12 teaspoon ground Allspice
0.5 teaspoon ground Cinnamon
0.25 teaspoon ground Black Pepper
0.25 teaspoon ground Ginger
0.5 teaspoon Lavender, crushed
0.5 pound Priming Sugar

Yeast
Wyeast 3787 Trappist High Gravity

Mash Schedule
Saccharification Rest 147°F 60 minutes

Brut du Faucon Noir

Where the original Brut is a pale beer with an aggressively dry profile, the Noir takes a rounder approach to the finish. The final clearing dryness is provided by a stronger carbonation (roughly 5.5 volumes as opposed to the original Brut's 3.5 volumes).

Style: Champagne Beer
Brew Type: All Grain
For 5.5 gallons at 1.084, 18 SRM, 18 IBUs, 12.0 percent ABV
90-minute boil

Directions

1. Follow the Single-Infusion Brew Process (page 284).

2. Make the priming sugar by bringing 1 cup of water to the boil, add the sugar, stir to dissolve, and return to the boil. Add the spices and boil for 15 minutes before straining through a coffee filter.

3. Follow the bottling instructions in text.

TIP

All wrapped up with their corks and cages and even foils if you choose, the Bruts make great gifts. Given at Christmas, they're perfect for that midnight New Year's toast.

Malt/Grain/Sugar
10.00 pounds Pilsner Malt
0.75 pounds Wheat Pils
0.50 pound Special B Malt
0.25 pound Carafa II Special Dehusked Chocolate Malt
2.00 pounds Light Sugar
0.50 pound Turbinado Sugar

Extract (for 16.0 pounds of Pale Malt)
12.50 pounds Pale Liquid Malt Extract (LME)

Hops
1.00 ounce Styrian Goldings (5.25 percent AA) Pellet for 60 minutes
0.50 ounce Czech Saaz (3.50 percent AA) Pellet for 20 minutes

Other Ingredients
1 tablet Whirlfloc
1 tablespoon Yeast Nutrient
0.12 teaspoon ground Allspice
0.5 teaspoon ground Cinnamon
0.12 teaspoon ground Mace
1.00 teaspoon Double Strength Vanilla Extract
0.75 pound Priming Sugar

Yeast
Wyeast 3787 Trappist High Gravity

Mash Schedule
Saccharification Rest 149°F 90 minutes

Bacteria: The Friendly Germs

Every cleaning and sanitation step you do serves the purpose of suppression of spoilage bacteria and wild yeast. Some brewers take a step outside all the chemicals and efforts to pursue a chance to add the funk to their beer. However, this isn't the wild and wooly world of lambic brewing they roam through. Both Wyeast and White Labs provide cultures of Brettanomyces strains, Lactobacillus, and Pediococcus.

Brettanomyces bring earthy, spicy, pineapple fruity flavors to a beer. Brett does better with a starter to build up their slow growing populations. With sufficient time and starter size, you can pitch a beer with nothing but Brett and attempt a full "wild" fermentation. It will take longer and be less active, but you get a remarkably aromatic character.

Brettanomyces save their biggest aroma and flavor show for their performances in secondary as backup singers. Flamboyantly wild earthy flavors spring forth along with a touch of acidity. To achieve this character, make a large, decanted starter and add a shot of food: sugar syrup, boiled DME, fresh starter wort, and so on, then sit back and wait. After a month, a slightly greasy white film (a "pellicle") will form and the Brett's real work begins. An additional six to nine months later your reward will be an off-kilter beer that surprises people.

Regarding equipment, keep track of what gear touches the wildlife. If you can, use separate fermenters, racking canes, tubing, and kegs for these beers. It will simplify your life. If that's not to be the case, super sanitize everything thoroughly unless you want the Brett to develop as a part of your house profile, like some Belgian breweries.

Tempting Fate

Inspired by Russian River Brewing Company's "Temptation," a golden ale aged in used Chardonnay barrels and funkified with the house's blend of micro flora. The Brett take their sweet time expressing themselves, but given time and a little food, they add a complex earthiness and spiciness that interacts beautifully with the spicy characters of the French oak.

Style: Belgian Specialty Ale
Brew Type: All Grain
For 5.5 gallons at 1.054, 4.3 SRM, 23 IBUs, 5.8 percent ABV
60-minute boil

Directions

1. Follow the Single-Infusion Brew Process (page 284).

2. After cooling, pitch only the Belgian ale yeast. Begin soaking your oak in Chardonnay.

3. Transfer the beer to secondary and pitch both Brettanomyces strains and add about a quart of basic starter beer to give it some extra food. Walk away for 6 months.

4. After 6 months, taste the beer, if there's enough "funkiness" for you, add the oak beans (sans wine) and age for 2 to 4 weeks and then package. Your beer should be at a low terminal gravity (around 1.008) to prevent bottle bombs. Carbonate highly and enjoy.

5. Remember to thoroughly clean and sanitize every piece of equipment used from secondary on before using it with your regular beers.

Malt/Grain/Sugar
10.00 pounds Belgian Pilsner Malt
0.25 pound Biscuit Malt
0.25 pound Caramel Pils (C8) Malt

Extract (for 10.0 pounds of Pilsner Malt)
7.50 pounds Pilsner Liquid Malt Extract (LME)

Hops
1.25 ounces Styrian Goldings (4.2 percent AA) Pellet for 60 minutes

Other Ingredients
2 ounces French Medium Toast Oak Beans Soaked in Chardonnay for 6 months
1 tablespoon Yeast Nutrient

Yeast
Wyeast 1214 Belgian Ale Yeast/WLP550 Belgian Ale Yeast
WLP645 Brettanomyces claussenii
Wyeast 5112 Brettanomyces bruxellensis/WLP650 Brettanomyces bruxellensis

Mash Schedule
Saccharification Rest 150°F 60 minutes

TIP

Want to tempt fate at night? Drop a pound of pilsner malt and add 1 bottle (1.5 pounds) of the dark Belgian candi syrup (D2 variety). Follow all the same instructions except age your oak cubes on Pinot Noir instead of Chardonnay.

APPENDIX A

Recipe Acknowledgments

Thank You

Many, many thanks go out to the following folks who, by donating their recipes and brewing techniques, broadened the number and depth of brewing projects and philosophies brought to you in these pages. Brew their beer and give them a silent raise of the glass. If you ever meet them, rest assured, they'll talk your ear off about beer and maybe even let you buy them a glass or two!

In addition, thanks to the many members of the Maltose Falcons who worked on many of these recipes including Cullen Davis, Kent Fletcher, Jim Kopitzke, and Jonny Lieberman.

Brewer Recipe Credits

Brewer	Recipes
John Aitchison	Brutal Bittered (page 249), Aichtie's Flemish Red (page 236)
Kevin Baranowski	Falconsclaws (page 214)
Bruce Brode	Falkenator Doppelbock/Eisbock (page 212)
Denny Conn	Denny's Bourbon Vanilla Imperial Porter (page 266), Nick Danger Porter (page 242)
Steve Cook	Abby Imperial UK IPA (page 269), Ball-a-Holic Hefeweizen (page 198)
Cullen Davis	Artemis Calliphygia Wit (page 219), Old Fuddy Duddy Old Ale (page 192)
Chris P Frey	Off-Kilter Strong Scotch Ale (page 185)
Kevin Grizard	Black Perle DIPA (page 254)
Tom Hamilton	Bombay Bomber IPA (page 252), Old Rasty Imperial Stout (page 245)
Doug King	Schutzen Lager (page 169), Dougweiser (page 241)
Bill Krouss	Bamberg Burner Rauchbier (page 215)
Jonny Lieberman	Arrogant Sombrero (page 204), Becky's Bootylicious Cinnamon Porter (page 243), Blackwine IV (page 270), Steve French Golden Strong (page 226), Texas Warrior American Brown Ale (page 246)
George Mahoney	Frankenale (page 271)
Todd Peterson	Black Sea Baltic Porter (page 213)
Mark Poliner	Coffee and Cream Stout (page 81)
Maribeth Raines	Anniversary IPA (page 170)
Richard Schmittdiel	Schmitty's Smoked Porter (page 261)
Curt Stock	Gatekeeper Memorial Porter (page 187), Walker Helles (page 206)
Gregg Van Citters	GVC's Imperial Chocolate Porter (page 79), Haarlem Bokbier (page 227)
Diane Van Wagner	Benton's Bitter (page 181)
Tom Wolf	Old Rasty Imperial Stout (page 245), Old Smokey (page 256)
Jamil Zainasheff	Evil Twin (page 247), Trigo Oscuro (page 199)

APPENDIX B

Additional Resources

Further Reading

You'll find a great number of books on beer and brewing on the market. Explore these books to learn even more! Even if they cover some of the same ground, every author's take is different enough to yield useful nuggets for your brewing.

General Brewing

The Complete Joy of Homebrewing by Charlie Papazian: The granddaddy of homebrewing books. Written by the founder of the American Homebrewer's Association. Learn what it means to "Relax! Don't Worry! Have a homebrew!"

How to Brew by John Palmer: Recent book that contains information for beginning, intermediate, and advanced brewers with an emphasis on the technical aspects of brewing.

New Brewing Lager Beer by Gregory Noonan: This is the advanced tome of craft and homebrewing. This book digs into the meat of brewing mechanics and chemistry.

Designing Great Beers by Ray Daniels: Using recipes from the National Homebrewing Competition, Daniels analyzes what makes an award-winning beer. The front of the book offers invaluable lessons in calculating everything you need to design your recipe.

The Compleat Meadmaker by Ken Schramm: The most complete treatise on meadmaking from an award-winning meadmaker. Includes information on different yeast strains, honey types, and effects of fruit in a mead.

Style and Recipe Books

Beer (Eyewitness Companions) by Michael Jackson: The final book from Michael Jackson, beer writer nonpareil. This pocket guide covers the major brewing centers of the world and key beers from each. There are no recipes, but the writing transports you to the café sharing a beer with the writer. Look for his other books, too!

The Classic Beer Styles Series by various authors: Each volume in the eighteen-book series tackles a different beer style in depth. They cover the history of the style, how commercial examples are made, and how that translates to success at home.

Brewing Classic Styles by Jamil Zainasheff and John Palmer: Zainasheff is the homebrewer's Babe Ruth. Winner of more medals than anyone else, Zainasheff presents his award-winning recipes for eighty different styles of beer. Includes recipes for extract and all-grain brewers alike.

Radical Brewing by Randy Mosher: In need of some inspiration? Want to find a different direction to take? Look no further than this book. Trawling through endless historical brewing volumes, Mosher resurrects obscure styles and encourages you to try unusual ingredients in your next batch.

Extreme Brewing by Sam Calagione: Dogfish Head Brewing is known for their take on extreme beers, laced with hops, unusual fruits, and wood. Owner Sam Calagione recruits fellow "extreme" brewers to present advanced extract-based versions of their famous beers.

Clone Brews and *Beer Captured* by Tess and Mark Szamatulski: The owners of Maltose Express in Connecticut formulated clone recipes of 300 famous beers for their customers. These two books cover all their experiments.

Brewing Magazines/Newspapers

Ale Street News—One of America's oldest beer rags, covers the world of American beer with a focus on the Mid-Atlantic and New England

Beer—A new monthly magazine dedicated to the younger, inexperienced beer enthusiast.

Beer Advocate: The Magazine—A monthly magazine dedicated to fostering greater public understanding of the beer world. Includes beer reviews, beer cooking tips, beer style, opinion, and homebrew columns. (N.B.—The BYOB column is written by the author).

Brewing News—A network of regional brewspapers with independent columnists covering their regional happenings.

Brew Your Own—One of two dedicated homebrewing magazines. Focuses on the practical project-oriented brewer.

Celebrator Brewing News—America's oldest brewspaper. Includes features on travels to smaller breweries around the world and a small flight of tasting notes per issue.

Draft—A bimonthly magazine dedicated to the beer lifestyle. Well produced with a celebrity interview per issue and beer lifestyle articles.

Zymurgy—The official newsletter of the American Homebrewers Association, the bimonthly magazine has numerous feature articles on brewing styles, Q&A, and beer news. Subscription comes with a free membership to the AHA and access to perks like their pub discount program.

Online Resources

Beer Review Sites

BeerAdvocate.com—Based out of Boston, MA, this is the world's largest membership-driven rating site with active forums and pub and beer reviews.

RateBeer.com—With the most beer ratings of any site online, the California/Canadian site produces regular ranked lists of members' favorite beers.

Discussion Forums

BeerAdvocate
(*http://beeradvocate.com/forum/list/2*)

Brew Board
(*www.brewboard.com*)

The Brewing Network
(*www.thebrewingnetwork.com/forum*)

Got Mead?
(*www.gotmead.com/forum/index.php*)

More Flavor
(*http://forums.moreflavor.com*)

Northern Brewer
(*http://forum.northernbrewer.com*)

Rate Beer's Forums
(*www.ratebeer.com/Forums*)

Recipe Sites

Beer Recipator (*http://hbd.org/recipator*)
The oldest-running-recipe calculator and database. More than 6,000 recipes!

BeerRecipes.org
A new recipe collection website with forums for discussing.

BeerTools.com
The most comprehensive recipe website out there. Helps users formulate recipes, analyzes where they lie in the guidelines, and allows users to review and update recipes over time.

Brewing Organizations

The American Homebrewers Association
Based out of Boulder, CO, this is the group looking out for the American homebrewer. Publishes *Zymurgy* six times per year, runs a pub discount program, rallies at craft breweries, sponsors National Big Brew and Mead Days, and more, including hosting the world's largest beer competition.

The Beer Judge Certification Program
Trains and certifies beer judges and registers competitions. The BJCP maintains and updates the large style guidelines used as a baseline for homebrewers everywhere.

APPENDIX C

Calculations

A note about units. If not specified otherwise, gravity is always calculated in "Gravity Units" = (Gravity − 1) × 1000. E.g. 1.050 = 50 gravity

Extract Calculations

Converting LME Amounts to DME and Back

$\text{Pounds Needed}_{\text{new extract}} = (\text{Pounds}_{\text{current extract}} \times \text{Gravity}_{\text{current extract}}) / \text{Gravity}_{\text{new extract}}$

Where Gravity = 37 for LME, 46 for DME

Extract for Grain

$\text{Extract}_{\text{pounds needed}} = (\text{Malt}_{\text{pounds}} \times 27) / \text{Extract}_{\text{gravity}}$

Where $\text{Extract}_{\text{gravity}} = 37$ for LME, 46 for DME

Remember when choosing extracts, stay pale and try and match base malts and country of origin.

Needed Extract for Partial Mash

Plug into the previous formula the amount of malt you can't mash to find out how much extract you need.

Recipe Calculations

Calculating Gravity

For gravity potentials, refer to the table on page 24 for grain and use either the generic 37 pppg for LME and 46 pppg for DME or your specific values. For unknown systems assume system efficiency of 75 percent

$\text{Gravity}_{\text{Malt}} = (\text{Potential}_{\text{Malt1}} + \text{Potential}_{\text{Malt2}} + \ldots + \text{Potential}_{\text{Malt N}}) \times \text{System Efficiency}$

$\text{Gravity}_{\text{Sugar/Extracts}} = (\text{Potential}_{\text{Sugar/Extracts1}} + \text{Potential}_{\text{Sugar/Extracts2}} + \ldots + \text{Potential}_{\text{Sugar/Extracts N}})$

$\text{Overall Gravity Potential} = \text{Gravity}_{\text{Malt}} + \text{Gravity}_{\text{Sugar/Extracts}}$

$\text{Original Gravity}_{\text{Predicted}} = \text{Original Gravity Potential} / \text{Batch Size}$

Calculating AAU (Alpha Acid Units)

AAU = Weight (hops) × AA percent (recipe)

Calculating IBUs

IBU (addition) = (AAU × Utilization percent × 7490) / Volume (beer)

TINSETH ALPHA ACID UTILIZATION FACTOR				
Boil Time	1.030	1.050	1.070	1.090
0	0	0	0	0
1	0.01	0.01	0.01	0.01
5	0.06	0.05	0.04	0.03
10	0.10	0.08	0.07	0.06
15	0.14	0.11	0.10	0.08
20	0.17	0.14	0.12	0.10
25	0.19	0.16	0.13	0.11
30	0.21	0.18	0.15	0.12
45	0.25	0.21	0.18	0.15
50	0.26	0.22	0.18	0.15
60	0.28	0.23	0.19	0.16
70	0.29	0.24	0.20	0.17
80	0.29	0.24	0.20	0.17
90	0.30	0.25	0.21	0.17

Calculating BU:GU

BUGU is a useful measurement for thinking about the amount of bitterness in a beer versus the maltiness. For more information see *Designing Great Beers* by Ray Daniels.

$BUGU = IBU_{batch}$ / Original Gravity Units

Calculating Color

Sum together for each malt, extract, grain, and sugar ingredient:

$Color_{Ingredient} = Lovibond\ Ingredient \times Weight_{pounds\ Ingredient}$

Divide the Color sum by the Batch Size for approximate color.

Example:

A 5 gallon batch consists of 5lbs Pale LME (Rated 3Lovibond) and ½ lb of Crystal 40L.

Color Sum = $(5 \times 3) + (½ \times 40) = 35$

Batch Color = $35 / 5 = 7L$

This is a very rough estimate.

Mash Calculations

Basic Mash Equation

$Grain_{Factor} + Water_{Factor} = Mash_{Factor}$

where

$Grain_{Specific\ Heat} = Weight_{Grain} \times 0.05$

$Grain_{Factor} = Grain_{Specific\ Heat} \times Temperature_{Grain}$

$Water_{Specific\ Heat} = Volume_{Gallons\ Strike\ Water}$

$Water_{Factor} = Water_{Specific\ Heat} \times Temperature_{Water}$

$Mash_{Specific\ Heat} = (Weight_{Grain} \times 0.05) + Volume_{Gallons\ Water}$

$Mash_{Factor} = Mash_{Specific\ Heat} \times Temperature_{Mash}$

Strike Water Temperature

$Strike\ Water\ Temperature = (Mash_{Factor} - Grain_{Factor})$ / $Volume_{Gallons\ Water}$

Example: Find the temperature needed for a mash with 10 pounds of grain, 12 quarts of strike water, and a desired rest temperature of 153°F

$Weight_{Grain} = 10$ pounds

$Temperature_{Grain} = 70°F$

$Volume_{Gallons\ Strike\ Water} = 3.0$ gallons

$Temperature_{Mash} = 153°F$

$Mash_{Specific\ Heat} = (10 \times 0.05) + 3$

$Mash_{Factor} = 3.5 \times 153 = 535.5$

$Grain_{Specific\ Heat} = 10 \times 0.05 = 0.5$

$Grain_{Factor} = 0.5 \times 70 = 35$

$Strike\ Water\ Temperature = (535.5 - 35) / 3 = 166.8°F$

Mash Infusion Equation:

How much boiling water is needed raise a mash to the next temperature? The equation depends on the differences in temperature between known temps.

$Temperature_{Mash-Grain} = Temperature_{Mash} - Temperature_{Grain}$

$Temperature_{Mash-Strike} = Temperature_{Mash} - Temperature_{Strike\ Water}$

$Temperature_{Boil-Mash} = Temperature_{BoilingWater} - Temperature_{Mash}$

$Total\ Heat_{Grain} = Grain_{Specific\ Heat} \times Temperature_{Mash-Grain}$

$Total\ Heat_{Strike\ Water} = Volume_{Gallons\ Strike\ Water} \times Temperature_{Mash-Strike}$

$Volume_{Boiling\ Water} = (Total\ Heat_{Grain} + Total\ Heat_{Strike\ Water})$ / $Temperature_{Boil-Mash}$

Example: Boost the previous mash to 168°F with boiling water (210°F for heat loss)

$Temperature_{Mash} = 168°F$

$Temperature_{Mash-Grain} = 168°F - 70°F = 98°F$

$Temperature_{Mash-Strike} = 168°F - 166.8°F = 1.2°F$

$Temperature_{Boil-Mash} = 210°F - 168°F = 42°F$

$Total\ Heat_{Grain} = 0.5 × 98°F = 49°F$

$Total\ Heat_{Strike\ Water} = 3.0\ gallons × 1.2°F = 3.5$

$Volume_{Boiling\ Water} = (49 + 3.5) / 42 = 1.25\ gallons$

Mid Brew Calculations

Calculating Dilution or Concentration

V1 = Volume you have

G1 = Gravity you have

V2 = Target Volume

G2 = Target Gravity

The basic equation

V1 × G1 = V2 × G2

If you want to know what your gravity will be after a boil or if you dilute, you can solve the equation as:

(V1 × G1) / V2 = G2

5 gallons of beer at 1.050 concentrated to 4 gallons will yield:

(5.0 × 50) 4.5 = 55.5 or 1.055.5

If you want to dilute a beer that's too high in gravity, you can calculate how much water is needed by

(V1 × G1) / G2 = V2

V2 − V1 = V (amount of water needed)

If you have 5 gallons at 1.060 and want a beer at 1.055, the amount of water needed to dilute is:

(5.0 × 60) / 55 = 5.45

5.45 − 5.0 = 0.45 gallons of water

Calculating Efficiency

$Original\ Gravity_{Expected\ Perfect}$ = Gravity calculated for ingredients at 100 percent efficiency

$Volume_{Recipe\ Size}$ = Gallons recipe was calculated for

$Original\ Gravity_{Observed}$ = Gravity measured by hydrometer

$Volume_{Observed}$ = Gallons of wort when measured

$System\ Efficiency = (Original\ Gravity_{Observed} × Volume_{Observed}) / (Original\ Gravity_{Expected\ Perfect} × Volume_{Recipe\ Size})$

Fermentation Calculations

Calculating Attenuation

Apparent Attenuation = 100 × ((Original Gravity − Final Gravity) / Original Gravity)

Calculating Alcohol

Alcohol By Volume = (Original Gravity − Final Gravity) / 7.5

Alcohol By Weight = (ABV) × .78

Unit Conversions

Plato / Brix to Specific Gravity

Specific Gravity = 1 + Plato / (258.6 − ((Plato / 258.2) × 227.1))

Convert Fahrenheit to Celsius and Back

Celsius = (Fahrenheit − 32) / 1.8

Fahrenheit = (Celsius × 1.8) + 32

Standard Brewing Processes

Steeping Grains and Extract Process

This profile covers the basic procedure used in brewing extract beer with steeping grains. The recipes in the book are converted for this procedure as well as all grain. To do so, use the amount of malt extract specified in the "extract" section of the recipe and subtract the specified amount of malt from the grain bill.

For instance, a recipe calls for 17 pounds of Maris Otter Malt. The extract section calls for 12.5 pounds to replace 16 pounds of Maris Otter. Use 1 pound of Maris Otter in your steep and 12.5 pounds of LME for the boil.

If you wish to use DME and LME is specified, remember you only need 80 percent as much DME. Multiply the LME weight by 0.8 to calculate the amount of DME needed. In the above example you could substitute 10 pounds of DME (12.5 pounds × 0.8 = 10 pounds).

Steeping Grains Instructions

1. Heat 3 quarts of filtered water to 165°F. Turn off the heat. Have 3 to 4 gallons of filtered water chilling in the fridge or freezer.
2. If using, place the crushed malt into a grain bag and submerge the bag in the steeping water. If not using a grain bag, stir the crushed malt into water. Steep for 45 minutes
3. While the grain is steeping, heat another 3 quarts of filtered water to 170°F
4. With loose grain, line a colander with several layers of cheese cloth or use a fine-mesh strainer. With a grain bag, put the bag in a colander. Suspend colander over your boiling pot (20 quarts or larger) and pour the steeping liquid through the colander.

5. Rinse the grains with the heated water. Remove the colander and grains and bring your boil kettle to a vigorous boil.
6. Remove the kettle from the heat and stir in the extract. Stir thoroughly, making sure that all the extract is dissolved and the pot bottom is free of any residue. Return to the boil.
7. Once at a boil, begin timing your boil and add hops as specified in the recipe. For instance add the 60 minutes hops when 60 minutes are remaining in the boil. (This is typically the start of the boil, but some recipes do specify longer boils of 75 to 120 minutes. Start counting down and when you hit 60, add the hops.)
8. At boil's end, add any last-minute hop additions. Vigorously stir the pot to create a whirlpool effect, place the lid on and wait 10 minutes. Chill the beer to 90°F to 100°F with a chiller or place the pot in a sink full of ice and barely running cold water.
9. Pour the lukewarm wort into your sanitized fermenter and add chilled water to bring to the desired volume (5.5 gallons typically). Seal the bucket or insert a sanitized stopper in the carboy and shake the beer for 10 minutes to mix.
10. Open the fermenter and grab a hydrometer sample to record your original gravity. Add the yeast to the fermenter.
11. Refer to the Fermentation and Packaging section of this appendix (page 285).

Late-Extract Variant

To brew a paler-colored extract batch, during Step 6 only add a third of the total extract to the kettle. When there are 15 to 20 minutes remaining in the boil, add the remaining extract, making sure to dissolve it completely.

Full-Boil Variant

For a major step up in attenuation and hop character, boil the full beer volume with a larger pot. After rinsing the grains with hot water, add enough water to the kettle to equal your target volume plus 1 gallon per hour of boil time. For example, in a recipe yielding 5.5 gallons with a 60-minute boil clock, fill the partially filled kettle to 6.5 gallons. For a 90-minute boil, fill to 7 gallons. The extra volume compensates for water lost during the boil. To chill rapidly, it is advisable to invest in a chiller instead of cold water baths

For extra-pale beer, you can combine the full boil and late-extract variants.

Single-Infusion Brew Process

Single-infusion mash is the simplest and most versatile mash schedule used extensively in the British and American brewing worlds. This mash regimen takes advantage of the complete conversion of modern barley malt. Before developing better strains of barley and malting techniques, more complicated mash regimens were needed to convert the mash.

Single-Step-Infusion Mash Instructions

1. Measure out strike water based on the amount of malt in the mash. The typical strike ratio used in the book's recipes is 1.25 quarts per pound of malt. (So, for a grain bill of 10 pounds you strike with 12.5 quarts of water.) In a separate vessel, measure an equal or greater volume of sparge water.

2. Heat the strike water to approximately 12°F above the desired mash rest temp. (For instance, heat to 164°F for a mash rest of 152°F). This dif-

ferential will vary from system to system. Also heat the sparge water to 170°F.

3. Mix the grains thoroughly and stir to break up any clumps. Rest for 10 minutes and take a temperature. Adjust with cold or hot water (or direct heat in a pot) to settle at the rest.

4. After 60 minutes, slowly drain a quart of cloudy grainy liquid and pour onto a plate or foil on top of the mash. Continue this process until the liquid runs clear.

5. Divert the runoff to the boil kettle and top up the tun with sparge water approximately 1" above the grain bed.

6. Collect enough runnings to equal the target volume plus 1 gallon for every 60 minutes of boiling (for example, 6.5 gallons for a 5.5 gallon recipe boiled for one hour). Check the runnings as you sparge and stop the flow if they drop below 1.010.

7. Once at a boil, begin timing your boil and add hops as specified in the recipe. For instance, add the 60 minutes hops when 60 minutes are remaining in the boil. (This is typically the start of the boil, but some recipes do specify longer boils of 75 to 120 minutes. Start counting down and when you hit 60, add the hops.)

8. At boil's end, add any last-minute hop additions. Vigorously stir the pot to create a whirlpool effect, place the lid on, and wait 10 minutes. Chill the beer to 60°F to 75°F with a chiller.

9. Transfer the beer to the fermenter and take a gravity sample. Add aeration or oxygenation and then pitch yeast.

10. Refer to the Fermentation and Packaging section of this appendix (page 285).

Multistep Brew Process

As mentioned above, older malts and the few under-modified malts left on the market require more complicated mash rests. Belgian breweries often employ a multistep mash to encourage more attenuative worts.

Multistep Mash Instructions

1. Begin as in the Single-Infusion process. Complete your first rest at the lower temperature (up to Step 3).
2. To raise the mash temperature by infusion, refer to Appendix C to calculate the amount of water needed to push the mash to the next rest temperature. Kettle mashers can raise temperature via direct heating. Fire up the burner and stir the mash continuously for 5 minutes. Turn off the heat, stir thoroughly, and check the temperature. Repeat until at target.
3. Repeat Step 2 for as many rests as required. When the last rest is completed, resume the Single-Infusion Process at Step 4.

Decoction Brew Process

Instead of relying on infusions of hot water or application of heat, the traditional decoction mash is the German way. The brewer takes a third of the mashed grains out of the tun and raises them to a saccharification rest temperature for a brief period. The grain is then boiled and added back to the main mash. Traditional schedules involve up to three different pulls to achieve final resting temperatures.

Decoction Mash Instructions

1. Begin as in the Single-Infusion process. Complete your first rest at the lower temperature (up to Step 3).
2. While the main mash rests, pull a third of the grain to a pot. Leave most of the liquid in the mash tun. Heat the pulled portion to saccharification temperature between 150°F and 156°F and rest for 10 to 15 minutes.

3. After the rest, ignite the heat and stir the mash continuously. Bring to a boil and boil for 10 minutes while stirring. Add this boiled pull back to the main mash, stir thoroughly to incorporate the heat, and raise the overall mash temperature to target.
4. Repeat Steps 2 and 3 for as many rests as required. When the last rest is completed, resume the Single-Infusion Brew Process at Step 4.

Fermentation and Packaging

1. For most normal-gravity beers, allow the beer to ferment in primary for a week or two until the gravity is no longer changing. Rack to secondary if desired or to dry-hop or spice the beer. Fermentation temperature should be varied to the optimum values indicated by the yeast manufacturer
2. To bottle, clean and sanitize fifty-four 12-ounce bottles. (To keg, follow instructions in text.)
3. Prepare a sugar solution of ¾ cup (approx 4.5 ounces by weight) Priming (corn) sugar and ¾ cup filtered water. Boil for 10 to 15 minutes and add to sanitized bottling bucket.
4. Rack beer onto sugar solution to mix thoroughly.
5. Fill each bottle to approximately 1.5 to 2 fingers' width from the top and cap
6. Store bottles in the seventies for two weeks. Chill one bottle and check the carbonation level. Wait one more week if carbonation is not as desired.

Extract Brewing Checklist

Beer Name:_____ Brew Day: _____ OG:_____

3 Days before Brew Day (for beers greater than 1.050)
- [ ] Prepare Yeast Starter (Swirl actively for 2 days)

1 Day before Brew Day
- [ ] Collect 6 to 7 gallons of water. Chill half of it overnight
- [ ] Chill the starter (or smack the yeast pack for smaller beers)
- [ ] Clean fermenters and kettles

Day of Brewing
- [ ] Remove yeast or starter from fridge
- [ ] Steeping (if using grains)
  - Bring 3 quarts of water to 170°F
  - Add crushed grain, stir thoroughly, and steep for 45 minutes. (If you have a grain bag, fill it with the grain and steep the bag)
  - Bring 3 quarts of sparge water to 170°F
  - Strain steeping liquid into 20-quart kettle
  - Rinse grains with sparge water, don't squeeze out the excess liquid, discard
- [ ] Boil
  - Add water to bring kettle to 3 gallons and put over high heat
  - Mix sanitizing solution to fill fermenter. Clean and sanitize airlock, funnel, hydrometer, thief, and foil
  - Warm LME container in a pot of hot water
  - Once boiling, pull the kettle and add the extract, stir thoroughly, and return to the heat
    - *For paler beers, add the extract after 50 minutes of boiling with the hops. (See Late-Extract Variant)*
  - Add the bitter hops and start the brew timer. Add the remaining hops at the appropriate time. Remember recipes always specify time as "Time Remaining." (For example, a 5-minute addition goes in with 5 minutes left in the boil, typically 55 minutes)
  - 15 minutes remaining, add yeast nutrient and kettle clarifiers (Irish moss, whirlfloc)

- Fill your sink with cold water and ice
- 0 minutes remaining, kill the heat and stir the pot rapidly to generate a whirlpool.
- [ ] Chill and Pitch (Everything's Sanitary Now)
  - Set the settling pot into the ice bath and wait until the wort temperature reaches around 90°F
  - Fill freshly sanitized fermenter with 2 gallons of chilled water.
  - Add the wort and top up with any remaining chilled water to 5 gallons.
  - Seal the fermenter and shake vigorously for 10 minutes to ensure complete mixing
  - Using the sanitized thief or turkey baster, withdraw enough wort to take a hydrometer reading.
  - Decant the spent starter liquid and swirl to suspend the yeast. Pour the yeast into the fermenter and seal the beer away.

Ferment (1 to 3 weeks after Brew Day)
- [ ] Ferment for 1 week at recommended temperature (generally 65°F to 70°F)
- [ ] Check the hydrometer to confirm completion
- [ ] For clearer beer, transfer to a sanitized carboy for 2 weeks of settling.

Bottle (3 to 5 weeks after Brew Day)
- [ ] Sanitize the bottling bucket, bottling wand, hoses, and spigots.
- [ ] Boil approximately ¾ cup of priming sugar in a cup of water for 10 to 15 minutes, add to the sanitized bottling bucket.
- [ ] Rack beer (via siphon) to the bottling bucket, allowing to swirl to mix with the sugar.
- [ ] Fill each bottle, cap, and set aside in a warm space for 2 weeks.
- [ ] Chill and test a bottle. If carbonated, you're ready! Otherwise, wait another week and repeat.

All-Grain Brewing Checklist

Beer Name:_____ Brew Day: _____ OG:_____

3 Days before Brew Day (for beers greater than 1.050)
☐ Prepare Yeast Starter (Swirl actively for 2 days)

1 Day before Brew Day
☐ Collect 7–8 gallons of filtered water
☐ Chill the starter (or smack the yeast pack for smaller beers)
☐ Clean fermenters and kettles

Day of Brewing
☐ Remove yeast or starter from fridge
☐ If your grain is not precrushed, crush the malt with your grain mill
☐ Mash
- Heat 1.25 quarts of water/pound of grain to around 12°F above desired mash temperature
  For example, heat 12.5 quarts of water (3 gallons) for 10 pounds of grain
- Start heating the sparge water (5 gallons) to 170°F. Hold there for the end of the mash
- While stirring vigorously, add the crushed malt to water. Stir thoroughly and break up any clumpy dough balls
- After the proscribed rest at temperature, if you're using a multistep mash, heat the mash to the next temp. If applying direct heat, stir constantly to avoid scorching. For boiling water additions, consult a calculation program for appropriate amounts of water
☐ Sparge
- Cover the top of the mash with aluminum foil. Punch numerous small holes in the foil
- After the final mash rest, open the mash tun drain and slowly collect the initial runnings. Add these runnings back to the top of the mash until the wort runs clear and free of grain, about 10 to 15 minutes
- Collect the runnings into the boil vessel

- Maintaining the slow flow rate, add sparge water to cover the grains. When the boil volume is at 5 gallons, stop adding water to the mash. Continue to runoff and collect 6.5 gallons of liquid. Aim for 60 minutes of sparge time
- Close the mash tun and move it off to clean
☐ Boil
- If extra burner space is available, begin heating the wort after the kettle bottom is covered by ½ inch
- As the beer comes to a boil, clean and sanitize the carboys, chillers, and airlocks for the batch
- Clean out the mash tun. Don't let it sit overnight!
- With a fine-mesh strainer, collect the scum that rises to the boil top until decently clear. Rinse the strainer in cold water between scoops
- Add the bittering hops and start the brew timer. Add the remaining hops at the appropriate time. Remember recipes always specify time as "time remaining" (for instance, a 5-minute addition goes in with 5 minutes left in the boil, typically 55 minutes)
- 15 minutes remaining, add yeast nutrient and kettle clarifiers (Irish moss, whirlfloc). If using an immersion chiller, add it to the kettle now to sanitize
- 0 minutes remaining, kill the heat and stir the pot rapidly to generate a whirlpool. Let rest for 10 minutes
☐ Chill and Pitch (Everything's Sanitary Now)
- Follow the instructions for your chiller and lower the temperature to 70°F or below.
- In mid-transfer to the carboy, grab a sample for hydrometer testing
- Either shake or use an oxygenation system to prepare the cooled wort for yeast
- Decant the spent starter liquid and swirl to suspend the yeast. Pour the yeast into the fermenter and seal the beer away

Ferment (1 to 4 weeks after Brew Day)

- ☐ Ferment for 1–2 weeks at recommended temperature (generally 65°F to 70°F)
- ☐ Check the hydrometer to confirm completion
- ☐ For clearer beer, transfer to a sanitized carboy for 2 weeks of settling

Bottle (3 to 5 weeks after Brew Day)

- ☐ Sanitize the bottling bucket, bottling wand, hoses, and spigots
- ☐ Boil approximately ¾ cup of priming sugar in a cup of water for 10 to 15 minutes, add to the sanitized bottling bucket
- ☐ Rack beer (via siphon) to the bottling bucket, allowing to swirl to mix with the sugar
- ☐ Fill each bottle, cap, and set aside in a warm space for 2 weeks.
- ☐ Chill and test a bottle. If carbonated, you're ready! Otherwise, wait another week and repeat.

OR!

Keg (3 weeks after Brew Day)

- ☐ Clean and sanitize a keg.
- ☐ Pop the lid (store in sanitizer) and cover mouth with foil.
- ☐ Rack beer into keg, seal, and add CO_2 pressure.
- ☐ Set your CO_2 tank to the recommended pressure (see table) for your temperature. Hook up the CO_2 and attach for a week.
- ☐ Alternatively, shake the chilled keg for 10 minutes and allow to settle for several hours before serving.

Index